America's Romance with the English Garden

❧ ❧

"Illustrated with colorful reproductions of original catalog artwork, this engaging book conveys a wonderful insight into how the catalogs of nineteenth-century seed and nursery companies had a profound and lasting influence on American garden design. There may be other books explaining America's enchantment with the English garden style, but none, I'm sure, match the scope or contents of this one."—Betty Earl, photographer and author of *In Search of Great Plants: The Insider's Guide to the Best Sources in the Midwest*

❧

"In the nineteenth century a confluence of mechanization and reliable propagation of seeds and plants brought the 'English garden' within reach of the wider American public. Thomas Mickey has pored over period nursery catalogs and other ephemera to prove his point that nurseries were catering to unspoken aspirations, a much more powerful advertising message than merely offering mundane seeds and plants. He tells a convincing story."—Judith M. Taylor, author of *The Global Migrations of Ornamental Plants: How the World Got into Your Garden* and coauthor of *Tangible Memories: Californians and Their Gardens, 1800–1950*

❧

"The American reverence for things English may be rooted in our national beginnings as the bumpkin across the pond, but our continuing fixation on English-style gardens, as Thomas Mickey lovingly demonstrates in *America's Romance with the English Garden*, can be traced directly to the illustrated seed catalogs that blossomed with the advent of cheap printing in the late nineteenth century. The catalog authors—nurserymen and women entranced with the growing prospects of the new nation—were the country's first garden writers, and their enthusiasm for the lawns and colorfully massed borders of English estates left residents of San Bernardino and Buffalo with the same idealized yen for vistas of water-hungry fescue and delicately trailing roses. Mickey is both a historian of public relations and a passionate Master Gardener, and his engaging book is full of colorful personalities—both plants and humans."—Ariel Swartley, Master Gardener, photographer, and writer, author of *In Xanadu: A Little Book of Poppies*

"I loved this meticulously researched guide through the history of American gardening. It's fascinating to discover how much has changed in our gardens over the last two hundred years, and how much has not."—Susan Harris, blogger, *Garden Rant*

"As Thomas Mickey supplies examples of developing methods for advertising seeds and plants in the nineteenth century, he suggests that such nationally distributed advertising across the United States made gardens themselves more uniform across region. *America's Romance with the English Garden* opens the door to a further exploration of the print culture of gardening." —Ellen Gruber Garvey, author of *Writing with Scissors: American Scrapbooks from the Civil War to the Harlem Renaissance* and *The Adman in the Parlor: Magazines and the Gendering of Consumer Culture, 1880s to 1910s*

America's Romance

WITH THE

English Garden

Ellwanger & Barry
ROCHESTER, N.Y.
"Crimson Rambler Rose."

COPYRIGHTED BY
ELLWANGER & BARRY
1894.

America's Romance

WITH THE

English Garden

Thomas J. Mickey (signature)

Thomas J. Mickey

OHIO UNIVERSITY PRESS

Athens

Ohio University Press, Athens, Ohio 45701
ohioswallow.com
© 2013 by Ohio University Press

To obtain permission to quote, reprint, or otherwise reproduce or distribute
material from Ohio University Press publications, please contact our rights and
permissions department at (740) 593-1154 or (740) 593-4536 (fax).

Printed in the United States of America
Ohio University Press books are printed on acid-free paper ⊗™

23 22 21 20 19 18 17 16 15 14 13   5 4 3 2

Library of Congress Cataloging-in-Publication Data

Mickey, Thomas J.
America's romance with the English garden / Thomas J. Mickey.
    p. cm.
Includes bibliographical references and index.
ISBN 978-0-8214-2035-5 (pb : alk. paper) — ISBN 978-0-8214-4452-8
(electronic)
1. Gardens, English—United States—History. 2. Seed industry and
trade—United States—History. I. Title.
SB457.6.M53 2013
635—dc23
                    2013000593

Contents

❧ ❧

1891

Cottage Rose Garden.
·COLUMBUS, OHIO·

Illustrations

✿ ✿

Featured Plants

Preface

In 1908, Chicago landscape designer Wilhelm Miller wrote a book called *What England Can Teach Us about Gardening.* He opened with these words: "The purpose of this book is to inspire people to make more and better gardens."[1] He then presented several chapters that reflected the gardening trends in nineteenth-century England, covering topics such as landscape gardening, formal gardens, borders, water gardens, wild gardens, rock gardens, and rose gardens. How had we come to look to England as inspiration for our gardens?

Martha Stewart once wrote an article about hydrangeas for her magazine. As the story goes, within days nurseries around the country sold out of hydrangeas. Gardeners everywhere wanted the hydrangea because Martha had recommended it in her publication.

Both stories illustrate the power of mass media such as books and magazines, coupled with advertising, to sell just about anything.

Nineteenth-century American gardeners were the first ever to experience the mass marketing of the garden. New communication technologies and the emergence of modern advertising created for the first time a mass-media-marketed garden; in this case, one modeled after the English garden that appeared regularly in such media forms as the seed and nursery catalogs. The image of the garden in the catalog appealed to a national audience, especially women, defined through advertising as shoppers.

For the first time, the advent of mass production of seeds and plants, reliably produced and distributed like any other product for the home, increased their demand across the country. Modern advertising sold the seeds and plants using the image of an ideal garden that would motivate a consumer. This idealized image was that of the contemporary English garden, often featuring a woman planting or gathering flowers.

For many years I have been interested in the study of the cultural values within public relations, advertising, and marketing materials. A product or service by itself is not what is being sold and promoted, but rather an image of a better life, a happier home, or a more fashionable garden. I believe that you can understand a culture better if you look at the way advertisers and public relations professionals promote products and services.

The goal of this book is to lead readers to an understanding of how the advertising and marketing of seeds and plants in nineteenth-century America encouraged a particular view of the garden. Styles of gardening such as the Italian, Dutch, Spanish, and French fashions were familiar but were not the image that company owners fostered in their thousands of catalogs and countless advertisements. That image was, instead, the English garden style.

This book had its start when I spent a year at the Smithsonian, reading dozens of American seed and nursery catalogs from the nineteenth century. I was looking for a link between marketing and the American garden in that period. From the first time I picked up a catalog, I was struck by the friendly words of the company owner, both in the introduction and in the articles. The catalog's illustrations only reinforced the words. After a while, what I found was that the catalogs sold a particular image of the garden.

I could see early on that the wealthy as well as the middle class in the nineteenth century had to garden in a particular way. Advertising material such as seed and nursery catalogs presented a view on how to use the seeds and plants so they would have meaning for the reader as a gardener who sought what was in fashion. It was no surprise to me that the same kind of English garden appeared from coast to coast, both in the catalog and on the ground.

In the nineteenth century, being modern—and the middle class valued modernity—meant you had an English-style garden, and especially a lawn. Perhaps that's why garden historian and landscape designer Wade Graham wrote that despite all the powerful environmental critiques of the lawn, the American garden cannot escape from turf.[2]

This is the story of American gardening as told through the words and images of the seed and nursery catalogs of the nineteenth century. Michael Pollan said that garden design remains the one corner of our culture in which our dependence on England has never been completely broken.[3] Perhaps because the nineteenth-century seed and nursery catalogs played no small role in creating that dependence, the publisher for Miller's book on the English garden knew there was an American audience, eager for its message.

PETER HENDERSON & Co's

MANUAL OF

EVERYTHING FOR THE GARDEN

PETER HENDERSON & CO.
35 & 37 CORTLANDT ST. NEW YORK.

1886

Acknowledgments

❧ ☙

IN MY YEAR at the Smithsonian, made possible by the Enid A. Haupt Fellowship from the Smithsonian's Horticultural Services Division, I read many catalogs from nineteenth-century American seed companies and nurseries at the National Museum of American History, the National Museum of Natural History, and the library of the Department of Agriculture, located in Beltsville, Maryland. This book is the result of that research.

Later, the following institutions proved essential for supporting material, including more garden catalogs: the Massachusetts Horticultural Society, the Boston Athenaeum, the Pennsylvania Horticultural Society, the Arnold Arboretum Library, Winterthur Library, Hagley Museum Library, the Bartram Garden in Philadelphia, the Marblehead Museum and Historical Society, the Dedham Historical Society, the Ethel Z. Bailey Horticultural Catalogue Collection at Cornell University, the library at Tower Hill Botanic Garden, and the Newton Historical Society.

Many people helped me as I wrote this book. At the Smithsonian I am indebted to Lauranne Nash from Horticulture Collections Management and Education, who believed in this work from the beginning. At Bridgewater State University I have to thank Howard London, Jabbar Al-Obaidi, Frances Jeffries, and my research assistant, Kelley Walsh. The Center for Advancement of Research and Teaching (CART) at BSU provided several grants for this book. Steve Hatch, former journalist and editor at the *Boston Globe,* suggested the preface. New Hampshire photographer Ralph Morang supplied the images of the plants from my garden for the Featured Plant sections. Special thanks for their advice to Jim Nau, Stephen Scanniello, and Cathy Neal.

Thanks to Elizabeth Eustis, Karen Madsen, and John Furlong from the Landscape Institute, now located at the Boston Architectural College. They encouraged me to ask the garden history research question that started me on this book's journey.

Finally, I am happy that Ohio University Press opened the door when I came knocking in search of a home for this book. Editorial director Gillian Berchowitz helped me with her endless patience.

Introduction

❧ ❧

Let us encourage our writers—and that can be
any of us—to write garden stories.

KENNETH HELPHAND

TODAY IN Doylestown, Pennsylvania, outside of Philadelphia, you can visit Fordhook Farm, bought by the seedsman W. Atlee Burpee in 1888. There Burpee spent his summers, on what he called his trial farm, to test seeds for his catalog. The two-story eighteenth-century farmhouse still stands, and in the first-floor study lined in mahogany panels near the fireplace you see the desk at which Burpee wrote his seed catalog.

At the corner of the room a door opens to steps that lead up to the bedroom on the second floor. If, in the middle of the night, Burpee got an idea for his catalog, he would descend the steps to his desk below and record his thought. He did not want to lose any inspiration, because seedsmen such as Burpee were serious about their business: helping the gardener grow the best lawn, flowers, fruits, and vegetables.

Burpee was only one of dozens of nineteenth-century seed merchants and nurserymen who were passionate about the garden and eager to spread the word about the importance of a garden for every home.

This book tells the story of how mass-marketed seed and nursery catalogs in the late nineteenth century told us what seeds to use, plants to choose, and landscape design ideas to employ. It is the story of how we became English gardeners in America because the seed companies and nurseries sold us the English garden.

They did their job well. To this day we love the English garden. Why is it that so many people stress over the perfect lawn? In the face of mounting questions about the sustainability of English-style gardens and their lawns —water shortages, chemical damage, and the use of demanding, exotic plants—we cling to the ideals sold by these merchants.

❧

Here, the meaning of the phrase "English garden" dates to the nineteenth century. Its landscape includes a lawn, carefully sited trees and shrubs, individual garden beds with native and exotic plants, and perhaps, out back, a vegetable or kitchen garden. The lawn and the use of exotic plants are relics of the English garden style we have loved for the past two hundred years.

The English style of garden began in its modern form after the reign of King Henry VIII, in the sixteenth century. Garden then meant a symmetrical layout, often with a well-trimmed knot garden, which you can still see at London's Hampton Court. By the early eighteenth century, the formal look was disappearing, replaced by a picturesque or more naturalistic view, with its signature feature, the long, sweeping green space devoted to lawn. By the early nineteenth century the garden had come to mean a gardenesque view— still a natural look but also with the careful grouping of exotic plants. Victorian gardens after 1850 meant carpet beds of annuals that the English usually first imported from a tropical climate and then cultivated in their conservatories over the winter. By the end of the century, the English garden included the wild garden, colorful perennial borders, and a return to a formal garden design.

❧

The first section of the book (chapters 1–3) deals with early British influence on American gardening. Beginning in the colonial period, British garden authors provided the books for American gardeners. Professional gardeners emigrated from Great Britain, and Americans hired them, or they came to own large American seed and plant companies in such cities as Boston, New York, and Philadelphia.

Like the English, horticultural societies appeared in major American cities, first along the East Coast. America followed the English format as well as content of garden journals, so it is no surprise that C. M. Hovey's *The American Gardener's Magazine* mirrored J. C. Loudon's *Gardener's Magazine.* The rural cemetery movement in major American cities corresponded with the British example of that time. If American businessmen with money to spend on their hobbies loved gardening, they collected plants, many exotic, and built their greenhouses, just as the English aristocracy had done before them.

We look at eighteenth-century Colonial Williamsburg, Virginia, where, as in the other British colonies, the Elizabethan-era English garden style became the model of what a garden should look like. The plant choices were limited, as were sources for those plants. It is worth noting that at a time when few seed and nursery catalogs appeared in America, the colonists engaged in a vigorous exchange of seeds and plants across the ocean.

Next follows a story of a mid-nineteenth-century country gentleman's landscape, dependent on the ideas of the English picturesque landscape garden. The country estate of Joseph Shipley, in Wilmington, Delaware, established in the 1850s, provides the example. Shipley could afford the leisure of gardening for pleasure, designing a landscape with the parklike style of the English design. Most Americans were farmers, and so more concerned with survival.

The second part of the book (chapters 4 to 7) develops the persuasive hold of the American seed companies and nurseries. The mass-produced catalog proved an important business decision because it was a way to connect with customers across the country. Seed companies, along with nurseries, had published catalogs of one sort or another for decades, but never had they produced the thousands of inexpensive copies that the new technologies of print and illustration made possible after 1870. Cheap newspapers, low printing costs, easy mail delivery, the railroad, and chromolithography, combined with an emerging middle class in the suburbs, contributed to the growth of the business.

The history of the seed and nursery industries of the nineteenth century comes through in the words of the company owners in the introduction section of their catalogs. The essays captured an owner's thoughts and hopes for readers. Here he (most owners were men, though not all) spoke in a friendly, colloquial way about the industry, about new seeds and plants, about how difficult the catalog was to put together, about how important the reputation of the company was, and about how gardening formed an important part of American life. As the Maule Seed Company from Philadelphia put it in its 1892 catalog, "Nothing represents the growth of this business so well as this book [catalog] itself."

The authors of horticultural literature in nineteenth-century America were often the owners of the seed companies and nurseries. They knew not only what the gardener had to plant but also how to plant it. The company owners followed with their own books, magazines, and articles. The catalog covered such topics as soil preparation, watering, bulbs, container planting, and landscaping. The company owner considered himself an educator, not just a purveyor of seeds and plants.

In the catalogs the companies frequently told their own stories of how they used the latest technological developments for printing and illustrating the catalog and also of the newest means of shipping their products. Major themes included the availability of novelty plants; the impressive size of company buildings, extensive trial gardens, and greenhouses; and the use of railroads for shipping. Addressing these themes both in words and in images, a company constructed its relevance to society. The reader could see that the company was progressive and thus surely deserved a customer's business.

This change in our garden story came with an increase in the numbers of newspapers and national magazines dependent on advertising, especially after 1870. The nineteenth-century seed companies and nurseries used the new mass media to sell a standardized garden—their version of the English garden of contemporary fashion—which their customers could easily recognize in articles, illustrations, and ads. For the first time, a mass-media-driven garden became part of the culture.

The third part of the book (chapters 8 and 9) examines the importance of a garden as part of the home landscape for the emerging middle class—but a garden reflecting the English garden style. The middle class, who were defined more and more as consumers by modern advertisers, wanted a standardized product. The gardener that catalogs sought to attract was the woman of the house, who made most of the purchases for the home, while the husband spent the day at work outside the home. Most women wanted a garden like the one that appeared in the catalogs. They would buy the seeds and plants as well as the books and magazines about gardening that came from the seed houses and nurseries, holding on to an ideal of a garden that one day might be theirs.

Philadelphia nurseryman Thomas Meehan wrote in his magazine, *Gardener's Monthly,* "The garden is the mirror of the mind, as truly as the character of a nation is the reflex of the individuals composing it."[1] He wrote what we still in some sense believe today: show me a garden, and I will tell you what class of people inhabits the home. The garden became a cultural symbol for the middle class. Today, lawns and yards may exist to fulfill some innate human love and need for beauty, but it is more likely that they announce the dignity and responsibility (or perhaps, in some cases, lack thereof) of their owners.[2]

When, as if in one voice, the catalogs recommended a plant, they exerted an influence unlike any in earlier times, because the production and mass circulation of the catalog made the company's message available across the country. In the mid-1890s, the catalogs trumpeted a novelty plant called the 'Crimson Rambler' rose, introduced from England. By the end of the century, most major catalogs listed this plant and included chromolithographs of its bright red color. The 'Crimson Rambler' soon became an important addition to the American garden and maintained its popularity for over thirty years.

The final section of the book (chapter 10) concludes with the home landscape, the embodiment of an enduring English garden style. The catalogs taught the middle-class reader how to landscape the home grounds. The landscape discussed in the catalogs included the lawn, curved walks, group-ings of shrubs, trees to line the property, flowerbeds of annuals, and, later, borders of perennials.

The English style of landscape appeared around the country. Horticul-turalist Denise Wiles Adams, in her research into heirloom plants from the nineteenth century, wrote, "As I studied the gardening practices of dif-ferent areas of the United States, it became increasingly clear that landscap-ing and garden styles remained fairly consistent and homogenous across the continent."[3]

♒

In nineteenth-century America, the seed and nursery merchants worked hard to publish catalogs that would both tell their story and sell their prod-ucts. They considered it their duty to endorse a particular style of garden, an English design, and so they wrote about and illustrated garden and land-scape ideals they thought would motivate their customers. They were just doing their job.

Seedsman and Civil War veteran Roland H. Shumway, in his catalog of 1887, discussed how he would like to be remembered: "Good Seeds Cheap! is my motto; and has been ever since I left the tented field as a soldier, and staked the few remaining years of my busy life, in an earnest endeavor, to place good seeds within reach of [the] poorest planters. I will further in-form you how we strive to do you good, and not disappoint you. From the beginning of the new year, until after spring planting, my industrious em-ployees work 16 hours, and myself and family 18 or more hours a day. Are we not surely knights at labor? How can we do more? Do we not deserve the patronage of every planter in America?"

Seed merchants such as Burpee and Shumway worked long hours to create a successful business, but they and their nurserymen brethren offered more than seeds and plants. This book tells the story of how the nineteenth-century seed and nursery industry sold the American gardener the En-glish garden.

Featured Plant

Each chapter concludes with a section called "Featured Plant," discussing a plant that I grow in my own garden. The image is also from my garden.

The plant choice is based on the discussion of that chapter, so it is usually an early plant variety, either native or exotic, though in some cases a newer variety is presented. These plants are still available to the gardener, thus linking the garden of the nineteenth century to today's home landscape. I give a history of the plant and instructions on how to care for it as well.

VOL. VIII.   SEPTEMBER   1892.

THE MAYFLOWER

FLORAL PARK
NEW YORK.

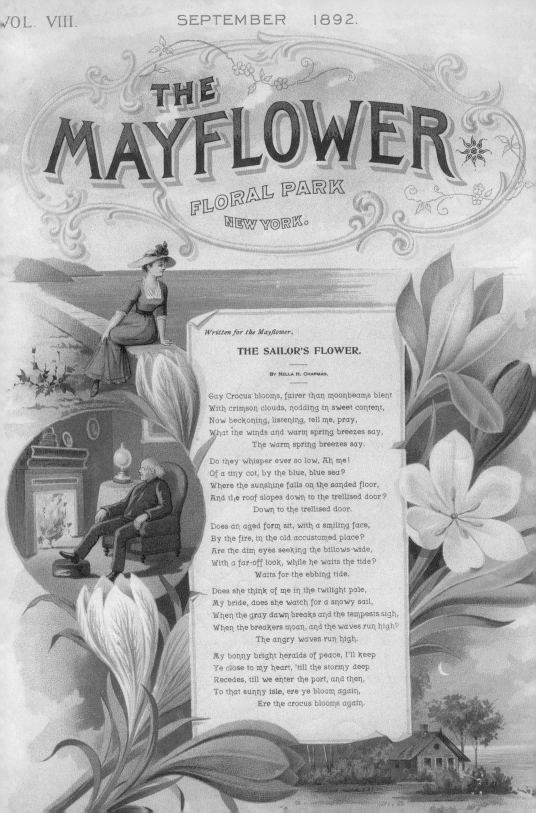

Written for the Mayflower.

THE SAILOR'S FLOWER.

BY NELLA H. CHAPMAN.

Gay Crocus blooms, fairer than moonbeams blent
With crimson clouds, nodding in sweet content,
Now beckoning, listening, tell me, pray,
What the winds and warm spring breezes say,
    The warm spring breezes say.

Do they whisper ever so low, Ah me!
Of a tiny cot, by the blue, blue sea?
Where the sunshine falls on the sanded floor,
And the roof slopes down to the trellised door?
    Down to the trellised door.

Does an aged form sit, with a smiling face,
By the fire, in the old accustomed place?
Are the dim eyes seeking the billows-wide,
With a far-off look, while he waits the tide?
    Waits for the ebbing tide.

Does she think of me in the twilight pale,
My bride, does she watch for a snowy sail,
When the gray dawn breaks and the tempests sigh,
When the breakers moan, and the waves run high?
    The angry waves run high.

My bonny bright heralds of peace, I'll keep
Ye close to my heart, 'till the stormy deep
Recedes, till we enter the port, and then,
To that sunny isle, ere ye bloom again,
    Ere the crocus blooms again.

The British Connection

AT THE AGE of fifteen, Charles Mason Hovey gardened in the backyard of his house in Cambridge, outside of Boston. In gardening he had seized on his passion. For the rest of his life he made a career in the nursery business and helped others find pleasure in gardening. He wrote in his garden magazine, "With respect to ourselves, Gardening is a pursuit to which we have ever been zealously devoted, and in which we have ever felt a deep interest."[1]

In 1831, Hovey went to Philadelphia to visit the Landreth Company, the first seed firm in America, probably to see how the seed business worked. The next spring, at the age of twenty-two, he began a nursery business in Cambridge and opened a seed store in the center of Boston, in partnership with his brother, Phineas Brown Hovey. He was on his way, but it was just the first step on a long journey: Hovey's lifework would ultimately lead him down a path that reflected his preference for the gardening style of England, and his influence on American gardeners would go far beyond selling them seeds and plants.

Perhaps the most visible manifestation of this influence is his publication *Magazine of Horticulture,* which became the longest-running nineteenth-century garden magazine in America. Hovey began the magazine in 1835, after reading the English publication *Gardener's Magazine* (first issued in 1826), which was edited by horticulturalist John Claudius Loudon. Hovey designed the layout and chose the editorial content for his magazine to resemble Loudon's. In addition, he often incorporated articles from English garden magazines such as *Gardener's Magazine,* so his readers became familiar with English plants as well as English landscape style.

The magazine, however, was only one way in which Hovey brought an English garden influence to America. Like many other seedsmen and nurserymen of nineteenth-century America, Hovey found the English garden a source of inspiration for learning about plants and cultivating them, but he did not limit his efforts to business ventures. For example, Hovey joined the new Massachusetts Horticultural Society, modeled after the English version. Moreover, he encouraged the development of public parks and rural cemeteries, supported early on by the English.

Though Hovey and other seedsmen and nurserymen encouraged all things English in horticulture, the English garden style was only one among several in early America. Different forms of gardening emerged, whether brought first by explorers and colonists or by later immigrants. Each of these groups would form a landscape and garden in a style familiar to them from their homeland.

Early American Gardening

Before 1900, America witnessed several gardening styles, each contributing to the garden palette of the country. During the 1700s, missions in Florida and California favored Spanish gardens. These were often geometric in layout, with water elements such as fountains serving as an important feature of the design.

In early eighteenth-century America, the French formal garden design dominated through the presence of vista gardens. This grand style appealed to colonial governors, who had the clout, as well as to southern planters and northern merchants, who had the money.[2]

In colonial New England, dooryard gardens predominated in the form of a fenced-in area that contained beds of herbs and flowers serving both the cooking and the medicinal needs of the family. An example of this English style can be seen in the restored colonial housewife's garden at the Whipple House, in Ipswich, Massachusetts. In this style, rows of plants were placed along straight paths running parallel to one another. Contemporary English garden writers, who proposed this symmetrical style of garden, were important to the early settlers in the New World.[3]

The Dutch settled New York in the early seventeenth century. At first, their gardens were small and geometric in design. The Dutch, whether rich or poor, always provided an array of flowers in their gardens.

By the time of the Revolution, the majority of the country homes of New York's wealthy citizens were situated on Manhattan Island, bordering the East and Hudson Rivers, though a few had also been established on Long Island.[4] In this environment, the naturalistic English garden style became popular, and by the end of the century it had come to be featured on several regional estates.[5] By then the middle-class landscape with its garden area would also reflect that same English picturesque view.

To the south, in the settlements of Maryland and Virginia, and along the James and other rivers, the geometric English style prevailed. Wealthier people chose to design elaborate gardens with more formal lines, rather than draw on the natural style. More money, as well as the help of slaves, enabled towns such as Williamsburg to showcase the geometric English garden style, with its trees, shrubs, straight walkways, parterres, and boxwood edging. This ancient English landscape garden style inspired such gardens in all the colonies during the second half of the eighteenth century but was especially favored on the southern plantations.[6]

At Middleton Place, in Charleston, South Carolina, an even more elaborate style of gardening emerged, with a lawn and an extensive collection of ornamental trees and shrubs. The garden was laid out in 1755; today it remains as an example of a combination of both the formal and the picturesque. The English garden style was at one time formal and geometric, and later naturalistic and picturesque.

Farther north, the William Paca house, built in Annapolis in the mid-1770s, likewise showcases a formal garden design, with parterres, walks, and a fountain. John Penn's estate in Philadelphia, another design of the same period (laid out during the 1780s), demonstrated a taste for the contemporary English fashion of naturalistic landscape gardening, which included the ha-ha to keep animals from the house, irregular flower gardens, and a vista south of the house. The design reflects the work of Capability Brown and his vision of the ideal English landscape garden of the period.[7] Other important estate gardens appeared in and around Philadelphia during the last decades of the eighteenth century.

Designed landscapes in America were not a priority in the colonial period, and certainly for decades after the revolution most people had to attend to the demands of farming just to survive. Few Americans were then familiar with the English picturesque style that had emerged in seventeenth-century England as the "modern" style. An English traveler who wrote about his visit in the first quarter of the nineteenth century said, "Ornamental gardening is an art at present totally unknown or at least unpracticed, in the United States."[8] Evidently, he had not visited Woodlands: William Hamilton (1749–1813) designed Woodlands, his property in Philadelphia, in the modern English style of the picturesque. Indeed, Woodlands was so well done that Thomas Jefferson visited the estate to gain ideas for his own landscape in Virginia. Woodlands, reflecting the English obsession with plant collecting, included ten thousand exotic plants, many of which had to be grown in the greenhouse.

Henry Pratt's Lemon Hill, likewise in Philadelphia, was another important estate garden. Three thousand plants, including the first gardenia in

America, were in Pratt's collection. Pratt had an even more concrete connection with the English garden: not only did he send his gardener to England to bring back exceptional plant varieties, but also nurseryman Robert Buist, who later became an influential figure in English-style landscape gardening in America, worked at Lemon Hill when he first emigrated from Scotland. Though Buist worked for only a year or two at Lemon Hill, considered one of the finest gardens in America at that time, he probably felt at home since the garden reflected a style that Buist knew from Great Britain.

However, not all gardeners had the funds or the space for estate gardens, and the Colonial gardening style remained strong until 1840. Gardens until that time were often developed by Europeans who had immigrated to the United States, and these gardens reflected the style of gardening back in the immigrants' home countries, with their focus primarily on vegetables and herbs. By the second half of the nineteenth century, though, colonial gardens had started to diverge from that model, edging toward a New World sensibility.

The gardens of German settlers in mid- to late nineteenth-century Wisconsin are a good example of this trend, showing the distinct influence of mainstream America in relegating the kitchen garden to the side yard and having plantings in neat rows (rather than the traditional rectangular beds). Row planting allowing for mechanical cultivation, with the tools suggested by the garden catalogs.[9] Indeed, the gardens took on the look presented in the catalog.

Middle-class gardens, too, reflected a more standardized form of gardening, which had swept the country largely in response to the advertising in seed and nursery catalogs. Along with popular garden magazines, books such as seedsman Peter Henderson's *Gardening for Pleasure* encouraged the same kind of garden, featuring flowerbeds and an extensive lawn.

Members of the growing middle class did not limit themselves to standardization and practicality, however. After 1870, the period of the Gilded Age encouraged large estates in which the landscape and gardening became a way to show off one's wealth. The middle-class Victorian garden included a lawn with flowerbeds and exotic plants, evoking the gardenesque view first introduced by Loudon. Boston nurseryman Marshall Wilder, president of the Massachusetts Horticultural Society, said in 1879 that the introduction of subtropical plants such as palms, agaves, musas, dracaenas, caladiums, and the many other ornamental foliage plants was the most characteristic feature of that era in horticulture.[10]

By the final third of the nineteenth century, the Victorian garden of exotic tropical annuals, popular in England and America, had come to require a greenhouse in which to start the plants and also to overwinter them. Rejecting beds of annuals for the landscape because they demanded too much time in maintenance, the English horticulturalist and writer William Robinson's new book *The Wild Garden* promoted the use of perennials in borders. Perennial borders were likewise a feature in the "cottage garden" look favored by English garden designer and artist Gertrude Jekyll, who influenced American gardening through her insistence on perennial borders in carefully orchestrated chords of a certain color that would bloom with season-long interest.

Still other influences came to bear in America. One of these, the Arts and Crafts movement, which developed at the turn of the century, focused on native plants such as grasses for the landscape. In midwestern states such as Illinois and Wisconsin, a new interest emerged in using prairie plants in the garden rather than exotics. Around the same time, an interest in Italian garden styles (inspired even by novelist Edith Wharton) became part of the American garden scene in the 1890s. More preference for the formal garden soon followed, promoted through the work of American landscape architects such as Charles Platt.

Because of all these influences, and more, the preferred garden style of the decades before 1900 fluctuated between formal design and a more natural and less geometric composition. The extent of variety in gardens of the period was readily apparent to the likes of Daniel Denison Slade (1823–96), a Boston physician and member of the Massachusetts Horticultural Society, who described the garden styles in his book on the evolution of New England horticulture: "Between the lawns, walks, and shrubbery of the Gardenesque, so often deemed 'artistic' and the only possibility for beautiful grounds—the wildness of the Picturesque, requiring little or no interference with nature,—the Geometrical style, so intimately connected with Architecture,—between these types, there are numerous modifications that are appropriate and will be adopted by those of refined taste."[11]

Despite all this variety, most of the American gardens of the time shared a common element: the influence of the English-style garden. As nineteenth-century Americans read English garden books and designed their landscapes in that style, the English garden became the fashion. England's reputation for having a developed sense of horticulture certainly played a role in making English design more prominent. Travel, too, to view English gardens firsthand helped make the English garden the preferred style among some Americans, including Thomas Jefferson. While Americans recognized the importance of English gardening practices and sought them out, the English were eager to spread their knowledge of horticulture on our shore as well.

Hovey wrote in *Gardener's Monthly* of 1876 of the influence of one English garden writer: "Loudon's books have molded and formed the present English taste for landscape art, as they have also influenced to a great degree the taste in our own country."[12] But Loudon was not the only writer to find an audience across the Atlantic. In the early nineteenth century, William Cobbett, a seedsman from Kensington, England,[13] visited America in search of new plants. In 1821, Cobbett published a book in America titled *The American Gardener,* an account of his trip along with some recommendations for the American gardener. He began by highlighting the English garden tradition: "The labourers of England are distinguished from those of other countries by several striking peculiarities; but, by none are they so strongly distinguished as by their fondness of their gardens, and by the diligence, care, and taste, which they show in the management of them."[14] That care of the garden was something he sought to instill in an American readership.

In the book Cobbett thanked his American hostess, Mrs. John Tredwell, of Salisbury Place, Long Island, for her hospitality and dedicated the volume to her. The purpose of the book, as he saw it, was to instruct American gardeners on the principles of gardening that he had learned in England. He, like nineteenth-century American seedsmen and nursery owners in their catalogs, set out to teach Americans how to garden in the English style.

And Americans were eager to learn. In the early 1800s, significant horticultural movements taking place in Great Britain appeared in American versions in cities such as Boston, New York, and Philadelphia. Hovey stood at the forefront, encouraging American gardeners to take up the English model of gardening as both an art and a science.

England's Garden Tradition

The training and support of professional gardeners shows the importance a nation places on its gardens. England's garden history illustrates the role of professional gardeners as well as an evolution of the meaning of the word *garden*.

Although in England gardening was an important occupation between the twelfth and fifteenth centuries at royal castles and manors,[15] monasteries were the centers of botany and horticulture. Behind the walls of their monastic enclosures, the monks cultivated herbs, vegetables, and fruits. That all changed when Henry VIII (1491–1547) confiscated the monasteries and gave or sold them to his lords; after that, the gardens of the monasteries became the property of the aristocracy and the landed gentry. Interest in gardens and landscapes spread among this wealthy and powerful group, expressed in the land they owned or confiscated, which sometimes became deer parks. Today at Hampton Court, for example, the park where the monarch and invited guests once hunted for deer still forms part of the landscape.

Thus, despite England's modern horticultural reputation for expertise, English gardening as an art and the aesthetic appreciation of flowers scarcely existed until the fifteenth or early sixteenth century.[16] (Not until the nineteenth century, especially in the gardenesque style of the Victorian period, would masses of flowers assume an important role.) Back in the seventeenth century, fruits were abundant and orchards grew throughout the country. Kitchen gardens were maintained for the table as well. Hired gardeners began to take over the daily tasks of caring for the crops of fruits and vegetables. Apprentice gardeners worked under a head gardener, who would teach the skills of horticulture while he bought, sold, and planted for the needs of the garden.[17]

English garden style evolved over a period of centuries. The English in the 1600s copied the elaborate symmetrical landscape designs of the French, particularly as expressed in the formal style of Versailles. Elaborate topiary, a garden style of the Dutch, followed, with clipped shrubs and trees in the landscape. The English also combined the French landscape style, with its more formal appearance, with the fountains and statuary of the Italians.

The definition of the garden changed again in the 1700s, when landscape designers, or "landscape gardeners" as they were called, proposed a view of landscape that required a more natural use of trees, shrubs, and extensive lawns. This design approach, called "picturesque," resulted in a landscape characterized by variation and irregularity.

By the mid-eighteenth century, England had begun to promote that more natural landscape, which included a lawn, winding paths, and the use of carefully placed trees and shrubs in groups similar to those one would, supposedly, find in nature. Flowers and flowerbeds were minimal or shunned entirely. This new approach was a reaction to the more formal landscape design that had dominated the English garden for over two hundred years. Advocates of the new garden design included landscape designers William Kent, Capability Brown, and Humphry Repton, each associated ever since with this naturalistic landscape. That view came to define the English garden by 1800. Today, the grand English landscapes like Rousham, Stowe, and Stourhead still embody that picturesque design.

By then the garden had ceased to be limited to an enclosure and instead approached the image of a park in the country.[18] The estates of the aristocracy included an extensive lawn to create that parklike setting. For over two centuries the lawn, the central feature of the park view, has probably been the most constant factor in English gardening.[19] Not that the lawn was limited to England. In 1864, Hovey, then serving as president of the Massachusetts Horticultural Society, praised the lawn in its picturesque style, as found on the Lyman property located in Waltham, outside of Boston, and he called it a fine example of the art of landscape gardening in America: "Who does not remember the once and yet elegant demesne at Waltham, where, years gone by, the beautiful deer might be seen bounding o'er the lawn, or gently reposing beneath some graceful elm?"[20]

By the end of the eighteenth century, landscape gardening in the natural design had become the recognized style of England and was reproduced on properties in Europe and America as well. Indeed, English gardens became the fashion. Old gardens were even destroyed to give place to the new style,[21] and books were written abroad extolling English taste and inviting other nations to copy it. One continental example of the new English naturalistic style of the time was Germany's Englischer Garten, in Munich.

Even today the grand estate gardens of eighteenth- and nineteenth-century England, such as Stowe, Stourhead, Rousham, and Chatsworth, serve as primary illustrations of the country's history of gardening. Thus, it is no surprise that the English garden, until Loudon attempted to appeal to an emerging middle class in his writing during the early 1800s, was restricted to the landscape of the wealthy aristocrat. Usually a team of gardeners took care of the property and looked at gardening as a profession, one in which they could advance to become head gardener one day, like the famous Joseph Paxton at Chatsworth.

Gardeners often came from families of professional gardeners, which instilled the importance of this work in their sons; of the young men who were accepted as apprentices in the school of the garden of the Horticultural Society of London in the 1820s, about half were the sons of gardeners.[22] By the mid-nineteenth century, England had long fostered a tradition of professional gardeners, who knew gardening both in theory and in practice. William Cresswell, one such English gardener, left a diary of his duties as a nineteenth-century gardener. His book provides insight into the levels of apprentice, journeyman, and finally professional gardener. Cresswell's goal was to make horticulture his life's career, as had his father before him.[23]

British Gardeners Journey to America

In the nineteenth century, some British gardeners, like many other Europeans, left to come to America to seek a new life. A few established their own seed or nursery businesses. They would, of course, also educate the American gardener about the English garden. The immigration of European-trained gardeners was an important factor in the early development of American horticulture.[24]

Some of this reliance on European-trained gardeners was born of necessity, because of the relative lack of professional gardeners in America. When John Bartram Jr., son of the founder of the Bartram garden and nursery in Philadelphia, died in 1812, his daughter, Ann, and her husband, Colonel Robert Carr, took over the business. In Loudon's *Gardener's Magazine* of 1831, Carr wrote an article in which he complained how difficult it was to find American gardeners: "We are very far behind you [England] in gardening, and willing to learn all we can from such as come here."[25]

However, not everyone who came from England and called himself a gardener was qualified. Cobbett wrote, "Every man, who can dig and hoe and rake, calls himself a Gardener as soon as he lands here from England. This description of persons are generally handy men, and, having been used to spadework, they, from habit, do things well and neatly. But as to the art of gardening, they generally know nothing of it."[26]

In addition, British and European gardeners did not necessarily have a lifelong passion for the craft. Englishman William Wynne visited Bartram's Garden in Philadelphia in the early 1830s. When he returned to England, he wrote, "Before I left London, several young gardeners begged of me to let them know what encouragement there is for such persons in this country.

Colonel Carr told me (with regret) that most of the European gardeners turned farmers soon after they came here. This speaks volumes. There are no American gardeners except amateurs."[27] So the owners of large estates with extensive gardens in America were left to fend for themselves, since there were no professional gardeners as there were in Great Britain. Decades later, the situation in America would not be much better. Meehan suggested in an 1874 edition of his *Gardener's Monthly* that the lack "of horticultural colleges is one of the principal reasons why there are few educated and really competent gardeners."

Although the meaning of *gardener* has a long history in English gardening, American professional gardeners before 1870 were to be found only on the estates of the wealthy, tending to the fruit trees, lawns, and greenhouses. In contrast to the British with their system for training gardeners, the free-spirited Americans most often sought work in factories in the city or working the fields on a farm. Until the last quarter of the nineteenth century, indeed the profession of horticulture did not attract many native-born Americans.[28] This disadvantage did not go unnoticed. As Andrew Jackson Downing wrote in his magazine *The Horticulturist,* in an article that compared American and British horticulture, "Rapid as the progress of horticulture is at the present time in the United States, there can be no doubt that it is immensely retarded by this disadvantage, that all our gardeners have been educated in the school of British horticulture."[29]

The need to train professional gardeners shows how important gardening and gardeners were to the British; they took their gardens seriously. Eventually, so would American garden lovers, who did not necessarily enlist professional gardeners but nevertheless came to view the garden as something worthwhile, especially for an emerging middle class with suburban homes. Though seed and nursery businesses such as Hovey's contributed to the growing importance of American gardening, the homeowner did not fear to take on the role of gardener.

Over a three-hundred-year period, England had evolved a definable garden style. It makes sense, therefore, that American seedsmen and nurserymen, eager to find an image to convey the message of the importance of the garden in their marketing, would rely on that tradition to teach their customers how to garden and to promote the sale of seeds and plants.

America Reflects English Horticulture

Garden historian Abigail Lustig has written that horticulture, as a new mode of gardening and botany, was an English invention, but it did not remain confined to Great Britain.[30] Nineteenth-century botany and horticulture in Great Britain would also have an impact on America, but not without the involvement of American seed and nursery industries.

Many horticultural developments in Great Britain were reflected on the American continent in the nineteenth century. To pursue his dream of educating others in horticulture, Hovey, seedsman and nurseryman, among others, took part in garden-related practices that reflected what the English had already introduced to the world of gardening.

Horticultural Societies

In 1804, English plant enthusiasts began the Horticultural Society of London, later to become the Royal Horticultural Society. The organization focused on plant science and exploration, and the members encouraged the development of gardens using the newest plants, whether imported from the Americas or from Asia. Members were primarily wealthy businessmen and aristocrats who had an interest in building greenhouses and cultivating exotic plants in the landscape. Exotic plantings were displayed in a range of specialized garden areas such as the American garden, which featured native American plants, and the pinetum, a collection of evergreens. Eventually, the horticultural societies appealed to the middle-class gardener, particularly in their yearly exhibitions of plants, which would attract hundreds of visitors.

The Pennsylvania Horticultural Society (1827), the Massachusetts Horticultural Society (1829), and the New York Horticultural Society (1855) came along shortly thereafter and modeled themselves after the Royal Horticultural Society. Like the English society, which was made up of the British landed gentry, at the start wealthy American merchants who were also avid gentleman farmers formed the membership of the horticultural societies.[31] Prominent American seedsmen and nurserymen were often officers of these societies, if not founding members, for nineteenth-century nurserymen and seedsmen founded horticultural and pomological societies wherever they had their businesses.[32] In Boston, for example, Hovey served as president of the Massachusetts Horticultural Society from 1863 to 1866. Boston nurseryman Marshall Wilder and seedsman Joseph Breck also served as president. Local nurserymen William Kenrick and Jacob W. Manning, along with seedsman James J. H. Gregory, were involved as well. Fruit grower Robert Manning, from Salem, was both secretary and editor of the history of the society.

At the laying of the cornerstone for the Massachusetts Horticultural Society's new building in 1864, Hovey, in his role as society president, said, "We erect this Temple to foster and extend a taste for the pleasant, useful, and refined art of gardening."[33] Thus, Hovey extended his passion for gardening by presiding over the premier horticultural society in the city as well as erecting a building for future lovers of gardening. Indeed, it was through Hovey's skills in fund-raising that the new building in Boston, at the corner of Tremont and Montgomery, saw the light of day.

Horticultural societies enabled middle-class gardeners to enjoy gardening in a way only the wealthy could before, particularly in the ability to collect plants and build greenhouses. Although a few people were collecting plants before 1800, the era of serious plant collecting, with an emerging botany as well, did not begin until 1805, with the Horticultural Society of London. Such horticultural societies had as their goal, as Hovey recognized, fostering a passion for gardening, which included bringing unfamiliar plants to a wide audience. As evidence of this broad interest, thousands attended the yearly exhibitions of fruits, flowers, and vegetables sponsored by societies, such as the Pennsylvania Horticultural Society, which held its first public exhibition (the precursor of the current annual Philadelphia Flower Show) in 1829.

Exhibitions were good for business not only in expanding the market but also in achieving higher visibility. Seed companies and nurseries collected, grew, and sold seeds and plants, especially novelties, to satisfy customer interest. Hovey, for example, grew hundreds of pears, apples, and plums, as well as camellias and chrysanthemums, after he expanded his nursery in 1840.

Parks

Loudon, in an 1833 issue of his garden magazine, defended the importance of parks for the health of all classes of people. He wrote, "The time is just commencing for the embellishments of public parks, and gardens adjoining towns, in which the beau ideal of this description of scenery will be realized, at the expense of all, and for the enjoyment of all."[34] The majority of the population, not just the monarchy and the wealthy, needed outdoor green space. Because Loudon's ideas on landscape inspired Downing, who in turn was an important influence for Frederick Law Olmsted, America's foremost park builder, it is no surprise that Central Park demonstrates the influence of the English view of the picturesque landscape.

Loudon considered the garden to be an agent of social change. He wanted green space or parks, especially in the cities, where people could enjoy fresh air. Many of his readers agreed. In London, Hyde Park and St. James Park were initially intended for wealthy aristocrats. In 1835, Regent's Park became the first important city park designed for public use. Regent's Park had a lasting and beneficial influence on park designers through the rest of the century and beyond.[35] In 1843, Joseph Paxton built Birkenhead Park, the first publicly owned park in Britain.

🙙 *Figure 1.1.* A view of St. James Park in London. This image appeared in James Vick's magazine, *Vick's Illustrated Monthly,* in January 1881. *Courtesy of the Five Colleges Depository at the University of Massachusetts, Amherst.*

The American seedsman James Vick, in 1881, included in his monthly magazine an illustration of St. James Park in London (fig. 1.1). He wrote, "The view here given in St. James Park, London, is of a very different kind, and no admirer of nature would hesitate to ascribe to it far greater merit as a pleasing work of art. What is meant as the natural style of landscape gardening is here made evident much more forcibly than is possible by words."

America would also build parks. Central Park, serving as a model in its use as public green space, was eventually reflected in similar designs around the country, often with the Olmsted firm hired as the designer. In 1888, the Mount Hope Nurseries, the premier nursery in the country owned by Ellwanger and Barry, in Rochester, New York, gave the city twenty acres not far from the nursery. That gift later became Mount Hope Park, which Olmsted also designed.

Rural Cemeteries

In Paris in 1804, Père Lachaise Cemetery had become an international model of the rural cemetery, inspiring the creation of garden cemeteries abroad.[36] Across the channel, in London, cemeteries had become a problem as the city's population increased dramatically in the nineteenth century. The amount of space available for burying the dead was diminishing in large cities, both in America and in England, creating the threat of health problems, including the fear of miasmas, for the urban residents. But more than fear of disease prompted calls for a new type of cemetery; aesthetic appreciation also played a role. Loudon, for example, proposed in his magazine a parklike cemetery with trees and shrubs in an extensive landscape that would ensure a natural, picturesque view of nature and also give city dwellers a chance to enjoy a Sunday stroll along the cemetery's winding paths and grassy hills, dotted with stately trees. England's first suburban, parklike cemetery in London was Kensal Green Cemetery, laid out in 1832.

At about the same time, Boston joined the movement toward the rural cemetery, a newly emerging style of burial ground. In 1831, with the support of the leadership of the Massachusetts Horticultural Society, Mount Auburn Cemetery was built in Cambridge in the manner of the rural cemetery of Europe. Hovey referred to Mount Auburn as "the sacred garden of the dead."[37] Later, in 1848, Boston's Forest Hills Cemetery was also built, as an expression of the best style of landscape or picturesque gardening.

Vick encouraged the rural cemetery, with its lawn, trees, and shrubs. Figures 1.2 and 1.3 show illustrations from his magazine. He wrote in 1878, "Although the laying out and general treatment [of a rural cemetery] should be as for a gentleman's ground or park, still the Cemetery may and must have a character of its own, not forced or artificial, or severe, but natural and graceful. This character can be expressed in no way so well as by judicious planting."[38] He thus encouraged the use of lawn, trees, and shrubs in a cemetery, much in the tradition of the English as represented in the writings of Loudon.

Figure 1.2. The cemetery as it existed in many areas. *Vick's Illustrated Monthly,* June 1878. *Courtesy of the Five Colleges Depository at the University of Massachusetts, Amherst.*

Plant Collecting and Greenhouses

As noted earlier, the English had been avid plant collectors since the 1700s, when English horticultural societies and botanic gardens hired plant collectors to search the world for plants. To a large extent, the work of plant collectors was what made fashionable horticulture possible, as they sent thousands of intriguing new species to the gardens and herbaria of Europe.[39] Plant collectors from England were representatives of the horticultural societies, of botanical gardens such as Kew, and even of British plant merchants such as Veitch Nurseries, which were always on the lookout for new plant varieties.

In America, the century began with the Lewis and Clark expedition to the northwest, which included a hunt for plants. Later, Asa Gray, the Harvard botanist, would provide a scientific listing of American plants. By the

Figure 1.3. The cemetery as it should be, with trees and shrubs in the English style of cemetery landscape. *Vick's Illustrated Monthly,* June 1878. *Courtesy of the Five Colleges Depository at the University of Massachusetts, Amherst.*

end of the century, botanic gardens such as Boston's Arnold Arboretum would sponsor their own plant collectors, who traveled to Asia to bring back plants suitable for the American garden.

Historian Philip J. Pauly has written that nineteenth-century nurserymen were deeply involved in the work of selection, hybridization, and improvement of plants.[40] For example, by the end of the century the Reasoner Nursery in Florida had made significant contributions to botany and agriculture by introducing plant varieties that are still grown in the mild climates of America.[41]

Hovey stands as a particularly good example of plant improvement, for throughout his life he sought better plant varieties. As he wrote in his nursery catalog of 1849, "From the best sources in Europe, all the new and choice varieties have been procured." Philadelphia nurseryman Thomas Meehan agreed, saying, "Numbers of the best new plants and fruits were first introduced to the public from [Hovey's] nurseries and seed house in Boston."[42] Hovey's own fruit, the 'Hovey' strawberry, held a prominent place in the market for thirty years. Some claim that it was the start of the commercial sale of strawberries in this country.

Owners of commercial nurseries were not the only source of plant selection and improvement, however. At the historic English garden Chatsworth, the Duke of Devonshire collected orchids, which were housed in a glass house built by Paxton in 1834. Several orchids were named after Paxton and the duke. The glass house still stands on the original site.

The glass house is the most characteristic garden structure of the nineteenth century.[43] Plants such as orchids and camellias became popular for greenhouse cultivation for the wealthy, but by midcentury the cheap price of glass had come to allow even the middle class to overwinter plants in a glass house. At the end of the century, Cornell horticulturalist L. H. Bailey wrote, "Even the humblest gardener, if he is thrifty, can afford a green-house."[44]

By 1848 Hovey had built four greenhouses on his nursery grounds. One visitor wrote, "He erected one of the largest span-roofed houses in the country, being ninety-six feet long and thirty feet wide, chiefly for the growth of specimen plants."[45] His camellia collection had its own conservatory, called the Camellia House, which was eighty-four feet long and twenty-two feet wide.

Garden Publications

The English published several popular garden magazines in the nineteenth century. As Meehan wrote in his *Gardener's Monthly* of 1878, "The Horticultural, or as they are justly more proud of saying, the Gardening press of England, is a great power. On the tables of the most intelligent, although you might not anticipate any gardening proclivities, you may not be surprised to see the Gardener's Chronicle."[46] In 1844, *The Gardener's Chronicle* was proposed as a new English garden journal by John Lindley, a garden writer and botanist who headed Chelsea Physic Garden in London. Lindley offered this editorial evaluation of his market: "Gardening is admitted to be better understood in Great Britain than in any other country, and the number of works on the subject prove the patronage it receives, and the desire there is to extend the knowledge of its various branches."[47]

Lustig considers Loudon, Lindley, and Paxton the three great horticultural writers of mid-nineteenth-century England.[48] Although England created a stream of publications for the middle-class gardener, Loudon's was the first and most famous. It was for the businessman who gardened on the weekend, when he, too, could enjoy the pleasures of botany and horticulture, once solely the domain of the wealthy aristocrat.

The English gardening press maintained its influence but not its exclusivity, however: garden publications in England were soon imitated in America, with American seedsmen and nurserymen providing the lead. Hovey's publication, with the original name *The American Gardener's Magazine*, was America's first magazine devoted solely to horticulture. It remained in publication for thirty years. Though America published its own garden magazines, the country still relished the garden instruction from England. American nurseries and seed houses looked to England for garden inspiration and then passed that experience on to their customers in the catalogs, articles, and books they wrote.

Botanic Gardens

The Worshipful Society of Apothecaries founded London's Chelsea Physic Garden in 1673. Today its research continues to promote the study of the properties and origins of over five thousand plant species and encourages their conservation. In the eighteenth century, Phillip Miller was the garden's director; in the nineteenth century, Lindley and plant collector Robert Fortune took that role. The garden's purpose was, from the time of its origin, more scientific, that is, to study a plant's possible medicinal uses. Nonetheless, it set the stage for what botanic gardens would eventually become: gardens to educate the public in horticulture and botany.

Another notable example of a public botanic garden is Kew. Princess Augusta and the Earl of Bute, in the late 1700s, began Kew, the royal garden in London, to house plants that had been collected around the world and then labeled in a scientific manner. It became a public garden in 1841. By 1848 Kew had built its Palm House, which demonstrated to the public the use of glass to cultivate exotic palms throughout the year.

From the beginning, America, too, had its botanic gardens. In the eighteenth century, the Bartram Botanic Garden, located in Philadelphia, and the Linnaean Botanic Garden, founded by William Prince on Long Island, illustrated the importance of collecting plants and using their scientific names to identify them. Nurseryman Dr. David Hosack saw the importance of gardening for the public good. In 1801 he began the Elgin Botanic Garden in New York, located where Rockefeller Center now stands. Hovey's nursery

A Furor for Plants from England

*I*N HIS *Magazine of Horticulture,* in 1868, Hovey wrote about the new hybrid coleus:

Since the introduction of Coleus Vershaffeltii, with its rich deep colored foliage, it has formed a prominent object for bedding purposes, especially in England, where the style of ribbon borders had extensively prevailed. The introduction of another kind, called C. Veitchii, increased the taste of rich foliaged plants, and by the skill of the hybridizer, a great number of new sorts have been raised between these two, which seem to have attracted unusual attention, amounting almost to a furor for these plants. The successful grower of these hybrids was M. Bause, of the Chiswick garden, who has raised twelve of these seedlings. . . . All of these, or a portion of them, will no doubt find their way into American collections.[49]

sat on Cambridge Street not far from Harvard College, where a botanic garden was set up in 1805 and then replaced in 1872 by the Arnold Arboretum.

Though there were several garden styles in early American gardening, the English style would dominate in the nineteenth century in the sale of garden products and in the ideas expressed in garden publications. The seed and plant peddlers, such as Hovey, would provide the voice for that garden fashion in their catalogs, magazines, and books.

Hovey remained at the forefront of the gardening movement in this country for half a century. Over that time, his magazine and his catalogs reflected the evolution of American gardening. In the December 1886 issue of his magazine *Gardener's Monthly*, Philadelphia nurseryman Thomas Meehan said of Hovey, "Horticulture on this continent is probably more indebted to him than to any living man."[50] By then Hovey's camellia 'C. M. Hovey'—of which the English journal *Garden* said, "It has no peer, whether we take into consideration its size, growth, floriferousness, or the size, form, and color of the flowers"[51]—was growing in the Camellia House at the Royal Exotic Nursery in Chelsea. A year later, Hovey died and was buried near his home in Cambridge, in Mount Auburn, the parklike cemetery.

❧ ☙

FEATURED PLANT

Podophyllum peltatum / Mayapple

BECAUSE MY PROPERTY includes many trees, I am always on the hunt for shade-loving plants. The mayapple fits that description well. I grow it along the back of the house, which the nearby trees shade most of the day.

English garden writer William Robinson included this plant in his nineteenth-century classic *The Wild Garden* in a list of plants for naturalizing beneath trees. Robinson attacked the Victorian style of carpet bedding, which demanded high maintenance from the gardener. He preferred a

garden style with perennials like the mayapple. American nurserymen soon adopted Robinson's ideas as well.

Liberty Hyde Bailey refers to the native American plant *Podophyllum peltatum,* or mayapple, as a most desirable plant for the wild garden when planted in a colony.[52] The plant is an herb common in woods throughout the eastern United States.

The mayapple is a perennial that blooms starting midspring and continuing to late spring. The mayapple requires part shade to full shade, a medium amount of water, and little maintenance. It will reach a height between six and eighteen inches.

The leaf arrangement is opposite with only one to two leaves. Each plant has a single stalk topped with one or two broad, deeply divided leaves that vaguely resemble umbrellas. The fruit of the mayapple, hidden under the large leaves, is a berry that resembles a lime in shape. It is edible when ripened, but all other parts of the mayapple are toxic.

Since 1820 the mayapple has been recognized for its medicinal value. Native Americans used the root of the plant as a laxative to treat worms and other diseases. It was also used as an insecticide on crops. Today the root of the mayapple is used in certain cancer medications.

⁊ *(facing page)*
Podophyllum peltatum, mayapple

The English Garden Influence at Williamsburg

RUSTRATED WITH HIS family problems and his business, tobacco grower and member of the Governor's Council John Custis (1678–1749), of Williamsburg, Virginia, took up gardening as his escape. He said, "I have a pretty little garden in which I take more satisfaction than in anything in this world."[1] Custis looked to England for plants for his garden. In the process he would develop a twenty-year friendship with Englishman Peter Collinson.

Like many other eighteenth-century English gardeners, Peter Collinson and his friend Lord Petre, who cultivated one of the largest collections of plants from around the world, sought to add more American plants to their gardens. Collinson corresponded with John Custis, and the two men exchanged plants for twelve years, from 1734 through 1746. Collinson shared the seeds and plants with Petre and his other "Brothers of the Spade," a name he used to refer to his fellow gardeners.

Williamsburg provides an early example of the English garden influence in America: English gardeners inspired the landscape design for the town and wrote the garden literature the town's citizens read. Additionally, gardeners in colonies such as Williamsburg came to depend on seeds and plants from England.

Collinson, for example, shipped the latest in English garden fashion, though often the seeds would not germinate or the ship captain killed the plants by overwatering. Custis's letters tell us that sometimes problems ranging from high temperature to winds to Williamsburg's proximity to the sea prevented the seeds from germinating. Indeed, the double tulips, the lily of the valley, and the crown imperials sent by Collinson failed to come up for Custis in the spring of 1738.

Despite such failures, Custis managed to cultivate a four-acre garden on Francis Street, where he grew the newest varieties of plants in an English garden style that was more formal than naturalistic. His gift plants from England included Chinese aster and globe thistle. Letters from Collinson often mention the seeds and plants shipped to Custis's garden, including a box of "Horse Chestnuts, and peach stones of the Double Blossoms."[2]

Custis wanted to keep his garden full of the newest plant varieties. For that he looked to England. In turn, he sent Collinson plants from Virginia such as the dogwood and laurel. And so Custis and Collinson, too, became "Brothers of the Spade."

The Landscape and Garden of the Colonies

Williamsburg exemplifies colonial gardening before the focal period of this book, the 1800s. The colonies along the East Coast shared a common heritage in their gardens, and so there were striking similarities.[3] Williamsburg illustrates for us the prevailing early colonial landscape design, the sources for seeds and plants for the garden, and the garden literature important for that time. Though seeds and plants in nineteenth-century industrialized America would come from commercial houses, whose owners would write garden books and publish garden magazines, the decades before the start of the nineteenth century showcase a garden style that was already dependent on English plants and English garden writers.

English colonists first arrived in Virginia in 1607, at Jamestown. By the eighteenth century Williamsburg had become an important political and cultural center as well as a center of gardening activity.[4] Although in the mid-eighteenth century the landscape design of England was changing to a more natural, picturesque style, the gardens of Williamsburg retained the older seventeenth-century English landscape style, which featured a more formal and geometric look.

Lieutenant Governor Francis Nicholson's plan for the original Williamsburg in the early eighteenth century is still largely intact. The town boasts a series of broad, straight streets with impressive public buildings, including the Governor's Palace and the Capitol. This material has been used to superb effect in the restoration of Colonial Williamsburg. This privately managed living museum today covers more than three hundred acres and includes about one hundred gardens. The gardens provide a key to understanding how later styles of nineteenth-century English picturesque American gardening contrast with the older formal English style of Williamsburg.

In the 1930s, Boston landscape architect Arthur Shurcliff, who previously had worked with American landscape pioneer Frederick Law Olmsted, re-created the landscape of the Governor's Palace. Its geometric garden runs along a central north–south axis. Today its restored landscape (fig. 2.1) includes rows of boxwood shrubs and other evergreens, perfectly pruned, reflecting the English formal style. Behind each of the houses that lined the streets is a series of gardens. The garden style is mainly one of linear symmetry.

The settlers did not choose the more open, naturalistic garden made popular through the influence of landscape designers such as Capability Brown, whose ideas dominated from the 1750s to the 1780s.[5] Brown's preferences replaced the more formal, geometric design the English had enjoyed for decades. John Custis, who took pride in his carefully trimmed shrub-

🌿 *Figure 2.1.* The formal landscape of the Governor's Palace at Colonial Williamsburg illustrates England's early eighteenth-century landscape design.

bery, admitted that his landscape taste was not the modern, or more natural, design.

A Williamsburg garden took on a more formal design, and like older English gardens, it had to be enclosed within a wall, fence, or hedge. In fact, colonial law eventually required that fences be built around each lot. While the garden plots throughout the town were limited in space because of the unpredictable and often threatening environment, an enclosed garden provided safety and gave the colonists more control over what they were growing.

Plants

The colonial gardener displayed his wealth through the number of English plants represented in the garden. The garden also demonstrated the gardener's identification with England, where the colonists felt the most important plants could be found. Donald Wyman, horticulturist at Boston's Arnold Arboretum from 1935 to 1970, wrote that before 1752 English plants such as the horse chestnut, European birch, cedar of Lebanon, English beech, English holly, Scotch pine, European linden, and English elm were thriving in Williamsburg.[6]

In the American colonies, the seventeenth-century gardens had been almost totally what garden historian Ann Leighton once called "relevant":[7] they existed to feed, clothe, clean, cure, and comfort the settlers. The primary way people engaged with plants was as a source of food and medicine. Farming and growing crops of various vegetables served the basic need for food. Until the late eighteenth century, the colonists seldom had time for more than utilitarian gardens with simple flower and herb beds.[8]

When the colonists arrived and settled in Williamsburg, they, of course, wanted to garden. The vegetation they encountered there, however, was unlike anything they had known in England. English gardens depended on the mild, damp climate of the British Isles,[9] and the look and style of these Old World gardens were rooted in a particular ecology. Although the climate of Virginia differed drastically from England's, that did not deter the colonists, for the English had long believed that their gardens were the best in the world.

The colonists wanted their plants from home—so they brought plants with them, such as the English ivy (though they also used the native plants found in the region). The dandelion, for example, came from Europe and was used as a green for cooking. Today's popular ground cover for shade, vinca, or creeping myrtle, was brought here as well.

The majority of fruit trees came to Virginia from the Old World, where they had been grown in English gardens for hundreds of years.[10] The fruits introduced from England included the apple, plum, pear, peach, cherry, apricot, nectarine, and quince. The quince, for example, was brought to Virginia from England in 1648. For a century it was a more popular fruit than apples or pears, which had been introduced by the French missionaries and then adopted by the Indians. Cultivating fruit would become the major form of horticulture for American gardeners in the early to mid-nineteenth century when C. M. Hovey's magazine provided an important resource for fruit growers, covering cultivation, insect issues, and the countless new varieties.

Europeans introduced peas, cabbage, carrots, beets, and most leaf vegetables. The potato, a South American native plant, is believed to have been introduced to North America from England in 1565, when John Hawkins brought it to Virginia. It eventually became popular in Europe when, in Germany in 1710, it became an important food crop. The story is the same with rhubarb and the strawberry, which were brought to North America from Europe. The tomato came to Virginia in the late 1700s from Jamaica. By the nineteenth century it had become a staple for the table. There were also marigolds, both the African and the French varieties, first brought to England from Mexico, and later to the colonies.

Conversely, Native Americans introduced many plants to the English colonists. Among these was tobacco, a native plant that by 1650 had become the major crop in Virginia; tobacco was harvested, dried, and sent to England. Native Americans also introduced the colonists to peppers, maize, beans, pumpkins, and squash.

Williamsburg today has over five hundred kinds of cultivated plants, either indigenous to Virginia or introduced from abroad during the seventeenth, eighteenth, and early nineteenth centuries.[11] Cultivated native trees included the catalpa and the black locust. Plants within Williamsburg sometimes came from nearby plantations, for there was a strong relationship between the horticultural practices on the plantations and the gardens of Williamsburg. Thomas Jefferson, for example, received swamp mallow from marshes near the town and a fine apple tree from the garden of George Wythe's house in Williamsburg.[12] The fruit of that tree, he wrote, "was the most juicy apple I have ever known . . . very refreshing as an eating apple."

The plants of colonial-era Williamsburg were thus a collection of both imported and native plants, reflecting the influences of English, French, and Spanish colonists as well as Native Americans. The gardens of Williamsburg were so distinctive that people even traveled to the town to see them.[13]

The Gardens of Williamsburg

In Williamsburg, raised beds were the preferred way of planting herbs and flowers because this was also the old method of gardening in England. In addition, the wealthy had extensive parterres, topiary, and terraces, as reflected in the garden design at the Governor's Palace. The lots at Williamsburg were half an acre, one acre, or two acres in size, with the landscape design extending in straight lines from the centrally located building. The straight lines catered to the practical needs of the gardener, especially in simplifying the maintenance of fruiting plants, vegetables, and herbs.

The influence of the English garden style held strong well into the nineteenth century, when Americans began to develop their own way of gardening while remaining dependent on the English style. Garden historian and landscape architect Rudy Favretti maintains that the formal geometric style of Colonial garden design can be dated from 1620 until 1840 because design did not change significantly during that period.[14]

After Richmond became Virginia's capital in 1780, Williamsburg, Virginia's previous capital, was forgotten until the early part of the twentieth century, when it assumed its role as an important site of America's history. In the 1920s, Williamsburg was, in a sense, rediscovered when the creation of Colonial Williamsburg was begun with the restoration of the buildings and the gardens. In the process, landscape architects researched what colonial gardens looked like. Their resources included letters and deeds but also incorporated garden designs from other cities of that period. The garden design of Colonial Williamsburg, though reconstructed in the twentieth century, displays distinct English characteristics from the earlier period.

Today a visitor to Colonial Williamsburg can see what colonial gardening was like for both the commoner and the wealthy class.[15] The style in the gardens, as well as the buildings, is called Colonial Revivalism, a reconstruction of the eighteenth-century design of the home and garden. Though the style was produced in the previous century, some have, perhaps rightly, criticized it as a twentieth-century interpretation.

Some of the colonial plants were native, but most were imported, primarily from England. There were no American seed companies or nurseries offering catalogs yet. If a seed company—such as the David Landreth Seed Company, which emerged in Philadelphia in 1794—printed anything for marketing its seeds, the document was usually a small circular or a handbill. The residents of Williamsburg might have purchased plants through the Prince or Bartram nurseries, two of the earliest eighteenth-century American gardening enterprises, but they had no involvement with the American seed companies and nurseries that would become national businesses in the nineteenth century. Any commercial seeds they planted, except for those few that they saved from the previous harvest, came mainly from English seed companies that exported to America.[16]

Commercial Sources for Seeds and Plants

America's additions to the gardens of England during the colonial period were mainly trees, flowering shrubs, and vines. The English perennial garden is also indebted to America for many of its plants, such as the black-eyed Susan (*Rudbeckia hirta*), bee balm (*Monarda didyma*), coreopsis, goldenrod, garden phlox (*Phlox paniculata*), and the cardinal flower, which Robert Beverley praised in his book on the history of Virginia. Eventually, these plants would return to become part of American perennial beds, but only after American seedsmen and nurserymen began to sell them. Early among these American commercial garden enterprises of the eighteenth century are Bartram's botanical garden at Kingsessing, near Philadelphia, and the Prince Nursery on Long Island.

Having been encouraged to collect native American plants, John Bartram in 1725 started a business selling his plants. The name "Bartram" was synonymous with botany and horticulture in the fledgling United States, and the Bartram garden became known around the world as a source for American plants.[17] Though most of Bartram's plant sales went to Europe, he insisted on the importance of his plants for American gardens as well, his belief serving as an early plea to American gardeners to use native plants. When the senior Bartram died in 1777, his sons continued the work to the end of the century, traveling the country to find plants and also carrying on their father's tradition of practical gardening. In 1783, the Bartrams produced a broadside, or catalog, of plants and seeds available for sale from their garden. The garden, referred to as "America's oldest botanical garden," can still be seen, along with the Bartram house.

One particular bit of travel, to visit John Custis in Williamsburg (encouraged by Collinson, who corresponded with Bartram and received plants from him), proved a gardener's delight for Bartram. He had been instructed by Collinson, who, because he wanted Bartram to impress Custis, made suggestions regarding what to wear and how to act. Custis received him with much hospitality, and Bartram, who would never forget that visit, spent two days and one night. Bartram found the garden to be one of the best he had ever seen. Later Collinson wrote to Custis, "Your Intended Kindness to J. Bartram on my accountt [*sic*] is an Act of Real Fr'ship."[18]

Prince Nursery, the second early American commercial source of plants that must be mentioned, was operated from 1737 to 1850 by successive generations of the Prince family. The company issued its first catalog of fruit trees and shrubs in 1771. Because imported stock was essential in the early nursery and seed trade, the firm sold imported fruit trees, ornamental woody plants, and bulbs.[19] The Prince Nursery supplied seeds and plants to cities and towns along the East Coast and also shipped them to Europe. Notables such as Thomas Jefferson made selections from Prince's extensive catalog. Among the items sold were fruit trees—including plum, apricot, nectarine, peach, pear, mulberry, and apple—some of which were propagated by Prince.

A few smaller seed and nursery companies at that time also made important contributions to American gardens. By 1790, the gardeners of Williamsburg had a local commercial nursery, Bellett's, where Jefferson bought plants. Bellett specialized in ornamental gardening, importing most of his plant varieties from London.[20]

While the rich of Williamsburg may have had plants shipped to them from England, the cottager, or working-class gardener, depended mainly on seeds. However, the American commercial seed business spread by the mid-nineteenth century, when printing, increased transportation, improved postal service, and the Shakers' invention of the seed packet enabled gardeners to order their seeds through a free catalog. The general availability of plants increased as more American seed companies and nurseries opened in the nineteenth century. By 1870, there were dozens of companies scattered along the East Coast, in cities such as Philadelphia, Rochester, and Boston, as well as new businesses on the West Coast, in cities such as San Francisco.

Garden Books

During America's eighteenth-century colonial period there were few garden books, except titles from English writers who discussed gardening in the soil and growing conditions of England, not America. Few American seed companies or nurseries yet printed catalogs; no American newspapers or magazines published garden articles.

A popular information source for gardeners was a friend, as with Custis and his correspondence with Collinson, or a family member with whom a person might trade plants or seeds. Any reading by the more educated was based on an occasional book written by an English author. Personal memories of gardening in England also provided inspiration to the colonists.

The landscape architect and Williamsburg scholar Ian Robertson compiled a list of important English garden books on which the American colonial gardener depended in the eighteenth century.[21] The books include

The Compleat English Gardner, published in 1670 (with many subsequent editions), by Leonard Meager (1624–70). Meager referred to himself as a practitioner of the art of gardening for thirty years. He wrote for "young planters and gardeners" and covered fruiting plants, trees, shrubs, and the kitchen garden, as well as the flower garden, which he called the "garden of pleasure."[22]

Philip Miller was another popular garden author in England. His book, *Gardeners Dictionary,* was printed in London in 1731 and was reprinted several times, with later editions including double the number of plants mentioned in earlier versions. Many considered it the most important garden book in eighteenth-century England; that it was also popular with American colonists is not surprising.[23] Miller covered many garden questions but also wrote about using American plants in the English garden. These included trees, because they were "useful and beautiful" when "added to our wildernesses and other plantations."[24] In 1768, the eighth edition, he mentioned the black-eyed Susan, or *Rudbeckia hirta,* which he wrote "grows naturally in Virginia, and several other parts of North America."[25]

Among the many who read the work of Englishman Thomas Whatley, author of *Observations on Modern Gardening,* published in 1770, was Thomas Jefferson. Whatley discussed the importance of the popular naturalistic view of landscape, which Jefferson later employed in designing Monticello. This same style would later become the primary English landscape design promoted in the American seed and nursery catalogs of the nineteenth century.

The English poet Alexander Pope (1688–1744) also inspired Williamsburg's gardeners. English views of the natural landscape were aligned with the arts of poetry and painting, and the English at that time particularly relished the horticultural and agricultural ideas of the classical Latin authors. In a 1713 article in the *Guardian,* Pope praised the Roman poet Homer's enclosed garden of four acres, mentioning the trees, the fruits that never failed, the vineyard, and, at the extremity of the enclosed area, the kitchen garden. Pope noted, "How contrary to this simplicity is the modern practice of gardening."[26]

For Pope the "modern" form of gardening included topiaries: the heavily pruned and unusual shapes of shrubs and trees. Using his own garden as an example, he indicated his preference for a natural look to the landscape. He wrote, "Persons of genius and those who are most capable of art, are always most fond of Nature."[27] Pope inspired English landscape writers and designers with his preference for the picturesque view. That view later became important in nineteenth-century American landscape design through the writings of Andrew Jackson Downing.[28]

English garden writers Robert Bradley, John Abercrombie, William Marshall, and Charles Marshall were also popular in the colonies.[29] The first edition of John Abercrombie and Thomas Mawe's *Every Man His Own Gardener* was issued in 1767. Mawe was "gardener to his Grace the Duke of Leeds" and Abercrombie a "gardener" in Newington, Surry.

The English books presupposed farms of large acreage with existing well-cultivated grounds and the services of at least one well-trained gardener. Many of the plants discussed, however, were not available; procedures advised were not appropriate for the soils and climates of North America; and many topics were simply of no value to settlers engaged in the struggles of colonizing.

For these and other reasons, the need for American works on gardening became more apparent during the late eighteenth century.[30] After 1820, farm journal publications began to appear in many states. Such journals were written for the dirt farmer and gentleman farmer alike, both of whom were facing a climate different from that of England. But a handful of American books that preceded those journals established the foundation for American farming and gardening literature.

The first American treatise on agriculture was written by Jared Eliot, a minister, physician, and farmer from Killingworth, Connecticut.[31] His book, *Essays upon Field Husbandry,* appeared between 1747 and 1759. He wrote in the preface, "There are many sundry books on husbandry wrote in England. Having read all on that subject I could obtain, yet such is the difference of climate and method of management between them and us, arising from causes that make them always differ, so that those books are not useful to us."[32]

A few decades after Eliot's book, circa 1788, John Randolph, a lawyer and resident of Williamsburg, wrote the first American book on kitchen or vegetable gardening, *Treatise on Gardening,* which became popular among Williamsburg colonists. Before he wrote the book, he practiced Miller's garden instructions for several years to adapt English methods to the Virginian conditions. The book is mostly a list of plants, primarily vegetables but also herbs such as mugwort and artemisia. At the end of his book, he included a calendar with garden duties for each month.

Samuel Deane, vice president of Bowdoin College, presented a dictionary of farming terms in *The New England Farmer,* published in 1797. He wrote, "Americans speak the English language, yet the diction peculiar to different farmers on the east and west of the Atlantick, and the manner of their communicating their ideas on husbandry are so little alike, as to render it highly expedient that we should be instructed by our own countrymen, rather than by strangers."[33] It seemed to him that English writers had instructed American gardeners for far too long. Deane focused his book on farming in North America, specifically in New England, to address the lack of such information. He wrote not for the wealthy landowner but for farmworkers, so they could understand the importance of applying certain agricultural techniques.

One of the most popular early nineteenth-century books on gardening published in America was John Gardiner and David Hepburn's *American Gardener* (1804). Hepburn gardened for twenty years in England and for the next twenty years in America. He partnered with Gardiner, who was skilled enough in horticulture to write this practical manual, which gave great detail about the kitchen garden and also discussed the importance of flowers for the home landscape. The book appealed to the American gardener who had a small home lot.

Not specifically a gardening book but showing the importance of gardening was *The History and Present State of Virginia, in Four Parts,* written by Robert Beverley, the son of a Virginia planter. His purpose in writing this book was to lure English citizens to the new land. In it he discussed the plants that were native to the area and their value, which included nuts, berries, flowering trees such as the tuliptree, muskmelons and watermelons, corn, and potatoes—all well known to the residents of Williamsburg. Beverley said, "A kitchen garden don't thrive better or faster in any part of the Universe than here."[34] The garden included herbs and vegetables from England, but he argued that they grew better in Virginia. These gardens also contained native Virginia fruits and herbs.

Although books to instruct the gardener in colonies such as Williamsburg were primarily the work of English authors, the nineteenth century opened the door for American gardening writers such as Charles Mason Hovey and Andrew Jackson Downing, who, like so many other garden writers of that time, were also the owners of seed houses or nurseries.

❦

Because of his wealth and connections in England, where he had attended school, John Custis was able to receive the latest seeds and plants for his garden, which many claimed was the best garden in all of Williamsburg. Though many of his imports failed to grow, he never gave up asking Collinson for the newest variety of plant. He imported more European plants into the Tidewater region of Virginia than anyone else.

Through several growing seasons, Custis learned the lesson important to every gardener: persistence and patience mark the journey. Custis enjoyed his garden, which, according to some, was graced with the best collection of lilacs in America. Custis wrote to Collinson, "I am att [sic] a loss what Returns or acknowledgements to Make you for your Many Favours." The plants Custis sent and the splendid garden he tended in Williamsburg were thanks enough to Collinson.

George Washington, who married John Custis's daughter-in-law, Martha, after her husband died, years later spent a night at the Custis home. By then John Custis was gone, but Washington, a gardener himself, likely enjoyed the plants, both native and from England, in a garden that many once considered the best in Williamsburg.

🌺 *Rudbeckia hirta*, black-eyed Susan

🌺 🌺

Rudbeckia hirta / Black-Eyed Susan

As I walk around my garden in late summer, I see the yellow flowers of *Rudbeckia hirta,* or black-eyed Susan, popping out of crevices in the rocks that form a wall near the lamppost. How they get there I do not know, but every year they appear.

From the seventeenth century on, the English perennial garden included plants from America. This plant is native to eastern North America and was first sent to England in 1714. It appeared in the Bartram listing of native American plants in 1783, which was during the period when colonial

Williamsburg's gardens attained their prominence. In the nineteenth century, *Rudbeckia hirta* returned to become part of American gardens when American seedsmen and nurserymen offered it in their catalogs. Philadelphia's Robert Buist sold it in his 1845 catalog for twenty-five cents.

Linnaeus, the Swedish naturalist, named the flower *Rudbeckia* after Olav Rudbeck and his son, who were both professors at the University of Uppsala. In 1918 the black-eyed Susan became Maryland's official flower when it was designated the "Floral Emblem" of Maryland by the General Assembly. The story is told that its common name, black-eyed Susan, may refer to a Susan in England searching for her long-lost love, William.

The word *hirta*, the designation of the largest group from the twenty-five species of *Rudbeckia*s, means "hairy" and refers to the short, stiff hairs on the stem. The black-eyed Susan is very easy to care for and has no special needs. However, it does best—growing two feet in height—when it is in well-drained soil and full sun. Its leaves are diamond-shaped, have three prominent veins, and reach four to seven inches in length. The yellow flower with the dark center blooms from June through August, and it can be annual, perennial, or biennial. It is often confused with the sunflower. This plant is usually found in dry fields, roadsides, prairies, and open woods.

Early Wealthy Americans and
Their English Landscapes

ANKER JOSEPH SHIPLEY felt the pain from gout run through his body. When confined in his chair near the window, he enjoyed looking out at the extensive lawn and trees in the picturesque landscape outside his Liverpool home. Though his English landscape gave him some consolation, his illness often made him think about returning to his native America.

Shipley wrote to his nephew, requesting that he purchase on Shipley's behalf the Weldin property in his hometown of Wilmington, Delaware. To his English friends it was no surprise, therefore, that in 1851, at the age of fifty-six, Shipley set sail for America, where he would retire and build the estate he called Rockwood.

After he arrived in America, Shipley could have read Cambridge nurseryman C. M. Hovey's 1850 seed catalog, for on the inside front cover Hovey recommended the English picturesque landscape style: "The cultivation of ornamental trees and shrubs is rapidly increasing, and with the increasing taste, a desire to possess a greater variety than has usually been enumerated in catalogues in this country. The publication of that magnificent work, the *Arboretum Britannicum,* by the late Mr. Loudon, has made known a vast number of trees and shrubs, which, through the exertions of foreign collectors, have been introduced into Great Britain and the Continent and have already added so much to the embellishment of their gardens and grounds. A great portion of these being perfectly hardy, their introduction into our grounds is an object of great importance." Hovey encouraged his readers to use exotic, imported plants in the home landscape to replicate the style of the English garden.

Shipley built his Delaware landscape in that English fashion. He provides an example of the early period of American gardening, when wealthy businessmen, with English garden books to guide them, chose to design their home landscape in the English manner. They would, however, buy their seeds and plants from an American company.

There had been no seed or plant catalogs in colonial Williamsburg, and inspiration for gardening came from English writers. That began to change during the nineteenth century, especially after 1870, when a large commercial trade in seeds and plants emerged, centered on the East Coast. While most Americans would continue to regard gardens primarily as a source of food and medical supplies, the wealthy could enjoy a landscape designed and planted as an art form. However, even though the words and images of the new catalogs opened up a world of possibilities to American gardeners, the inspiration remained the same: the tradition of the English garden.

The English Picturesque Design Comes to America

Eighteenth-century English garden designers such as William Kent, Capability Brown, and Humphry Repton promoted landscape designs that rejected the earlier formal geometric plan. Their encouragement of the naturalistic, or picturesque, garden design was widely accepted in England. The word *picturesque* refers to a painter's view of the landscape, and such a landscape was intended to resemble what a landscape painter would put on the canvas: a glimpse of untouched nature. These landscape designers' rejection of earlier garden fashions went beyond the figurative; in an act that angered some clients who had spent considerable money on a formal garden design, Brown often leveled a garden to make the land conform to this more naturalistic view—for example, adding grading for terraces and an expansive lawn.

James Kornwolf divides the picturesque landscape into three phases, which appeared one after another in eighteenth-century England. The first phase emphasized formal features and a variety of garden buildings in numerous styles, such as temples and grottos (for example, Alexander Pope at Twickenham, William Kent at Rousham Park); the second phase featured clumps of trees, artificial knolls, and serpentine ponds or lakes, often with islands (Capability Brown at Blenheim); the third phase generally stressed very natural settings and sweeps of turf with a minimum of "artificial" features.[1]

The picturesque style did not remain in England, however; wealthy Americans such as Joseph Shipley used its design principles to inspire their own gardens, designed and built in the manner of an English country home, with a lawn, trees, and shrubs. Such an estate sometimes served as a second home for a wealthy merchant who lived most of the year in the city.

The French immigrant Andre Parmentier, both a nurseryman and a landscape designer, was particularly notable in introducing the English style of landscape on the East Coast during the first part of the nineteenth century. Parmentier chose that design for his clients with properties along the lower Hudson River, outside New York City. He said that in America the landscape for the home needed to be more natural, not focused on an undue regard for symmetry: "Our ancestors gave to every part of a garden all the exactness of geometric forms. They seem to have known of no other way to plant trees, except in straight lines, a system totally ruinous to the beauty of the prospect. We now see how ridiculous it was."[2] His was an early voice for the naturalistic English picturesque style of landscape and garden on American soil.

The Gardenesque Style

English plantsman, designer, and writer John Claudius Loudon first used the term *gardenesque* in 1832, in his garden journal *Gardener's Magazine.* After traveling to France and Italy, he realized the importance of plant collections and wanted to accommodate such plants in the landscape. He proposed a style of gardening that would show off a collection of plants and also allow for a bit of formality.

Though Loudon originated the term *gardenesque* to describe his modern view of landscape, English landscape designer Edward Kemp also used it in his own book, written in 1850. Loudon wrote that there were three kinds of landscaping: formal, gardenesque, and picturesque.[3] For the rest of the nineteenth century, several American seed companies and nurseries used the same threefold division in their annual catalogs to instruct readers in how to landscape around the home.

In the gardenesque style, trees, shrubs, and flowers—often nonnative —would be planted carefully, so that one plant did not touch another. The idea was to create informal gardens that were, however, as obviously manmade as were formal gardens, so that the landscape would appear as a work of art. The landscape became an artistic display for a collection of plants that were often assembled from around the world.

Joseph Shipley of Delaware

Shipley, a member of one of the leading Quaker families of Wilmington, sailed to England in 1823 to run the Liverpool office of a banking firm called James Welch (the name would later change to Shipley, Welch, and Co.) that financed the shipment of cotton to England. Shipley remained in England for over twenty-five years, at a job that created enough wealth to purchase the land in Delaware and to design and build the house and landscape of his dreams. His home and landscape at Wyncote, whose design featured the parklike, more naturalistic use of trees and shrubs, clearly show that Shipley had firsthand experience of the modern English garden.

The British architect George Williams designed Shipley's house. Williams had earlier worked with the horticulturalist and landscaper Joseph Paxton on Liverpool's Prince's Park, designed by Paxton in 1842. Additionally, he had worked with both Paxton and Kemp on Birkenhead Park. He too was familiar with the current fashion of landscape gardening.

Shipley purchased the Levi Weldin farm in Wilmington, a property with distinctive cliffs, trees, and a view of the Delaware River. He also bought adjoining parcels, creating an estate of 382 acres. He named his new estate Rockwood. The house, built between 1851 and 1857, was both a re-creation of his English home and an expression of the Rural Gothic style, popular in the United States after 1841 (fig. 3.1).[4] That style, associated also with the picturesque view of nature, had been important in England earlier, when the Gothic Revival formed an expression of the Romantic age. The house featured a conservatory, a gate lodge, an extensive lawn, a kitchen garden, a carriage house, an orchard, a gardener's cottage, and acres of farm and woodland.

Shipley's Garden Books

Shipley's garden books included works by landscape designers Edward Kemp and Andrew Jackson Downing. While the wealthy in Europe were educated about landscape through reading and travel (including visiting gardens), wealthy Americans, too, traveled to Europe with the same intention. They also read English garden books.

Kemp's landscape ideas inspired the design of Rockwood. Kemp became superintendent of Birkenhead Park, which impressed Frederick Law Olmsted on his travels to England well before his Central Park picturesque design took shape. Borrowing ideas from Kemp's book *How to Lay Out Home Gardens,* Shipley transformed Rockwood into an English country estate in an English garden setting.

Figure 3.1. Rockwood was built in the Gothic style, popular in the first half of the nineteenth century.

Kemp would continue to be an important voice influencing landscape in America for decades. In 1877, Meehan wrote in his magazine *Gardener's Monthly,* "We would particularly recommend at this season of the year a consultation of works on taste in landscape gardening with a view to improvement in this respect. Of these there are Downing, Kemp, and Scott, within the reach of every one."[5]

Born to a small community, early on Kemp showed interest in designing gardens. When he was old enough to work, he started training under Paxton. In 1858, Kemp judged the New York Central Park Competition, selecting the now-famous Olmsted and Calvert Vaux design. With his book, Kemp made Paxton's ideas available to the masses. Paxton, first a rival and then a friend of Loudon's, published the magazine *Garden,* which was read by American seed and nursery owners, who would sometimes refer to it in their catalog.

Downing also inspired Shipley, who owned two copies of Downing's book *A Treatise on the Theory and Practice of Landscape Gardening.* Downing devoted a section of the book to the Gothic style of home building, which he admired as beautiful and picturesque.

Downing distinguished between landscape design for a cottage and for a villa, representing different social classes: one for the middle class and the other for the wealthy. Though he sought to provide inspiration for the emerging middle class, his appeal throughout the century would be to the wealthier estate owner. The rural architect Lewis Allen wrote, "Mr. Downing's Designs and Plans are too expensive for general use among this class [the mechanic and farming community] of persons; they will do for what are termed gentlemen farmers, and mechanics, who work, if at all, in gloves."[6] The wealthy could afford their own landscape designers, such as William Webster of Rochester, New York; Jacob Weidenmann from Hartford; Olmsted and Vaux; and, later in the century, Charles A. Platt.

Shipley was familiar with the landscape design principles of Loudon's *Encyclopedia of Gardening.*[7] Loudon made collecting plants for the landscape an important part of gardenesque design. Rockwood's historian Lawrence Elliott Lee referred to the estate's style of gardening as a gardenesque landscape.[8]

Sources for Rockwood's Plants

Even while in England, Shipley had known the value of American trees for the landscape, and he had planted several of them in his Wyncote landscape. He later purchased trees and shrubs for his Rockwood landscape from several East Coast nurseries. The orders, placed in 1857, included plants from the Robert Buist Company of Philadelphia. More were ordered in 1852 from the Mount Hope Nurseries, owned by Henry Ellwanger and Patrick Barry of Rochester, New York. The majority of the plants for the Rockwood gardens were obtained from American sources.[9]

Nursery receipts show that Shipley ordered his plants in two stages. First, he chose the plants for the landscape away from the house. Later, after the house was built, he ordered plants for the area around the house. By 1861 the gardens were well established.

The nurseries Shipley used featured both native and exotic plants from around the world. Because the companies offered such plants and encouraged patrons to use them, they encouraged the English gardenesque design, which featured collections of plants.

A bill dated 1852 from Ashton Nurseries listed the plants the nursery supplied to Shipley. The trees and shrubs numbered 103, along with twenty-five yards of dwarf boxwood, probably used for bordering the beds of the kitchen garden. The trees ordered included sugar maple, mahonia, willow, American linden, Norway spruce, and American holly. Shrubs chosen were viburnum and American arborvitae. The total bill came to $75.10. The owner, Hancock, in handwriting at the bottom of the bill, apologized to Shipley that he was unable to supply white oak, pitch pine, and cherry trees.

The orders from Ashton Nurseries also included the European larch and the Norway spruce. Today an old *Viburnum prunifolium* still stands on the property. A European larch and a Norway spruce, two large trees, stood near the terrace at the side of the house until twenty years ago.[10]

The Ashton plants also included the shrub *Weigela rosea,* a plant native to China and introduced to England in 1845 by the Scottish plant collector Robert Fortune. Downing recommended it in his magazine *The Horticulturist* in both 1848 and 1850. Because Shipley wanted colorful shrubs for his landscape, it is no surprise that he ordered four *Weigela rosea* shrubs. Though newly arrived from England, the weigela proved a popular landscape shrub for the American Victorian garden.

Shipley also ordered *Robinia hispida,* or rose acacia, also called bristly locust, a native plant that had been used by the colonists. It was listed in Bartram's 1783 broadsheet of native plants.

In 1838, the Philadelphia, Wilmington and Baltimore Railroad opened. By 1852 the Delaware Railroad Company had its tracks ready for the new rail cars. Shipley's plants were thus delivered to Rockwood by wagon, boat, and rail.

Laying Out the Grounds at Rockwood

Shipley developed a passion for his plants. At a time when horticultural societies were growing both in England and in America, Shipley was elected second vice president of the Delaware Horticultural Society, just one year after he returned to the country.

He knew the plants he wanted and where they were to be placed in the landscape. The trees and shrubs were grouped in the Rockwood landscape by species and size. The form of the tree, whether round or oblong, was placed to achieve a desired effect. Plants with various colors and types of leaves were arranged to produce complementary patterns throughout the season.[11]

Rockwood had several flowerbeds around the house, including outside the library. Thus, people from inside the house, as well as others in the garden area itself, would be able to enjoy the color of the flowers. The kitchen garden, located north of the kitchen entrance, was laid out in geometric form, much like the English-style colonial kitchen gardens at Williamsburg. An orchard was laid out north of the Rockwood kitchen garden. Here Shipley produced fruits, as well as grapes with which to produce wine for the table.

Just as Hovey had suggested, Shipley took inspiration for his landscape from the predominant English gardening style. Shipley brought Robert Salisbury, his gardener from England, to maintain the landscape. In keeping with the English style represented at Wyncote, a ha-ha was constructed near the house.

A ha-ha is a containing wall made by mounding earth to create a dip in the grading of the land, prohibiting any animal from coming close to the house or garden. Grass was planted in the dip and on the mound, which from a distance then gave the illusion of an unbroken line of lawn. Charles

Bridgeman of Stowe, England, an eighteenth-century garden designer and a pioneer of the English naturalistic school, is credited with the concept. Loudon, Kemp, and Downing mention the ha-ha as a solution to a problem area on the lawn. Although such a grass fence is quite common in England, it was apparently unique in Delaware.[12] The large, sweeping lawn, however, was an integral part of the then-fashionable English design.

Though Rockwood included a lawn, Middleton Place in South Carolina claims the first American picturesque lawn, installed in the eighteenth century. The use of the lawn as a more accepted landscape element for the middle class did not appear much before the Civil War in America.[13] When it did appear earlier as part of the landscape, it was most often seen in the Northeast on the property of the wealthy, such as the Lyman property near Boston that Hovey praised for its modern design.

Rockwood likewise received praise. The 1859 edition of Downing's book *A Treatise on the Theory and Practice of Landscape Gardening* included this brief mention: "Near Wilmington, Del., is the fine place of Mr. Shiply [*sic*]."[14] A few years later, *Gardener's Monthly,* Meehan's journal, featured a glowing review of the Rockwood gardens: "Without the aid of photographs, an artist, and an engraver, we could scarcely hope to convey any just idea of it. The estate comprises some five hundred acres of romantic hill and valley, mostly covered with natural trees, and apparently surrounded by forests."[15] Shipley must have been delighted when Meehan recognized its English inspiration. Meehan wrote, "It is the most splendid specimen of the English park-like style of landscape work that we have ever seen."

Other Estates and Landscapes of the Wealthy

Downing, in his book on landscape design, said, "The number of individuals among us who possess wealth and refinement sufficient to enable them to enjoy the pleasure of country life is every day increasing. And although, until lately, a very meager plan of laying out the grounds of the residence, was all that we could lay claim to, yet the taste for elegant rural improvement is now advancing rapidly."[16] At the same time that Shipley designed an estate and landscape in the new form of rural art, other Americans were planning for their own properties. In Missouri another wealthy businessman, Henry Shaw, also designed and built an estate whose landscape embodied the English garden style.

Shaw, an Englishman who settled in St. Louis, became an American citizen in 1843. His business importing English tools, along with his real estate investments, made Shaw a rich man. His gift to St. Louis, located not far from downtown, was his nineteenth-century country estate, including the house (fig. 3.2), the garden, and other buildings, which together now constitute the Missouri Botanical Garden.

Before he drew up his plan for the garden, Shaw traveled to England to visit famous gardens. During the hot month of August 1851, he toured the historic landscape of Chatsworth, Derbyshire, with its many gardens, water features, rockeries, shrubs, and extensive lawn. The experience was a turning point for him. Shaw decided to build a garden back home much like Chatsworth.

To this day, Chatsworth, with its three-hundred-year-old history, remains an important garden to visit. Head gardener Joseph Paxton rose to fame after his work there for the sixth Duke of Devonshire. Many other garden lovers, like Shaw, have ascended its grassy stretches, climbed the rockeries, and stood in amazement before the estate's waterfall.

Shaw's plan included Loudon's suggestions for the landscape, which meant flower gardens, an arboretum (or collection of trees), and a fruicetum (or orchard). The ideas in Shaw's landscape, like Shipley's, originated in the English gardenesque view, proposed by Loudon and prominent in Victorian America.

The garden and landscape were Shaw's pride and joy. He designed and supervised the planting to create a garden whose purpose, Shaw said, was to educate the public about horticulture and botany.

ᵈᵉ *Figure 3.2.* Henry Shaw built his house in the style of a country gentleman, with a Gothic design.

Shaw's first encounter with a landscape that included plants from around the world was at Mill Hill School, in England, where he studied as a young man. The school was previously the home of Peter Collinson, the eighteenth-century English plant collector who corresponded with Bartram in Philadelphia and Custis in Williamsburg. Perhaps Shaw saw the native American plant called trumpet vine, which was sent to Collinson from America. In that garden, Shaw could see firsthand the plant exchanges between Bartram, the American plantsman, and Collinson, the English plant collector.

Between 1859 and 1860, Shaw ordered his plants from various companies around the country, including some on the East Coast. Ellwanger and Barry, from their Mount Hope Nurseries in Rochester, supplied him with

The Trumpet Vine Returns
to American Gardens

*T*HE TRUMPET VINE, or *Campis radicans,* draped the walls of the greenhouse in Peter Collinson's garden in eighteenth-century England. The younger John Tradescant had introduced the plant, with its bright, cone-shaped orange flowers, in 1656. In the next century, it became one of the most popular plants for the English garden.[17] The trumpet vine is an example of how the English coveted American plants.

Though English explorers returned with plants from America as early as the late 1500s, not until well into the nineteenth century did American gardeners themselves treasure native species as important ornamental plants. The English referred to many of the American plants they used as "exotics," a name to indicate that a plant was suitable for the garden but came from another part of the world, sometimes America. So it was with the trumpet vine.

John Bartram listed *Campis radicans* in his catalog of 1783.[18] It was an American plant that eventually came back to American gardens, but only after the English had cultivated it for over a century in their own gardens.

Figure 3.3. Henry Shaw built this greenhouse, called the Linnean House, for his camellia collection.

three hundred hemlocks, fifty Norway spruces, and fifty black Austrian pines, as well as the weigela shrub. The seed merchant Robert Buist, in Philadelphia, supplied roses, grapevines, and pears, along with seeds of *Ageratum mexicanum, Mimosa pudica,* and petunia.[19]

Shaw's St. Louis landscape included both exotic and native plants. The garden is an important example of both nineteenth-century American plant collecting and the interest in botany in America. Plant collecting had become a hobby in America, especially for the wealthy, though the English had been collecting plants for two centuries. Shaw built a greenhouse he called the Linnean House to overwinter more tropical plants (fig. 3.3).

In 1859, Shaw opened his seventy-nine-acre garden as a public garden for all of St. Louis to enjoy. Meehan wrote in his *Gardener's Monthly* of 1868,

"Mr. Shaw's . . . Botanic Garden and residence at Tower Hill is unequalled by anything of the kind in the United States, and indeed by few others in the world."[20]

Today the garden attracts visitors, as well as scientists from around the world, to continue Shaw's legacy of a public garden centered on the landscape, botanical research, and education.

On the East Coast, other wealthy Americans also built country homes with extensive English landscapes. Jurist William Lewis Morris constructed Ward Hill beside the Hudson River in the Bronx. The grounds offered dramatic views of the Hudson. In 1834, William Rotch Jr. constructed a Greek Revival–style home in New Bedford, Massachusetts, with gardens facing south. Rotch, a founding member of the New Bedford Horticultural Society, employed an Irish gardener. In Wellesley, Massachusetts, in 1866, Horatio Hollis Hunnewell planted a large collection of evergreens, called the pinetum, modeled after the English evergreen collections that the English gentry cultivated.

❧

Today Rockwood is a public garden, where a visitor can still enjoy Joseph Shipley's home and stroll the landscape. The drive up to the house entrance features trees that hide the mansion from view, embodying the feature of the unexpected, which is an important element of picturesque landscape design. After the road curves at a rocky ridge, the walls of the gray-black mansion come into view. The broad vistas offered by the lawn with its large trees contribute to the naturalistic landscape design of Rockwood.

The American seed and nursery industries that Shipley dealt with began in the nineteenth century. By 1850 there were several important companies, especially on the East Coast, but the Robert Buist nursery, twenty-five miles away in Philadelphia, was the most famous. Thomas Meehan considered the Buist nursery the most popular on the East Coast in the first half of the century. It was no surprise, therefore, that Shipley turned to Buist for plants.

🌿 *Weigela florida* (or *Weigela rosea*), old-fashioned weigela

Weigela florida / Old-Fashioned Weigela

When we bought our house twenty-five years ago, on the lawn outside the front door we found a *Weigela florida* shrub. I am happy that it has survived in that spot. Since then each year it has offered a welcome display of pink flowers every June.

Robert Fortune (1812–80), the Scottish plant collector, introduced it in 1845 from China to England, where it first grew at the Gardens of the Horticultural Society. This shrub, with reddish-pink bell-shaped flowers, was named after the German botanist Christian von Weigel. Soon American nursery catalogs listed it as the newest exotic plant from England. In 1848, *Curtis's Botanical Magazine* wrote that it grew in the Royal Gardens of Kew and other botanical gardens in Great Britain.

This shrub could well represent the Rockwood landscape. When Shipley ordered it in 1852, it was still considered a new exotic plant from England and was therefore quite desirable for his landscape built in the English garden style. It eventually became a standard in American gardens.

Weigela florida grows four to five feet high and just as wide and is valued as a specimen or a border plant. The leaves are two to five inches long and usually have one end narrower than the other, a pointed tip, and a notched edge. The flowers measure an inch and a half in length. The inner envelopes of the flowers are usually a white, pink, or red color. The fruit of the flower is a dry pod containing small seeds. This shrub does well in most fertile soils but prefers a moist, well-drained soil in sun or partial shade. It blossoms in springtime, mostly during April, May, and June. This shrub is sometimes referred to as *Weigela rosea* or by the old garden name of diervilla.

A Short History of the Nineteenth-Century Seed and Nursery Industries in America

N 1832, when the book he wrote with Thomas Hibbert, *The American Flower Garden Directory,* came out, Robert Buist knew that he had arrived. Since emigrating from Scotland to Philadelphia four years earlier, at the age of twenty-three, he had worked pulling weeds for the David Landreth Seed Company, the oldest American seed company, and as a gardener for Henry Pratt, a wealthy merchant, at Lemon Hill, Pratt's summer estate in Philadelphia. Gardening was what Buist knew.

It was in the nursery business, however, that Buist sought to make his mark. In 1830, he partnered with Hibbert to buy Bernard M'Mahon's nursery, a business well known since the early 1800s. Buist grew roses for the new business and sold them on the streets of Philadelphia, practicing what some would later call market gardening.

Born near Edinburgh, Buist trained at the Royal Botanic Garden Edinburgh. His father, also a professional gardener, was his inspiration. In the introduction to his book, Buist wrote, "All that is asserted is the result of minute observation, close application, and an extended continuous experience from childhood."[1]

After Hibbert's death in 1833, Buist bought his late partner's share in the business and formed Robert Buist's Seed Store, which developed such a following that it eventually demanded new quarters. By 1837 it had moved to Philadelphia's Twelfth Street. The store included a seed division and a nursery that sold potted plants, fruits, and roses, as well as a greenhouse. For decades the company served as a primary source for seeds and plants in the Philadelphia area, as well as around the country. Even Henry Shaw, in Missouri, ordered from Buist.

Like other nurserymen and seedsmen, Buist sent out a yearly catalog of his seeds and plants to his customers. Such a catalog, though not completely new (for example, William Prince, of Flushing, Long Island, published an early catalog of fruit trees in 1771), did not become a significant part of the nursery and seed business until the mid-nineteenth century, when faster printing and expanded mail service for catalogs made them increasingly effective at reaching customers. From then on, the catalog served as a major tool in the establishment of seed companies and nurseries as important national businesses in nineteenth-century America.

The Business of Seeds and Plants

The trade of nurseryman in the modern sense had existed in England since the eighteenth century.[2] America was not far behind in adopting elements of the nursery trade, including the catalog.

Seed and nursery catalogs in America were based on the British practice of issuing a catalog of the goods that were available to the customer.[3] The golden years of American gardening catalogs extended from the 1850s into the 1890s. In this period, company owners sought to attract customers around the country with ever-larger and more colorful catalogs.[4]

Although determining a precise date for the beginning of the modern seed and nursery industries in America is impossible, there certainly were companies before 1850. The largest number appeared after 1870, and by 1900 the number of firms was in the hundreds.[5] The agricultural periodical *Farm and Garden* wrote about the seed industry in 1881: "For more than a half a century the seeds grown by Philadelphia houses have had a world-wide reputation for their high qualities, in consequence of which the seed trade of that city has been more than double that of any other city in the Union."[6]

Focusing on new seed companies rather than established ones, the agricultural newspaper *Practical Farmer,* discussing the seed business the following year, wrote, "The vast extent and resources of our country, the hundreds of thousands of immigrants annually seeking our shores, new lines of railroads opening up millions of acres of new lands, all these have tended to build up and foster a business which until recently has been in the hands of and controlled by a very few [seed] houses. The success and growth of these has invited competition and new firms have sprung up, and by their push and energy have taken a front rank in the business enterprises of the country."[7]

But essays and articles in such periodicals are not the only sources to be consulted in re-creating the history of American gardening in the nineteenth century. The products sold in the company catalogs tell their own story, and the catalogs are informative in other ways as well.

Charles Van Ravenswaay, the historian and former director of Winterthur, once wrote that the most neglected segment of America's horticultural literature had been the gardening catalogs published by the seed houses and nurseries.[8] Since then, researchers have studied the texts and images of the catalogs. Garden historian Cheryl Lyons-Jenness, for example, in her history of gardening, uses illustrations of nineteenth-century American landscapes, some from garden catalogs. She says, "Americans knew about the formal, geometric garden designs of the seventeenth and early eighteenth centuries, and followed the evolving English concern with naturalism and the picturesque landscape ideals."[9] The catalog, for her too, is thus much more than a collection of seeds and plants.

But it is not only our contemporaries who recognize the importance of the catalog. Thomas Meehan, the nurseryman from Philadelphia, wrote in his magazine *Gardener's Monthly* in 1860, "To those anxious to know the rapid progress horticulture is making on the American continent, the catalogues of the nurserymen are very instructive."[10]

One valuable piece of information that can be gleaned from these catalogs is the concentration of seed companies and nurseries in certain cities and the eventual expansion of the business into new regions around the country. After examining the major collections of early American catalogs of plant and seed companies in the United States, horticulturalist John T. Fitzpatrick and literary scholar Judith Ho concluded that the East Coast was the location of the majority of companies during the years 1771–1832.[11] Robert Buist joined the ranks of seed company pioneers, since his American seed business began in the Philadelphia area. By 1870, Rochester, New York, had become the home of the largest concentration of seed companies.[12]

The seed and nursery business spread to the West Coast, as well. After California became part of the United States in 1846, local nurseries imported plants from states in the Northeast and Europe. California garden historian Thomas Brown wrote, "Virtually ninety-five percent of the plants seen today are introduced species and varieties, and a great percentage of these were introduced before 1900."[13] As was the case across the country, most of the nurseries in California developed after 1880.

The Catalog

In the early 1800s, some of the British seed companies and nurseries that produced catalogs sent them to America.[14] It did not take long, however, for American garden businesses to produce their own sales catalogs for seeds and plants. Through concerted efforts of the seed and nursery industry, with the assistance of these sales catalogs, the nineteenth-century American garden expanded beyond the standard kitchen garden composed of well-established crop varieties, coming to include an ornamental garden and lawn, as well.[15]

The early nineteenth-century companies frequently printed a broadsheet of available seeds and plants, but by the end of the century a more elaborate catalog with color illustrations had begun to appear. Throughout the century merchants used the catalog, of whatever size, as the major vehicle both to sell their seeds and plants and to keep in contact with their customers. In the process, company owners also told the story of American gardening.

Seed companies and nurseries took pride in presenting their yearly catalogs. Seedsman John Lewis Childs, in 1896, told his customers in his catalog, "One of the pleasures which the first of each year affords is the presentation of a copy of our new catalogue to each of our customers, and we do it believing that they find pleasure and profit in receiving it. It is no small task to supply half a million books like this, and it necessitates an enormous outlay of labor and money."

The size, number of pages, text, images, and advertising of the seed and nursery catalog provide some insight into what the owners thought important for the industry. They began with an introduction or message from the company owner. Before 1860, the introduction might be called "Advertisement," and a bit later "Preface," but the writing always discussed the seed or plant business.

Before 1870

Meehan's *Gardener's Monthly*, in 1883, wrote about the Landreth Company, America's pioneer seed business, "The noise of the guns of the Revolution had hardly died away, when in 1784 the first seed establishment in America was founded at Philadelphia by David Landreth."[16] In 1826, Landreth offered in the catalog fruits, greenhouse plants, ornamental trees, flowering shrubs, bulbous roots, and seeds.

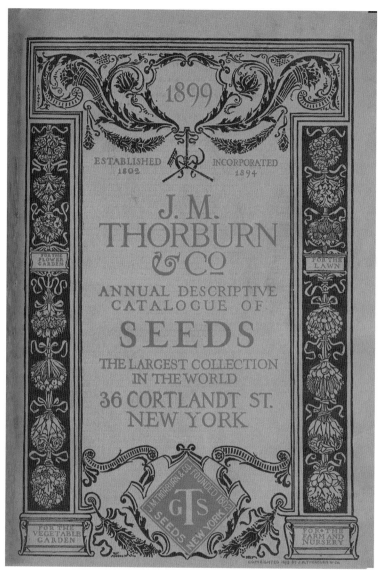

Figure 4.1. The Thorburn Company was one of the early seed companies. By the end of the nineteenth century, the catalog cover had become more elaborate and colorful. *Courtesy of the Bailey Hortorium, Cornell University, Ithaca, New York.*

Bernard M'Mahon opened his seed store in Philadelphia in 1806, shortly behind Grant Thorburn's shop in New York, which restarted in 1802 (fig. 4.1). Similar seed stores appeared in other towns, but there probably were not more than one hundred in the early nineteenth century.[17] M'Mahon, in 1804, said in his catalog that he had "for sale, an extensive variety of Asiatic, South-Sea Islands, African, and European seeds of the most curious and rare kinds" and that he was expanding his collection to include items from all parts of the world.

In 1818, Joseph Breck formed his seed company in Massachusetts, where he was also the president of the Massachusetts Horticultural Society. In the English tradition, many seed companies and nurseries linked their business with efforts to educate the customer about horticulture. Breck took great pride in the look and presentation of the seed catalog his company distributed. The company said in its 1886 catalog, "We have aimed to make our book a 'thing of beauty.'"

It was not uncommon for catalogs before 1850 to be a simple list of seeds or plants for sale. The William Booth catalog of 1810 was just that. Initially, so was that of American-born William G. Comstock, whose Connecticut seed business began in 1838. Comstock took his seed packets by wagon to sell in country stores. He said, "I laid out the first route myself going up the Connecticut River as far as Springfield, Vermont. We had little competition. Sales were good, the Shakers being about the only ones in the trade."[18] Comstock's 1846 catalog was modeled after that of the Shakers: a simple listing of plant seeds available for sale. Later, Comstock included in the catalog more about cultivation of the plants, a feature most seed and nursery catalogs adopted.

Similarly, Cherry Orchard Nurseries, of Cleveland, was proud of its simple listings, stating in the 1850 catalog, "This establishment . . . has so long enjoyed the confidence and patronage of the public, without the aid of puffs or long catalogs."

By 1859, Robert Buist had expanded into a three-story seed company in Philadelphia (where Joseph Shipley, of Delaware, quite possibly paid a visit, because Wilmington was not far away). Until about 1870, Buist's catalog was simple, listing just the plants available. By the end of the century, however, his son, who had taken over the business after the death of the elder Buist, was issuing thick catalogs with brightly colored covers.

Sometimes the catalog sold plants and seeds that were not in stock. Customers did not always appreciate that, and so in 1862 Morrison and Ball touted their catalog's accuracy: "We publish our descriptive catalog as an exact inventory of what we now have under cultivation, and for sale; thus hoping to avoid the annoyance arising from ordinary advertised things that only have a place on paper."

Illustrations in the catalog, though at first only black-and-white engravings, were important because they sought to persuade the reader that the company was modern, using the latest format for images in the catalog. The company owners, however, were not always enthusiastic about colored images. In 1869, Landreth said, "We may state for the information of the uninitiated, that colored drawings (illustrations we believe they are termed) of garden flowers, are not always reliable expressions. On the contrary, the attractive features are in some cases grossly exaggerated."

The catalogs from the seed and plant industries proved successful as a sales tool, mainly because the catalog was an advertisement of their products for sale, mostly seeds and plants. The companies knew it, and so did the customers. Later, more companies appeared, only to increase the number of catalogs.

After 1870

After the first two-thirds of the nineteenth century, the sales approach of the catalog changed. While some companies continued with broadsheets or simple lists of plants sold, others began to offer larger catalogs with articles and illustrations.

The last third of the century brought intense competition among the many seed and plant merchants, who used their elaborate catalogs to attract customers. Bold colors in detailed drawings became a standard feature used to show new plants, especially on the cover but also in the first pages of the catalog.

The names of the catalogs often reveal how the owner wanted to portray the business. In 1872, the Washburn Company of Boston called its catalog the *Amateur Cultivator's Guide to the Flower and Kitchen Garden*. The name of Peter Henderson's catalog for 1886 was *Everything for the Garden*. Lewis Templin named his 1887 catalog *Beautiful Flowers* and called his 1898 catalog *Bargains in Seeds, Plants, Vines, and Bulbs*.

Benjamin K. Bliss singled out the three groups of readers who used the seed company catalog. He wrote that his 1873 catalog was "useful alike to the amateur, professional florist, or the market gardeners." Later, other seed and nursery catalogs used the same threefold division of their customers. The amateur was usually someone who had a garden at home. The professional florist was one who made a business out of growing and selling flowers. Like Buist, the market gardener grew and sold mostly vegetables at outdoor markets, usually in or around a large city.

In its 1879 catalog, the Landreth Company detailed the marketing importance of its publication: "It is not an easy task for the same hand to write an Introduction to an Almanac for thirty-two successive years, and each time say something of interest to the reader; and that is exactly what the present writer is called upon to do. When, in 1847, the first number of Landreth's *Rural Register and Almanac* was printed it was a novelty, it afforded us an opportunity to come in closer communication with our customers than had previously existed."

Despite the link to the customer that the catalog afforded, many seed companies and nurseries wondered about the value of the catalog, even while issuing one or more each year. Seed company D. M. Ferry's catalog of 1882 included the following passage: "Is the trade so enormously profitable that they can afford to distribute gratuitously so beautiful and costly a book simply as an advertisement? That we, in company with every other seedsman in England and America, find it necessary to annually send out such a book indicates that there is something in the trade which demands it." The catalog had evolved into an essential ingredient in the seed and the plant business, especially because the majority of the country lived on farms and could not consult with the owners or examine the offered products on-site.

However, to publish two, three, or sometimes four catalogs a year was a tedious and time-consuming job. In 1885, Storrs and Harrison said, "Few realize the amount of care required to get up a presentable catalog, with reliable descriptions and cut and correct the typography."

Other aspects of preparing a catalog were also of uncertain value. A. D. Perry and Co., located in Syracuse, New York, in 1886 questioned the worth of writing the required introduction for the catalog: "We often wonder if all the fine print preface is read by one in a thousand of those who receive the catalog, for in these times printer's ink is spread very thin, and competition in that line is as great as in any trade."

Some businesses, in minimizing the advertising aspects of the catalog, deliberately pursued a different course. For example, Frank Finch, from Clyde, New York, produced the kind of catalog in 1889 that would save his customers money. He wrote, "I do not publish a costly catalogue, printed in colors, and charge my customers for it, but send a plainly printed, inexpensive one free of charge. I do not think it would be just right for me to charge my customers for the privilege of sending me an order, and then take the amount and give it to some lithographer to pay for getting up the catalogue."

Offerings in the Catalog

Plant collectors who traveled the world in search of plants, many representing English gardens like Kew, enabled American seed companies and nurseries to offer nonnative or exotic plants, as such plants often later came across the ocean to the United States. Companies took pride in such plant sales. Lines and Coe, from New Haven, Connecticut, wrote in 1894, "Through the zeal of the collectors, 'nature's scattered excellencies' are now available.

Instead of being restricted to the varieties that grow native about us, we have the whole flora, practically, of the world at our command, as well as the greatest number of the varieties that have been fostered into existence by much care and painstaking." Many exotic plants, such as certain rhododendrons, came from China or Japan through England.

Although native plants were offered, they were often considered less desirable. This attitude has not disappeared; recently, landscape architect Darrel Morrison wrote that native landscape proponents in this country have been viewed with a certain skepticism and even suspicion in some quarters.[19] It should be no surprise, therefore, to see a lack of interest in native plants in the nineteenth century.

Such an attitude was not universal, however. The Harlan P. Kelsey Company, from Linville, North Carolina, like a lone voice in the wilderness, made a plea that expressed the sentiment of botanist John Bartram about the importance of native plants for the American garden. Kelsey wrote in its 1892 catalog that "the whole earth outside the United States has been searched and explored to obtain the choicest trees and plants for beautifying our American parks, lawns, cemeteries, and gardens, yet the more beautiful American plants are rarely seen in cultivation, and, as a rule, are unknown to Americans."

Some seed companies and nurseries made available plants and seeds from their own trial gardens. When such plants were grown on-site, that fact served as a way for companies to differentiate themselves. Charles Wright, from Delaware, wrote in his 1894 catalog, "When purchasing nursery stock would you not prefer to deal with a practical fruit grower? Many men engaged in the nursery business have not a single specimen, much less an orchard on their grounds."

By the late 1800s, companies were specializing in certain plants, such as rock garden plants and evergreens, and even vegetables such as potatoes. D. Hill, who owned an evergreen nursery, wrote in his 1895 catalog, "The growing of evergreen from seed is my specialty. . . . For the past six years I have been testing and experimenting with these wild evergreens, under the most favorable conditions and the best possible care and cultivation. . . . Try nursery grown trees, if only a few, and you will become convinced that evergreens can be as successfully transplanted as apple or any other tree."

Among Hill's evergreens was the white pine, or *Pinus strobus,* a native American tree that Bartram had sold to English gardeners a hundred years earlier. The white pine, called in England the Weymouth pine, became a required plant in the English landscape. By the end of the nineteenth century, native American plants such as the white pine were beginning to find a place in the American home landscape.

The following account by F. Parkman, from Boston, about a tall plant with yellow flowers appeared in Meehan's journal *Gardener's Monthly* of 1875:

> As I write, a mass of golden yellow, 6 to 8 feet in width, and as many feet above the ground, rises in the herbaceous garden against the green wall and trees beyond.
>
> Two years ago, I imported from England an insignificant looking plant in a four-inch pot, a native, I believe, of this country, emigrating to the old world, where his merits found a recognition, which they had never found at home. Having thus reclaimed him, I planted him in a good soil at the back of a wide bed of perennials, where, this year, he made the display described above. Rudbeckia nitida is the name of the plant; and where a grand blaze of yellow is wanted on the lawn, or at the edge of the shrubbery, it would be hard to find its equal.[20]

Competition

The seed and nursery businesses were engaged in a struggle, and the owners knew their competition (fig. 4.2). The Ferry Seed Company said in its 1893 catalog, "Nearly every seed buyer examines during the year from one to several dozen of the catalogues issued by various seed houses." Because the

Our Native Rhododendron, Not Welcome at Home

*P*HILADELPHIA nurseryman Thomas Meehan wrote in *Gardener's Monthly,* in the June issue of 1870, "It has often been a source of wonder, that the idea that the most beautiful of all American ornamental plants—the Rhododendron—could not be grown in its native country, should ever prevail; yet so universal is this belief, that though persistent efforts have been made by enthusiast nurserymen, like Parsons of Flushing, and Hovey of Boston, to introduce it to public notice, and to show that they can be as well grown as any other plant, only a few yet realize the fact; and thousands of our readers do not know what a rhododendron is."[21]

editorials and articles presented the editorial views of the owner, many opinions appeared on important issues related to the business. As many businesses still do, the owners sometimes criticized other companies to put themselves ahead of their competitors.

The Landreth Company warned its readers not to believe everything they saw in a catalog. The company's 1890 catalog suggested, "It really seems as if the creature man was as anxious to be deceived in seeds as in quack medicines, for we do not hesitate to declare upon our reputation as seedsmen of repute that nine-tenths of the so-called new sorts advertised at high prices are, so far as merit goes, rank humbugs, and it is time the public were told so."

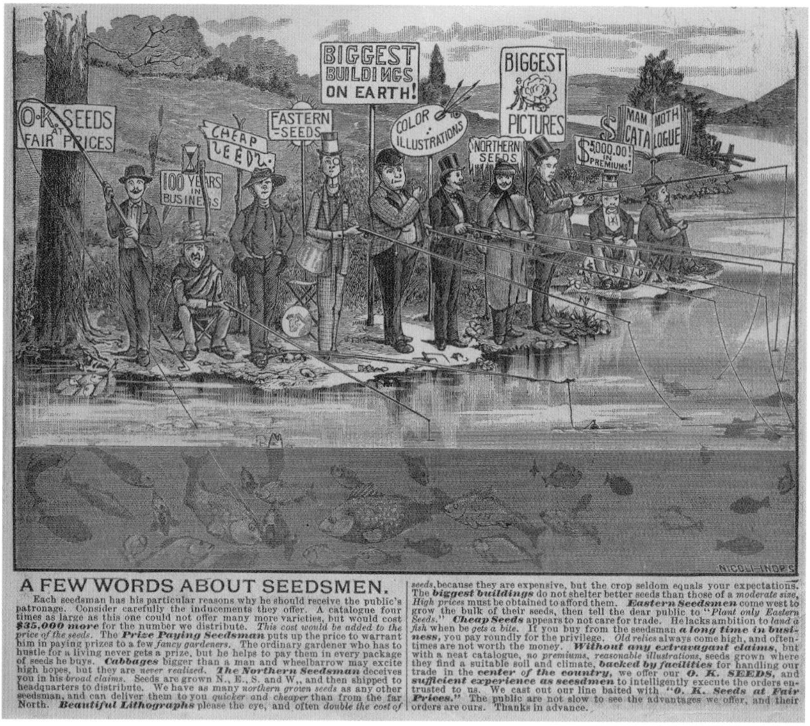

Figure 4.2. This ad from the Everitt Company in its 1892 catalog illustrates the competition among the seed merchants. *Courtesy of the Bailey Hortorium, Cornell University, Ithaca, New York.*

The catalog was also a place to boast of accomplishments, to prove to the reader that a company was the best and deserved the customer's business. The Goodell Seed Company, begun in 1875 in Dwight, Massachusetts, said in its 1890 catalog, "Beginning with less than two hundred customers the first year, I had several thousands the second, and it has gone on increasing rapidly until now Goodell seeds are not only planted in thousands of gardens in all parts of America, but orders are often received from many other foreign lands."

In 1890, John Lewis Childs, of Floral Park, New York, let his readers know how difficult the seed business was: "To become a successful seedsman and florist is a much more difficult task than gaining success in most any other business. More than a hundred start and fall where one succeeds."

A company's location in a large city was no guarantee of quality for the customer. F. B. Mills, from Rose Hill, New York, whose company was in a rural area of the state, wrote in 1893, "Nearly all the Seedsmen of America who do a large business are located in cities, paying enormous rents and spending from $25,000 to $100,000 annually, issuing expensive catalogues in colors, and sending out enormous advertisements. My establishment is located in the country, and is just the place where such a business should be."

The trust of the customer was essential for success. Companies sought to establish a bond with their customers through the catalog and so increase subsequent sales. Seed company and nursery owners certainly showed a sharp marketing skill through the catalog.

To convince readers of their reputation, many companies claimed that the number of their customers surpassed that of other establishments. Joseph H. Black, of Hightstown, New Jersey, wrote in 1891, "None can boast of a longer list of regular yearly customers. These men have dealt with us year after year, and it seems unnecessary for anyone to attempt to explain why. It is simply a self-evident truth. They must have been well treated in their dealings and were satisfied with our stock and trees."

John Lewis Childs emphasized fellowship with the gardening community: "Between people who love and cultivate flowers and gardens there is a bond of friendship and sympathy. They are never strangers; they are ever ready to assist each other; they rejoice in the success of each other and deplore each other's failures. Buying and selling between our customers and ourselves has never seemed to be merely a matter of dollars and cents."

When a company had been in business for many years, mention of that fact in the catalog was essential. Older companies often urged their customers to place trust in a company with a long history of customer service. Not to be outdone, newer companies promoted their "new kid on the block" image as their best feature. The E. M. Sherman Company, from Charles City, Iowa, wrote in 1894, "We would say that we do not come to you with the hoary head of antiquity; we were not established in the year one, nor were we established in the year 1801, but what we do have to say is, that since our establishment we have been up and doing."

The Peter Henderson Company catalog of 1895, published five years after the founder's death, describes the growth of the company in a way that links the business to the development of gardening in America:

> If it were possible to obtain a complete set of all the catalogues issued by us since the business was established, such a collection would not only be symbolical of our business development, but it would also be a faithful reflection of the wonderful progress American horticulture has made in the last fifty years. The first catalogue sent by Mr. Peter Henderson in '49 or '50 was a modest sheet of four pages, without cuts, and of which were 100 copies. This year [1895] the catalogs, general and special by Peter Henderson & Co. will aggregate 850,000 copies (an increase since 1885 alone of 450,000 copies).

Many nineteenth-century seed companies and nurseries referred to themselves as the "biggest." When W. Atlee Burpee died in 1915, an obituary in a trade journal said his mail-order seed business was probably one of the largest in existence.[22] Briggs, too, claimed that his own company was "the largest in the world." The meaning of the terms *big* and *large* was not always clear. The terms could indicate the number of buildings on the site, total years in business, the amount of acreage for trial and display gardens, the number of customers, or the amount of money spent in advertising—all may have contributed to the decision to highlight a company as the "biggest." No matter what the basis for the claim, what owners meant was that their business was important, both for them as individuals and for the country as a whole.

Seedsmen and nurserymen thus used whatever means necessary— boasting, comparing themselves with other companies, detailing their business growth—to impress customers and improve sales.

The Catalog Was the Salesman

Many nurseries chose to hire salesmen, or enlist tree peddlers, as they were called, to sell their plants; but for seed companies the catalog was the primary means for making a sale. Green's Nursery in Rochester said in its 1901 catalog, "Our catalog is our salesman. We employ no agents, nor any person to travel for us to sell our stock, since we have for twenty years found a ready sale by simply sending out our catalog with prices to people who apply for it."

The catalog was such an important business tool that some companies considered it the only way to sell seeds. Storrs and Harrison, from Ohio, wrote in 1892, "Our seed trade is entirely through this catalogue." That same year E. W. Reid, also from Ohio, wrote, "Through our catalog we can talk direct to the grower and planter. He can buy what he wants direct from the nursery, making his selections in the quiet of his own fireside—not buying from an agent." Such companies defended the importance of the catalog as a sales tool, well before Sears and Roebuck and others would later adopt it.

The seed houses and nurseries of the nineteenth century presented many challenges to their owners. They had embarked on a new kind of business that demanded a regular catalog printed in the hundreds, then thousands, then tens of thousands. No one had done that for seeds and plants in this country before; that made them pioneers. Some companies flourished, others disappeared.

Within the opening pages of the catalog, the seed companies and nurseries told the story of their industry, tracing the history, problems, and joys of the business. Their work was intimately connected with the success of gardeners, who looked to the industry not only for seeds and plants but also for information on how to garden and develop a home landscape. The authors of the catalogs did not disappoint them.

The seed companies and nurseries enjoyed the status of a substantial and effective business, which first was regional, then national, and became international by the end of the century. The customer welcomed the catalog's words of advice on how to garden and design a landscape because the seed company and nursery were seen as modern, progressive industries in a society that was moving toward a consumer-driven way of life. The catalog as a business tool sold seeds and plants but also a model for a modern way of gardening. This model would turn out to be the English style of gardening, a theme the seed companies and nurseries would also address in extensive articles, journals, and books.

Buist's Poinsettia Travels to Great Britain

Buist's early training at the Royal Botanic Garden Edinburgh gave him the opportunity to meet James McNab, a scientist and artist who eventually became the garden's director. McNab and Buist were the same age when they went to Edinburgh to learn about horticulture at the dawn of the career in gardening each of them envisioned.

In the early 1830s, McNab traveled to America with retired nurseryman Robert Brown to learn about the plants of the United States. He visited his friend Buist in Philadelphia. That visit is now forever linked to our celebration of Christmas.

Dr. Joel Poinsett, botanist and diplomat, served as the first United States ambassador to Mexico. While there in 1825, he came upon a plant that so impressed him that he had it shipped to his home in Charleston, South Carolina. Buist later bought the plant from him and grew it for a couple of years, naming it *Euphorbia poinsettia.* The first word indicated the plant's milky sap, a trait shared by other varieties of *Euphorbia;* the second term honored Dr. Poinsett.

The bright red bracts were what made the plant so special to Buist. He wrote later that it was "truly the most magnificent of all the tropical plants we have ever seen."[23]

The new *Euphorbia* appeared for the first time at the Philadelphia Flower Show in June 1829. Poinsett had also given a sample of the plant to Robert Carr, the director of Philadelphia's Bartram garden at that time, who agreed to display it.

When McNab visited Buist in 1834, he gave the plant to McCabe to take back to Scotland. The garden's director, Dr. Robert Graham, renamed it *Poinsettia pulcherrima* and introduced the plant into British gardens. Till the end of his life, Buist was upset that Graham changed the name.

We owe Buist a debt of gratitude for making the poinsettia available to the world. Buist introduced the poinsettia to the plant trade, and it became the essential Christmas decoration.

In 1879, a year before he died, Buist closed his Roseland Nursery. His seed business continued under the leadership of his son Robert Jr. Buist had found his way in America and achieved his dream of a life as a gardener.

FEATURED PLANT

Pinus strobus / Eastern White Pine

A FEW YEARS ago I decided to fill in a gap along my property line with three white pines. Today they are about twenty feet tall and have done a superb job of forming a border. What I liked most about these trees is how fast they grew.

The white pine is the only five-needle pine indigenous to eastern North America. Lord Weymouth introduced it to England in 1705, after the English colonies were established in America. From that time on, English gardeners have included it in their collection of American plants. English garden writer Horace Walpole wrote in 1771, "The Weymouth pine has long been naturalized here; the patriarch plant still exists at Longleat [Lord Weymouth's estate]."[24]

During the eighteenth century, white pines in New England forests provided materials for building houses and furniture. It is the regional tree of Ontario, Canada, and the state tree of both Maine and Michigan. Other common names for the species are northern white pine and soft pine.

Twigs of the tree are slender, flexible, and usually a pale red or brown. The needles are soft and flexible, two to four inches long, green in color, and three-sided; they come in bundles of five. The cones are slender, thornless, and three to ten inches long. The cones usually take two seasons to mature to full growth. Some white pines live to exceed four hundred years in age, but most generally live two hundred years. Mature trees are 80 to 110 feet tall.

White pines live in a variety of soils, from wet bogs and moist stream bottoms to dry sandy plains and rocky ridges. Most white pines are tolerant of intermediate amounts of shade.

ᏋᏋ (facing page)
Pinus strobus, eastern white pine

Garden Writing from the
Seed Companies and Nurseries

N HIS *American Gardener's Magazine,* in 1836, Charles Mason Hovey praised the then-current interest in cultivating mulberry trees that could be used as the food source for silkworms in the production of silk, most of which at that time was shipped to the United States from outside the country. He wrote, "We are every day more convinced of its practicability and its importance."[1]

He could not have been more wrong. Though some gardeners agreed with Hovey, the silk business in the United States never succeeded. Even Newton, Massachusetts, nurseryman William Kenrick (1789–1872) tried his hand at growing mulberry trees for a silk trade, but as it turned out, in America the silk business had no future.

Kenrick enjoyed a successful plant business in the early nineteenth century—that is, until he decided to invest in mulberry trees to support silk manufacture. He even wrote a book on the mulberry, in which he described how the silkworm ate the mulberry leaves as a step in the process of producing silk. An 1834 article in the journal *New England Farmer* took note of his interest: "I observe with much pleasure that the Chinese Mulberry, or Morus Multicaulis, has engaged the attention of Mr. Kenrick of Newton, an enlightened and enterprising cultivator of trees and plants."[2]

When the mulberry craze ended badly, Kenrick lost everything. He turned to real estate, selling off portions of his land for housing lots. Today his house still stands on a corner lot in Newton, near a street named after him. The property features large trees, including a beech that stands in command over a sweeping lawn.

Like many other seedsmen and nurserymen, Kenrick wrote what he knew about horticulture as a way to educate the gardener. Although perhaps few read *The American Silk Grower's Guide*, his book on the mulberry and silk cultivation, Kenrick's earlier (and most popular) book, *The New American Orchardist*, would remain a classic on fruit culture for decades. Indeed, at the height of its popularity there were eight editions in circulation. He propagated the fruit plants that arrived for his garden from his friend Thomas Andrew Knight, president of London's Royal Horticultural Society from 1811 to 1838, and also those from Chiswick Gardens, which was, according to some, the birthplace of the English landscape movement.[3] In *The New American Orchardist*, Kenrick also acknowledged the help he received from Salem, Massachusetts, fruit grower Robert Manning, who soon after published *The New England Book of Fruit*. Both writers and nurserymen were founding members of the Massachusetts Horticultural Society.

In the *Orchardist*, Kenrick included a section on landscape gardening, in which he recommended the then-modern picturesque landscape style rather than the old geometric style. He clearly drew on English authors, including making reference to Bacon and Milton as the inspiration for the modern, natural landscape.

Gardening books by nurserymen such as Kenrick had a long-lasting influence and still find a limited readership. Among those who appreciated such books was New Jersey book dealer Elizabeth Woodburn, who owned an antiquarian bookstore that specialized in old and rare books in the fields of horticulture, landscape, and gardening. Woodburn, who died in 1990, once wrote that it was American nurserymen who, in the nineteenth century, developed and taught their countrymen horticulture.[4] They were America's first garden writers for a mass audience.

Nineteenth-century seed companies and nurseries thus published catalogs, magazines, and books, offering both inspiration and instruction. Their writing illustrates the important role the company owners played in teaching the importance of the garden and the landscape while often following the principles of English design.

Articles in the Catalogs

The seed catalog, which was more than a list of seeds and plants, included essays and notes about the culture of the plants: instructions on how to plant them, how to care for them, and how to harvest their fruit. The catalog also sometimes contained general articles on gardening, farming, and landscaping. Over the long, cold winter nights, a faraway customer could read the catalog not only to discover the latest seeds but also to learn more about gardening and the landscape. M. O'Keefe, Son and Company, from Rochester, New York, stated in its 1870 catalog that the publication was full of advice "so that the most inexperienced may not fail."

In 1890, Richard Frotscher, from New Orleans, called his seed catalog *Almanac and Garden Manual* and equated it with an instructive book on gardening, intended to be useful like those catalogs of O'Keefe and Park, though not fancy: "For the looks of my work, it cannot be compared with the elaborate issues of my northern competitors, which are full of colored plates, and with gilded covers, resembling more a series of 'Mother Hubbard' than an instruction book on gardening; but I flatter myself, that it is the most useful for this section."

Mere information, however, was not all that the catalog articles provided: some had an even greater impact, in developing the gardening hobby. Ulysses P. Hedrick, historian of American horticulture, wrote that the catalogs and advertisements of Grant Thorburn's seed company and nursery contributed greatly to the formation of a taste for gardening.[5] Thorburn was more than a seed peddler: he taught Americans how to garden.

Similarly, Carrie H. Lippincott, from Minneapolis, the "Pioneer Seedswoman of America" as she called herself, directed her 1897 seed catalog, titled *Floral Culture*, at beginning gardeners. The first twenty pages were instructions on choosing and growing seeds. In the introduction, she offered counsel to the gardener in these words: "A little light and information for the flower lover, but not a scientific treatise on the cultivation of flowers. This little book does not pretend to know it all, it only aims to help the amateur who wishes to successfully grow flowers from seed." The remainder of the catalog was a "bargain collection of flower seeds."

George W. Park, from Fannettsburg, Pennsylvania, expressed a similar goal in his 1885 catalog: "To aid my numerous patrons in the selection of bulbs and seeds for fall planting, as well as to give some general instructions in regard to their management and culture, I issue this little pamphlet, and trust it will be carefully perused." Because American gardeners enjoyed planting bulbs, just as the English had done for a hundred years before them, a close association developed with the Dutch bulb industry, and by the end of the century, the planting of bulbs, which every seed company sold, made America one of the Dutch bulb growers' largest markets.

Prior to the Civil War, fruit trees were a dominant item for sale in the catalogs. Gradually, however, more vegetables were added. Seedsmen, through the company catalog, introduced the gardener to vegetables that have now become standard for the American table. The Vick Company, in its 1891 catalog, talked about the long tradition of gardening with vegetables, which was made possible by the valuable information presented in the annual seed catalog: "The improvement of all kinds of culinary vegetables has been very great, and the emulation in raising new and improved varieties was never higher than it is today." By the final third of the century, catalogs had also come to include a large collection of flowers. The readers depended on the company catalogs to learn not only what seeds to plant but also the choicest plant varieties available at a particular time.

The sons of James Vick, who took over the company after the senior Vick died in 1882, recalled the origins of the company in their catalog of 1898, noting especially the writing skill of their father: "There are now probably but few who can remember our honored father, the founder of the business, or his first writing about flowers in the old publication, the *Genesee Farmer,* published in this city half a century ago." It is more accurate to call Vick first a writer and then a seedsman, since he also took on the publisher role for Downing's *The Horticulturist* and wrote for agricultural journals long before he had his seed company. Vick was not the only seedsman, however, to pick up his pen for a garden paper or journal.

Magazines

Magazines were the first mass medium in the United States, though they did not become large-scale operations until the 1890s.[6] In the first half of the century there were few horticultural magazines in America. Most were farming or agricultural periodicals, which sometimes discussed horticulture.[7] They covered topics such as gardening, as well as home landscape design for the rural residence. The magazine became a popular medium and, like newspapers, by midcentury enjoyed a mass readership due to expanded mail service, which made sending catalogs as well as magazines to rural areas reasonable.

The first American magazine devoted to agriculture, called *Agricultural Museum,* appeared in 1810.[8] In 1834, Downing began his career with an article in the *New England Farmer* about planting ornamental trees.[9] In the same year, Judge Jesse Buel, from Albany, who was considered the most prolific farm writer of the nineteenth century, became the editor of a farm

VOL XXI.   FANNETTSBURG, PA., JUNE, 1885.   No. 6.

PARK'S FLORAL MAGAZINE.

THE OLDEST AND MOST POPULAR FLORAL MONTHLY IN AMERICA.

Figure 5.1. The Park Seed Company published its own magazine. Here is the masthead from its June 1885 issue. *Courtesy of the Bailey Hortorium, Cornell University, Ithaca, New York.*

journal called *Cultivator.*[10] Buel also wrote for Loudon's English horticultural journal, the medium through which Loudon spread his gardenesque ideas about landscape.

The nineteenth-century seed and nursery industry produced two kinds of horticultural journals. First, there were independent horticultural magazines, such as those written and edited by Downing, Landreth, Hovey, and Meehan. Then, by the end of the century, several seed companies and nurseries published their own in-house, company garden magazines (fig. 5.1). These were often produced throughout the year on a monthly basis, as was the case with Vick's *Illustrated Monthly.* The back pages often contained listings of seeds and plants for sale.

The two David Landreths of the Landreth Company began *Floral Magazine and Botanical Repository* in 1832. The publication was an eighty-page journal featuring descriptions and illustrations of thirty-one plants. The Landreths produced everything except the illustrations themselves.

In the 1835 first issue of his *American Gardener's Magazine,* Hovey wrote, "It cannot but be gratifying to every lover of gardening, to perceive that a rich fund of information has been gathered together. . . . We possess gardeners who know how to write as well as practice."[11] The magazine, which was the first form of national communication among American horticulturists, became an important nineteenth-century source for learning about horticulture.[12] It continued publication until 1868.

Similarly, Downing founded *The Horticulturist* in 1846; Benjamin K. Bliss started the quarterly *American Garden;* and Thomas Meehan's publication was *Gardener's Monthly,* later changed to *Meehans' Monthly.*[13] Meehan's 1894 catalog offered the magazine to its readers in these words: "A real lover of gardening is usually one of the best informed on general topics in the whole community. *Meehans' Monthly* devotes its energies to the cultivation of this general intelligence, and the publishers endeavor to make it of such a character that no one who has a library of any pretension can afford to be without it."

Hovey inserted advertising for his nursery along with other ads in the opening pages of his magazine, not an uncommon practice. Advertisers helped pay for the magazine. Meehan often wrote about the important division between editorial content and advertising, since sometimes he would get letters complaining that he favored those who advertised in the magazine. He responded that his office was located a distance from the advertising office and one never interfered with the other.

At times a company owner used the offer of a subscription to garden publications to motivate the reader to purchase seeds or plants. In 1893, Hastings and Co. from Interlachen, Florida, promised the farm journal called *Southern Ruralist* if the customer would buy its seeds.

While independent garden magazines might feature a nursery owner such as Thomas Meehan as editor, and correspondents wrote most of the articles, some seed companies and nurseries released their own publications, in which the company owner acted as the publisher, editor, and sole writer.

The John Lewis Childs Company produced its own garden magazine, called *The Mayflower* (fig. 5.2), which featured large colored chromos to illustrate vegetables and flowers. In 1892, the Childs seed catalog offered its readers incentives to subscribe to its magazine: "It has always been our study

Figure 5.2. The Childs Seed Company published *The Mayflower* garden magazine to send to its customers. This is the issue from September 1892. *Courtesy of the Bailey Hortorium, Cornell University, Ithaca, New York.*

to see how much we can give for a dollar, how much we can please purchasers and how much we can help them towards attaining the greatest possible success in their efforts to make home and the world brighter, happier, and better. It is not a matter of value for value when we offer the *Mayflower* for one year and its premium of 5 bulbs and 5 packets of seed for only 35 to 50 cents. The premium alone would cost, were one to buy it, over $1."

In the Childs Company's 1893 catalog, Childs boasted about his magazine: "It is the leading horticultural publication in the world, having over 300,000 subscribers." The catalog featured an illustration of the seed company's facilities in Floral Park, New York, which included one building called "the Mayflower printing office." By then, the magazine had become a significant part of the daily business of the seed company.

Green's Nursery, of Rochester, New York, advertised its magazine in its 1891 catalog, describing the magazine as "an early riser," just like the gardener: "Do you take *Green's Fruit Grower*? This is a live, wide-awake journal, gotten up to suit the market grower, the pleasure and home gardener, and it will suit you."

Vick began publication of his company magazine, *Vick's Illustrated Monthly,* in 1878, after many requests for advice. Since he could not personally answer the great volume of letters he received, Vick considered the magazine a means to speak to his customers. The monthly magazine, with a circulation of two hundred thousand copies per month, included sections on landscaping, garden travel stories like Vick's sojourns in England, and gardening for children. The magazine's publication demanded no small effort on the part of the seed company, especially when the circulation was so large.

Agricultural and horticultural magazine editors looked to seedsmen and nurserymen to write articles. The writers for Hovey's magazine included seedsmen and nurserymen Grant Thorburn, William Kenrick, and Robert Manning, as well as Andrew Jackson Downing, who also wrote articles for Loudon's *Gardener's Magazine*. Like Hovey's, Loudon's goal for his magazine, begun in 1826, was to appeal to middle-class gardeners. The magazine "was originally undertaken principally for the benefit of gardeners in the country, in order to put them 'on a footing with those about the metropolis,' but it soon became the universal means of communication among gardeners."[14]

Joseph Harris wrote about his extensive garden writing experience in his first seed catalog of 1879. He used his garden writing to establish a sense of credibility as a seed merchant. He wrote in that year's catalog, "It is sixteen years since I commenced to grow seeds. I have been an agricultural writer for twenty-nine years. My first article was written on this farm and appeared in the *Genesee Farmer* for October 1850. I have been connected editorially with the *Genesee Farmer, The Rural New Yorker, Albany Cultivator and Country Gentleman, Hearth and Home* and *The American Agriculturalist*."

Some company owners doubted the value of a nursery or seed business publishing its own magazine. In 1895, the W. W. Rawson Seed Company, from Boston, criticized other seed companies for publishing their own magazines, arguing that these were simply a way to sell more seeds. Rawson's approach was to offer *American Gardening,* begun fifty years before as Downing's *The Horticulturist,* rather than publishing his own journal.

Nevertheless, magazine publishing became a normal business practice of nineteenth-century seed companies and nurseries, and for some, publishing even expanded into books.

Books on Gardening

In his *Standard Cyclopedia of Horticulture,* written at the end of the nineteenth century, Cornell's L. H. Bailey listed many of the book titles mentioned below.[15] In noting them, he pays tribute to the contribution the nineteenth-century seed and nursery industries made to the growth of horticulture in American.

American Nurserymen
Recognized as Writers

PHILADELPHIA nurseryman Thomas Meehan wrote in his magazine *Gardener's Monthly*, in 1874, "At times, when reading in English horticultural magazines the immense amount of interesting matter freely contributed to the great cause, and which has been the great means of making English horticulture the great power it is to-day, we have wondered whether the time would ever come when American horticulture would ever be blessed by the same true love. This issue of the *Monthly* gives us hope. So many distinguished names, as well as matter from less known but not less valued contributors, have never appeared in one number before."[16] His contributors to that issue of the magazine included nurserymen Peter Henderson, Charles Mason Hovey, and Franklin Reuben Elliott.

Loudon realized that a gardening book was infinitely more influential and invariably more effective than even the most renowned garden.[17] Perhaps that is why he wrote so extensively throughout his life.

The English wrote most of the garden books read in America during the colonial Williamsburg era, but by the early nineteenth century more garden books from American authors were appearing, many produced by seed company and nursery owners. Book publishing was a way for a seed company or nursery to extend its message about horticulture to an emerging gardening public. Almost as soon as these companies started in America, in the early nineteenth century, their owners wrote books on how to garden. There simply were too few American titles, and their books filled that niche.

Seedsman Bernard M'Mahon's 1806 book *The American Gardener's Calendar* remained for fifty years the best American book on gardening.[18] M'Mahon copied English garden writers; he divided his book by the months of the year, specifying the work that had to be done in the garden or field for a particular month. M'Mahon borrowed particularly from John Abercrombie, author of *Every Man His Own Gardener,* which was first published in York in 1767 under the name of Thomas Mawe, the Duke of Leeds's gardener, who let Abercrombie use his name as author.[19]

M'Mahon also listed the seeds he had for sale. He promoted the kind of garden that his seeds would provide. Thus he became one of the early seedsman in America who both wrote about horticulture and promoted his own seed business in the same volume.

The first early American garden writer to address the issue of landscape design was M'Mahon. He wanted his readers to think about the art form associated with their home grounds and to pursue the use of space and plants to create a tasteful effect. The landscape he recommended for the home had sweeping views and even massive plants. He thought that nature should dictate the way plants were arranged, and so he preferred the more picturesque view, which by that point English landscape gardeners had advocated for several decades. M'Mahon wrote that there were two kinds of landscape design: the ancient style and the modern style. According to M'Mahon, the American gardener ought to prefer the new English style—the picturesque, or the modern.

In 1820, the Prince Company, one of the oldest nurseries in the country, published one of the earliest books on horticulture, *A Treatise on Fruit and Ornamental Trees and Plants.* Another Prince publication, *A Short Treatise on Horticulture,* from 1828, became the first garden book in America that broke from the English custom of treating horticulture in the calendar style used by M'Mahon, and earlier by Abercrombie and Mawe.[20] In 1846, Prince published one of the first books in America on roses, called *Manual of Roses,* which appeared at the same time that roses were beginning to become popular in American gardens.

American garden writers borrowed from European horticultural magazines and books. In his 1835 book *The New American Gardener,* Thomas Fessenden wrote, "The above directions are mostly copied and abridged from European writers on horticulture, of established reputation."[21] Nathaniel Hawthorne praised Fessenden as a man of genius. Though he depended heavily on English horticultural writing as his source, Fessenden did not shy from including American writers as well. In the same volume he wrote, "Mr. A. Parmentier of New York [referring to the American landscape pioneer who promoted the English picturesque style] wrote the article ['Landscapes and Picturesque Gardens'] for this work."[22] As indicated previously, Parmentier was the first to make a mark as a professional landscape gardener on this side of the Atlantic.[23] Unfortunately, the only writing by Parmentier that has survived is the article in Fessenden's book.

The Philadelphia seedsman Robert Buist was also a talented writer. U. P. Hedrick wrote that Buist was probably the most prolific horticultural writer in America in the first half of the nineteenth century.[24] In later editions of his 1832 book *The American Flower Garden Directory,* the first American book on flowers for gardeners, Buist wrote, "We boldly and fearlessly say that no country has made such rapid advancement in the art and science of horticulture in so short a period as the United States."[25] Other books by Buist include the *Rose Manual,* the first American book on roses, first released in 1844 and published in four editions, and *The Family Kitchen Gardener,* in 1847.

The Robert Manning Company, from Salem, Massachusetts, sold more than two thousand different kinds of fruit plants. That background in growing fruit trees provided Manning with the experience to write *Book of Fruits,* first published in 1838, and *New England Book of Fruit.* With the inspiration of Manning and other fruit growers, Hedrick said that no part of the country had produced so many good apples as New England.[26] Not only did the nurseries grow fruit, their owners also wrote books about fruit growing.

In 1843, Downing introduced fruit trees for sale in his catalog with these words: "In the present edition of our catalog we have the pleasure of offering (for the first time in this country) carefully prepared descriptive lists of all the most desirable sorts of fruit now in cultivation." Then on the inside back cover he advertised his own books, *A Treatise on the Theory and Practice of Landscape Gardening* and *Cottage Residences.* These were books that Joseph Shipley had in his library when he built Rockwood. They were the earliest books on landscape design by an American author. The English picturesque school of landscape design inspired Downing's writing as it did Parmentier's.

On the back cover of their 1867 Mount Hope Nurseries catalog, Ellwanger and Barry, from Rochester, New York, offered a book by co-owner Patrick Barry. The catalog described the book, *The Fruit Garden,* in these words: "A treatise intended to illustrate and explain the physiology of fruit trees; the theory and practice of all operations connected with the propagation, transplanting, pruning and training of orchard and garden trees."

The book added to Barry's list of publishing credentials. He was also the editor of the horticultural section of the *Genesee Farmer.* When Downing died in 1852, Rochester seedsman James Vick bought Downing's publication, *The Horticulturist,* and hired Barry, his friend, as its editor, thus keeping this important journal in the hands of the seed and nursery trade.

James J. H. Gregory, a seedsman from Marblehead, Massachusetts, introduced the Hubbard squash to the American garden. In his catalog of 1887, he listed the books he had written for the gardener: *Fertilizers; Onion Raising; Cabbages and How to Raise Them; Squashes and How to Grow Them;* and *Carrots, Mangold Wurtzels, and Sugar Beets.*

The success of Gregory's books is evident in this letter, dated 1886, written by F. T. Fleisbein, a customer from Atlanta: "Bought one of your books on fertilizers lat [*sic*] spring, Quite a no [number] of my friends wish to have one. I think I could sell a good many. Give me your lowest price."[27]

Like so many other seedsmen and nurserymen, Peter Henderson, from New Jersey, also an author, wrote the horticultural information that was necessary to become a successful gardener. From the beginning of the nineteenth century on, books were the liaison between nurserymen and the emerging middle-income class.[28] Henderson offered several gardening books free in his seed catalog of 1888. The customer who bought seeds would receive one or more books, depending on the amount of money spent.

Henderson wrote his garden books over a long career in the seed business. His titles include *Gardening for Profit, Practical Floriculture, Gardening for Pleasure, How the Farm Pays, Handbook of Plants,* and *Garden and Farm Topics.* When he died in 1890, his obituary referred to his garden books as being popular because they were eminently practical.[29]

The W. Atlee Burpee Company also published a series of garden books. In its 1894 seed catalog, the company explained why they published such books: "In the success of the planter is the germ of our success. First, the best seeds, bulbs, and plants; next, the plainly told practice of accepted experts in gardening." The company received a favorable response from readers for the books they published—over 73,000 copies sold—and so the books continued.

In one Burpee book, *Flowers for Every Home,* the author, E. D. Darlington, who was Burpee's grower in the trial gardens at Fordhook, said in the introduction, "Our book is intended more for beginners in flower gardening. The first steps are always the most perplexing and difficult, and the beginner invariably likes to know why he is told to do things in a certain manner."

The audience for books from seed companies and nurseries was made up of middle-class home gardeners. Americans were moving out of cities into suburbs and villages, where a small garden and lawn were seen as essential to a new home. Through their books, the writers provided what middle-class America needed to know about the landscape and the garden.

Recommended Reading

Garden catalogs often endorsed magazines and books written by seed company and nursery owners. In 1848, McIntosh and Company, from Cleveland, Ohio, made this comment in its plant catalog: "It is not enough for the planter to learn that raising fruit is pleasant and profitable; he should extend his inquiries further—read carefully horticultural books and journals, (such for example, as Downing's *Fruit and Fruit Trees, The Horticulturist,* and *Hovey's Magazine* [sic],) collect and compare statistics and thereby qualify himself to discriminate between varieties that are choice, hardy, and productive, and those that are inferior or worthless."

The A. R. Whitney Company, from Franklin Grove, Illinois, in 1858 also recommended the books of Downing and Barry: "Every man who sets a tree or plant should first procure some treatise on fruit raising, such as Downing on *Fruit,* Thomas' *Fruit Culturist,* or Barry's *Fruit Garden,* and there he will find everything in the line of fruit raising satisfactorily explained."

In 1890, the B. A. Craddock Company catalog, from Tennessee, offered at a discount price two important books by fruit grower Franklin Reuben Elliott, whose books covered the care of orchards and the design of a home landscape, including instructions for installing a lawn. The titles were *Elliott's Hand Book for Fruition Growers* and *Elliott's Practical Landscape Gardening.*

"Gardeners Who Can Write as Well as Practice"

The seed company and nursery owners often said that they were writing because they had the expertise, whether in greenhouse, garden, orchard, or field. They shared an ability to write down their experiences. Readers learned that know-how through the words on the page. That was a combination that the reader could not resist, making garden writing from the seed and nursery industries some of the most important horticultural literature of the nineteenth century.[30]

The inspiration for much of the writing of the American seed companies and nurseries was the English garden and landscape literature of the time, especially the writing of Loudon, who published an important magazine and several books. Loudon, called "the father of the English garden," often wrote for the weekend gardener who just wanted to grow something as simple as annuals in flowerbeds.[31]

American gardeners bought seeds and plants because the writers of the articles in the company catalog, along with horticultural magazines and books, told them how important the garden was to a society that called itself progressive and modern. To be progressive meant to be up-to-date in the garden with the current fashion. That included the newest seeds and plants. As the number of homesteads outside the city increased because trains and new roads made commuter access possible, America's middle class chose the kinds of grass, trees, shrubs, flowers, and vegetables recommended by the nineteenth-century seed and nursery companies. In the process, they followed an English style of gardening because American garden writers such as Downing, Hovey, and Vick had themselves long looked for inspiration in English garden writing.

American nurserymen and seedsmen of the nineteenth century left a marvelous horticultural heritage.[32] Their writing, whether in catalogs, magazines, or books, stands as their legacy to American gardening.

William Kenrick published *The American Silk Grower's Guide* in 1835, two years after the success of his volume on fruits. Shortly after that, a severe winter freeze as well as a disease that attacked the mulberry trees prevented his dream of a thriving silk industry in America from becoming reality. Kenrick would never recover from the setback.

In April 1844 he auctioned off many of the plants from his nursery. In 1845 another auction sold forty-two lots from the nursery. The trees he planted there, as well as those planted by his father before him, provided a picturesque setting for the landscape of the new home lots.

A year later Kenrick wrote a book to promote a railroad between Boston and Ogdensburg, New York. He said at the end of the book, "A company is formed, to which I would respectfully invite the attention of our citizens."[33] His name appeared simply as "William Kenrick, Newton, near Boston."

Kenrick closed his nursery in 1850, just four years later. He died in 1872, "having lived to see the orchards planted from his nursery come to full fruition and every part of New England made more beautiful by the ornamental trees and shrubs grown under his care."[34]

♣ ♣

FEATURED PLANT

Ipomoea lobata / *Mina lobata* / Firecracker Vine

THIS IS ONE of my favorite annual vines. I first saw it on a visit to Burpee's Fordhook Farm in Pennsylvania. The next summer I planted it out front at the lamppost, which was soon covered in red and yellow flowers.

The plant arrived in the United States in 1887. According to the Currie Brothers Seed Company magazine, *Currie's Monthly* of 1888, "The plant must have been flowering in the garden of the Royal Horticultural Society of London by 1841, when it first came to England from Mexico."[35]

We looked to England for this plant, and the plant merchants eventually sent it to the American garden. *Currie's Monthly* summed it up: "This is one of the most beautiful climbing plants we are acquainted with and one that is well worth the attention of all plant lovers."

Seed catalogs, as well as other garden magazines such as *Garden and Forest,* wrote about this new plant. The Dreer catalog of 1890 listed it as a novelty plant in these words: "Half-hardy Mexican climbing annual. The buds are, at first of a vivid red, but turn to orange yellow immediately before they open, and when fully expanded the flowers are of a creamy white shade. They are freely produced from the base to the summit of the plant, which attains a height of from 18 to 20 feet, and constitutes a strikingly beautiful object."

In his 1899 catalog, New York seedsman Peter Henderson sold a *Mina lobata* seed packet for ten cents. It was described there as a vine that "fits into almost any garden."

The growth of *Mina lobata* closely resembles that of morning glory, so it needs room to climb on a trellis or fence. It blooms from the middle of summer to early fall. *Mina lobata* does well in full sun or partial shade and survives best in a well-drained, moderately moist soil.

The flowers of the mina lobata are unusual. They are a shade of red, orange, yellow, and white, but as the buds mature the bright colors of the flower begin to fade to a lighter hue. The leaves are two to four inches in length and have five to seven lobes.

&2 *(facing page)*
Mina lobata (or *Ipomoea lobata*), firecracker vine

The Impact of Social Changes on the Seed and Nursery Industries

WEET PEAS had become the craze in gardening by the 1890s. The English, who called this flower the "Queen of Annuals," had by then provided the gardening world many wonderful varieties, but Silas Cole, the Earl of Spencer's head gardener, changed the sweet pea world forever when he introduced a bigger and brighter sweet pea, a flower gardeners everywhere coveted. The Spencer variety, as it is still called today, remains available through many seed catalogs.

W. Atlee Burpee, owner of the Philadelphia seed company, who recognized that the sweet pea mania had also spread to American gardens, brought the Spencer sweet pea to America to see how it would grow. Burpee had the sweet pea planted for testing at his new trial garden, called Floradale Farms, in Lompoc, California. An improved sweet pea followed, and soon the English presented Burpee with the only award for a sweet pea grower based outside England. A sweet pea craze swept America, thanks largely to Burpee, who, as an internationally renowned grower of this flower, became vice president of England's National Sweet Pea Society.

Burpee's interest in breeding plants began as a teenager in Philadelphia. In 1876, the year of the Philadelphia Centennial Exhibition, he disappointed his parents when he announced, at the age of eighteen, that he wanted to begin a chicken and livestock breeding business rather than pursue a medical career like that of his father. Within a couple of years he decided to focus only on plants, and the W. Atlee Burpee Seed Company was born. The name "Burpee" continues today in this long-running seed business, even through changes in ownership over the years.

Beginning in the early years, new plant varieties such as 'Surehead' cabbage and bush lima beans became staples in the annual Burpee catalog. Burpee traveled throughout the United States and Europe during the summers in search of new plant varieties. At Fordhook Farm, his home and experimental farm in Doylestown, Pennsylvania, he would evaluate vegetables and flowers for the catalog.

The business became an important late-nineteenth-century American seed company, eventually mailing out one million catalogs a year. His son took over the company when Burpee died in 1915.

A firm believer in the emerging modern form of advertising, Burpee wrote his own copy for the catalog even though he had an advertising department within the company. Burpee, like many other seedsmen and nurserymen, embraced nineteenth-century social changes so that the business would not merely survive but thrive in a competitive market.

Seed companies and nurseries became modern businesses selling products that were often identical to those offered by other companies, including the same seeds and plants. The new consumer culture, driven by advertising, demanded such standardization. The home gardener felt more comfortable buying from a company that was in line with its competitors. In the Victorian culture of late-nineteenth-century America, that meant that any product, from clothing to furniture, had to conform to a familiar style or fashion: mass production meant that everybody bought the same thing. The garden was no different. Seed and nursery catalogs had to offer similar seeds and plants and a common form of garden design. The English style, with its recognizable lawn and carpet bedding, became the garden fashion.

The nineteenth-century gardener lived in an increasingly industrialized age; the period was also a time of change for businesses and the goods they sold. Seed and nursery catalogs detailed the impact of modernization on their industry and reflected on how the country as a whole was changing.

The seed and plant industries took advantage of the growth of the railroads, the increase in the number of newspapers and magazines, and an expanding postal system. That openness to change made the seed companies and nurseries an important part of nineteenth-century America. The seed and nursery businesses grew, becoming bigger and more powerful. By the end of the century there were hundreds of such companies from Massachusetts to California, ready to fulfill their customers' hopes and dreams of a modern garden and home landscape that were promised in the words and illustrations of the catalogs.

Railroad

The Long Island Rail Road opened in 1836, enabling the gardeners and fruit growers who served New York to ship their produce to market in hours instead of days.[1] After seeing twenty years of growth in rail service, nurseryman C. M. Hovey said in his catalog in the 1850s, "Plants are now disseminated as rapidly over half the Union as they were in former years in the immediate vicinity of our large cities."

In Rochester, New York, on May 28, 1873, the city commissioners gathered at the site of the new city hall to lay the cornerstone. They buried a copper time capsule containing a document that told of the city's growth, so that future generations would know how progressive a city Rochester had become. The document read: "The railroads of Rochester, completed and in progress, are excellent, and now begin to be in keeping with her importance."[2] At that same time, Rochester seedsman James Vick, singled out in the same document for his business, which had attracted a national customer base, bought his own freight car so he could deliver his seeds on the tracks of the city's modern rail system.

Vick was not the only plantsman to take advantage of the emerging nineteenth-century rail service. Riverside Nurseries in Harrisburg, Pennsylvania, could ship live plants anywhere in the state within hours of receiving an order because there were forty-nine passenger trains leaving daily in every direction.[3]

By 1874, Burrow, Wood, and Co., from Fishkill, New York, were able to advertise in their catalog how the railroad had proved to be an asset to the business: "Our nurseries are located in the village of Fishkill, within five minutes walk of the New York, Boston and Montreal Railroad." Any interested customer could also quite easily come by rail to visit the nursery.

In their catalog of 1883, Miller and Hunt, in Chicago, included a black-and-white drawing of workers loading a railcar with nursery stock from the company. The caption under the image said, "The improvements that have been made within a few years in the preparation and care given to plants thus forwarded, together with the rapidity with which they are transported and delivered to their destination, no matter how distant, has reduced the percentage of loss to a minimum, so that we guarantee their safe arrival to all parts of the country."

In 1887, the S. Y. Haines Company, from Philadelphia, boasted of both its modern building and its accessibility by rail service, while Bragg and Co., from Springfield, Massachusetts, acknowledged in its 1889 catalog that the rail service helped the business with its very low freight rates. Green's Nursery, in Rochester, New York, discussed the revolution of rail service in its 1898 catalog, writing, "This has been called the iron age. It is the age of railroads, of steamboats, and of the bringing the ends of the earth together by means of rapid transportation."

By the end of the century, rail service stretched from coast to coast. By then the South, too, had its own seed industry. No longer did gardeners in the South have to depend on seeds from northern growers. H. G. Hastings and Company, from Interlachen, Florida, in its 1889 catalog wrote, "We are the only firm engaged in specially selecting and growing seeds for the southern states, and the high reputation already enjoyed by us is fully appreciated."

Roses, an important plant for the nineteenth-century garden, were often grown in England and shipped to America. In his 1899 catalog, Charles Dingee, from the Dingee and Conard Company of West Grove, Pennsylvania,[4] talked about the changes the rail service and the post office had brought to American rose gardeners:

> Nearly fifty years ago three young men bought out a small nursery here and went to work determined if possible to succeed. I was then thirty-three. Our post-office was served only once a week—Saturday. Our nearest railroad station was fifteen miles away. Now our post office is served four times daily and our railroad station is within a quarter of a mile of our office. Forty years has wrought some changes. We needed roses for our customers; they were hard to get, mostly English grown and budded. No dream then of growing them on their own roots by present methods and sending them safely in a growing condition by mail from the Atlantic to the Pacific, from the Saint Lawrence to the Gulf. Out of this want, and determined to supply it, the Dingee and Conard Company was born.

The fact that the seed and plant industries employed the railroads to ship products to customers also appeared in advertising. Images of railcars and their tracks within the pages of the catalog (fig. 6.1) told the reader that he or she was dealing with a modern company that employed the latest means of transportation. Surely, the customer would prefer to deal with such a progressive company.

Advertising

By the late 1700s, American newspapers were displaying ads for seeds, providing a new and wider reach for sales. Nathaniel Bird, a bookseller from Newport, Rhode Island, offered seed packets in an ad published in 1763. Samuel Deall and William Davidson, New York dealers in general merchan-

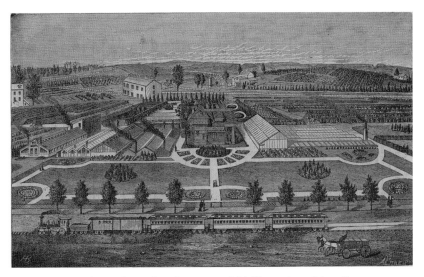

&e *Figure 6.1.* The modern railroad was part of this illustration of the office, green-houses, and fields that belonged to the Hoopes Nursery in Pennsylvania. *Courtesy of the Warshaw Collection of Business Americana—Seed Industry and Trade, Archives Center, National Museum of American History, Smithsonian Institution.*

dise, advertised seeds in 1776. A few years later, in Philadelphia, Pelatiah Webster, a writer on economics, advertised clover and duck grass seed.[5]

During much of the nineteenth century, the text in advertising was usually just product information with the name of the business and sometimes a black line drawing. In 1808 Landreth Seeds advertised in *Relf's Philadelphia Gazette,* using the following copy: "David and Cuthbert Landreth, seed and nurserymen, beg leave to inform the public that they continue to carry on their business as heretofore at their seed store in Market St., near 12th, at their nursery, Federal St., near Arsenal, and at their stall in the market, S.E. corner of the Old Court House every forenoon, Sunday excepted, where they have constantly for sale a general assortment of garden and flower seeds."

The increase in newspapers, made possible after 1830 by faster and cheaper printing, affected advertising as well. In the 1860s, the James Vick

Seed Company of Rochester, New York, advertised in over three thousand newspapers nationwide.[6]

By the end of the nineteenth century, advertising had been transformed into the most important marketing tool for any business, changing the business focus from simply selling a product to creating a consumer need for that product. Images, often illustrated in color by then, had become an integral part of the ad. A lithographed three-by-five-inch give-away card called a trade card, with an ad on one side and the business address on the other, represented the kind of advertising common by 1900.

In 1864, James J. H. Gregory, from Marblehead, Massachusetts, began advertising his seeds in newspapers. He said in one ad, "As the original introducer of the Hubbard Squash, Marblehead Mammoth Cabbage, and other choice vegetables, I invite the patronage of the public." The wording was simple and direct, with the emphasis on the most elementary information a gardener would need. Such was the style of most product advertising at that time, which served as an appeal to a rising middle class.[7]

After 1870, as competition became more intense, advertising in newspapers and magazines took on a more important role for the seed industry and nurseries. Sometimes the business would offer incentives to the newspaper editor to run an ad, such as the seeds that the Hiram Sibley Seed Company offered the newspaper in which it advertised. An 1887 letter addressed to newspaper editors, from the advertising department at the Sibley Seed Company, said, "Our advertising season has rolled round again and if satisfactory to you we are now prepared to make an arrangement for the insertion in your paper of our two inch, single column electro. This we should like inserted in your next issue to run sixteen weeks. Payment will be made in vegetable or flower seeds, of your own selection, from our Annual Catalogue, to the value of $7.00."

Not every seed company or nursery considered advertising essential for the business, however. As late as 1892, J. M. Philips Sons, from Mercersburg, Pennsylvania, thought simply giving out the catalog, as a listing of seeds, was enough to encourage business. In that year the catalog said, "We feel no need of extravagant announcement, special pleading, claims that cannot be verified or promises impossible of fulfillment; simply calling your attention to the following pages for prices and descriptions of what we believe to be one of the best assorted stock of 'Seeds' in the United States."

Owners who were not fans of advertising often said in their catalogs that customers paid for any advertising for a product, and indeed, doing business with a nineteenth-century seed company or nursery, including access to its catalog, generally meant that advertising costs were added to the prices. But some wondered why the customer should have to pay for advertising. Templin and Sons Company of Ohio questioned the value of advertising in its 1897 catalog: "[A] prominent seedsman, we are told, last season paid $30,000.00 for advertising, and nearly as much for catalogues. Did you ever stop and think who pays for all these expenses? Certainly those who purchase their goods must pay it, by giving more than the actual value for the plants and seeds purchased."

Burpee nevertheless believed that advertising was necessary for any business to succeed. In his 1897 catalog he wrote, "Advertising is as necessary an annual expenditure as the payment of taxes or rent. . . . Intelligent buyers realize that a good thing is worth advertising, and thus, making more sales, instead of increasing, advertising actually reduces the cost of goods."

Some nurseries and seed companies urged only truthful advertising. George Thompson and Sons, of Louisville, Kentucky, said in its 1892 catalog, "We do not advertise in these pages any such miserable 'novelties' that are displayed in catalogs of the trashy order—'Roses of Jericho,' at which a Syrian camel-driver would scorn to look twice, or any 'Boss' watermelon of impossible size."

Regardless of what position a company took on advertising, by the end of the century advertising had grown bigger and bolder. From 1880 on, advertising was used to introduce new products, homogenize tastes, and create a demand for new products.[8] *Ladies' Home Journal,* the most successful magazine in the country in the 1890s, achieved that status through its pages of ads for personal and household products that would make a middle-class woman's life easier. The financial success of *LHJ*, like that of other national magazines, emerged mainly from its advertising, not from its subscribers.

Before 1900, advertisers had to answer to no one. A company could say almost anything in an ad. So P. T. Barnum promoted the greatest show on earth and Ayer's patent medicine promised a cure for an assortment of medical problems. The seed and nursery industries likewise wrote what they wanted in their catalogs. Advertising historian Jackson Lears has observed that at that time there was a tendency to see selling as seduction.[9] What happened in the seed and nursery national advertising might be called a seduction by the images and words about the English garden.

Post Office

"Wherever the mail goes, our roses go and bloom," the Dingee and Conard Rose Company, of West Grove, Pennsylvania, wrote in its 1892 catalog.

By the 1850s, the United States mail service was cheaper and more efficient than ever before, and seed companies began to multiply. While the success of the mail-order seed and nursery businesses depended on the selling force of the catalogs, without question the post office was critical to the success of the seed industry in the nineteenth century. Later, many other businesses followed the industry's lead in using the postal system to ship catalogs and their products.

As a result of the Post Office Act of 1792, a new form of the post office became a vital communication link for the nation, carrying not just private correspondence but also newspapers, which were allowed in the mails at a low rate to promote the spread of information across the states. These newspapers also contained the advertisements of the few seed and plant companies.

America's population was predominantly rural for most of the nineteenth century, and so mail service was the best means for reaching the home gardener. The mail-order catalog became the primary method of advertising to the gardener, who eagerly awaited the arrival of the yearly catalogs for the newest information on seeds and plants. During the nineteenth century, the post office was truly an agent of change.[10]

By the late 1840s, postal rates had become affordable for businesses and opened the door to a potentially lucrative mail-order market. The mail quickly became an efficient dispenser of seeds and plants.[11]

By 1849, Henry Dreer, from Philadelphia, had begun to send his company's seeds through the mail. Denise Wiles Adams, who has done extensive research on heirloom plants, suggests 1850 as the year when mail-order purchase became a common form of seed catalog sales.[12]

In 1863, new postal rates enabled seed company owners to send four ounces of seeds for two cents. The companies thus enjoyed an inexpensive, dependable, and extensive system for delivering seeds to their customers and, in addition, could distribute the catalogs with a new third-class postage rate.[13] Philadelphia nurseryman Thomas Meehan wrote in his *Gardener's Monthly* in 1873 that wise post office laws were intimately connected to horticultural progress.[14]

Benjamin K. Bliss, a seedsman and florist from Springfield, Massachusetts, boasted of his early use of the mail service. He wrote in his seed catalog of 1865, "In the year 1854 we commenced putting up select assortments of flower seeds for sending by mail, that those who reside at a distance might enjoy equal facilities for procuring a fine display of flowers, at a moderate cost, with those who are nearer market. These collections are now favorably known in every part of the United States and Canada."

Bliss was certainly not the only seedsman to take advantage of the mail in expanding his customer base. The Gregory Company, for example, wrote in its 1872 catalog, "This [post office] law, in effect, brings my seed to every man's door."

Those who lived far from rail service could still receive packages from the seed and nursery companies through the mail. Ellwanger and Barry, of Rochester, New York, let their customers know in their catalog of 1881 that a popular rose could be easily received by mail: "There is a large number of our customers who, living at remote distances from the railroad or Express offices, cannot conveniently receive packages by Express. There is another and larger class, whose means do not admit of expensive purchases, but who cannot and will not be without flowers, and particularly without Roses. To such we are pleased to offer special inducements in the shape of Roses by Mail, at very low prices, thus enabling all to provide themselves with the most beautiful flowers."

By the end of the century it was not uncommon for large seed companies or nurseries to have their own post office. In 1886, John Lewis Childs announced in his seed catalog, "In consideration of the enormous mail business done at our place, the Post Office Department thought it necessary to establish a new post office in our seed store." In 1888, the Childs Company post office was renamed Floral Park Post Office. The railroad also changed the name of the local station. Thus, a local seed company started a Long Island town through the growth of its business.

Though this may be hard to believe, not every company endorsed the mail service for shipping plants. In 1888, the Good and Reese Company, of Springfield, Ohio, wrote in its catalog about a controversy over sending plants through the post office: "The same mail brought us last year catalogues denouncing the whole practice of sending plants by mail as wrong, and warning their customers against this method of transportation, while another contained the statement that they assured their patrons that they understood the art of mailing plants, and still another claimed that the mailing of plants was a great discovery, and that they had reduced it to a science. Now, some one of these statements was wrong, and they confuse the novice."

The mail-order business provided the inspiration for a new warehouse for Maule's Seeds, in Philadelphia. In his 1889 catalog Maule said, "Three years ago I had especially built for me the finest warehouse in America for conducting the mail-order business. I have devoted my entire attention to furnishing the gardens of America with my seeds direct, with the aim of doing the largest mail-order business on the continent."

Even when a seed company was located outside a city, it could still have easy access to its customers through the mail service. Joseph Harris, in his

1891 catalog, wrote of the new post office at Moretum Farm, his trial farm near Rochester, New York, "Hitherto we got our letters at Rochester, but we have now a Post Office on our own farm, and in our own seed house. In fact our facilities are far better in every respect than if we lived in the heart of the city."

As subscription magazine prices increased and businesses sold more through the mail, the early 1890s brought new postage rates that were favorable to business owners, including plantsmen. The Gregory Company made reference to the "New Postage Law" in its catalog of 1893: "Thanks to the persistent efforts of the Seedsmen's Association, Congress has reduced the postage on seeds one-half; viz., to one cent for two ounces, instead of one cent for an ounce, as formerly."

The Rural Free Delivery Act, which went into effect in 1896, allowed customers living on farms, in villages, and in suburbs to receive mail without charge. Until then, only city dwellers had enjoyed that privilege. Although two-thirds of the country still lived on farms at that time, the mail ensured the delivery of the seed and nursery catalog, along with the products advertised in it, to every rural mailbox.

In 1898, the Childs catalog said it was not uncommon during the busy months of the business "for Mr. Childs to receive as high as eight to ten thousand letters in a single day, including hundreds of Registered letters and thousands containing Money Orders." The mail delivery of seeds was so successful for the seed trade because the seed companies had learned that the seed packet, originally developed as a marketing strategy, made shipping seeds around the country easy. The business was truly a modern, efficient enterprise.

Usually a seed company located in the center of a city, would, like Vick's in Rochester, include several floors. The first floor would be a seed store where customers could walk in off the street to purchase seeds and bulbs. The second would be for the incoming mail. The third might be the packing department. The fourth would be the shipping department, where the seeds were packaged and mailed around the country. How impressive it must have been for a rural customer to see in the catalog how efficient and up-to-date the seed company was. Thus, a customer eager to be modern dealt with a company that displayed progressive values. The seed companies and nurseries did not fail to recognize the marketing strategy in that image and made a point of portraying themselves as modern, efficient enterprises.

Newspapers / Magazines

Just as the postal service benefited from changes in legislation in the late eighteenth century and into the nineteenth, so did the press. The ratification of the Bill of Rights in 1791 guaranteed freedom of the press, and America's newspapers began to take on a central role in national affairs.[15] By 1814, there were 346 newspapers. Newspapers throughout the country numbered approximately 1,000 in 1830. That same decade witnessed the development of a cheap newspaper, called the penny press. The term indicated a product that embodied the newest methods of papermaking, printing, and circulation. The penny papers, sold on city streets by newsboys rather than by subscription, were at the leading edge of journalistic innovation.[16] By 1895 there were approximately 20,000 newspapers in America.

The movement to create a more literate society accompanied the innovation in the printing industry. Books, newspapers, and magazines increased in number in the nineteenth century because of a literacy movement made possible by new press technology and cheap printing. In 1873, when Rochester's town fathers were laying the cornerstone for their new city hall, Rochester enjoyed five daily newspapers and a much larger number of weekly papers.

The seed and nursery industries early on recognized the important role of the newspaper for their business. Vick wrote in his catalog of 1874, "The influence of the press for good or evil is great in all civilized countries, but greater in America than in any other, because here everybody reads and takes the papers. The editors of newspapers sometimes give nurserymen and seedsmen a good deal of trouble. They are so anxious to furnish their readers the news, that if, by any chance, a report gets into any paper of a new shrub, or flower, or tree, it is copied into nearly all the papers of the country, causing a demand which it is impossible to supply." The newspapers were truly a mass medium of communication for cities and towns, enabling for the first time a garden and landscape described and illustrated by mass media.

In 1881, a new strawberry variety called 'Manchester' became available to the gardener. J. T. Lovett, in his nursery catalog of the following year, wrote about how news of this strawberry spread through the horticultural press: "Think of it! Formerly it took a quarter of a century to introduce a fruit, while now, the Manchester Strawberry, which I first offered to the public but a year ago, is now growing in almost every country on the face of the earth, even on the opposite side of the globe in New Zealand, where it is fruiting successfully."

Advances in printing also increased the number of books published, including horticultural titles. Newspapers carried ads for such books. Such advertising is alluded to by the Benjamin A. Elliott Company from Pittsburgh in its 1888 catalog: "The fifth edition of our book is now presented to our patrons and others, in the belief and hope that it may suggest ideas that may be of use, and that may be practically carried out in the making of gardens that must be a source of delight. We are also much encouraged to continue our efforts in behalf of hardy plants by the attention recently given the subject by the horticultural press, as well as some of the leading literary periodicals."

The seed and plant industries took advantage of the new printing technology as well to publish their own company magazines. Dingee and Conard, in their 1891 catalog, mentioned how their *Success with Flowers* had become possible: "A few years back a magazine like *Success with Flowers* could not be gotten out profitably under $1 a year subscription price; now marvelous paper-making machines and fast perfect printing presses, and above all, large circulation, give it to you for only 25 cents a year."

Chromolithography

Black-and-white woodcut engravings appeared in daily newspapers for the first time in the 1850s. By the end of the century, photographs would be used. Meanwhile, an important art form used for illustration in magazines and catalogs emerged called chromolithography.

Color lithography began in Europe in the early 1800s. Lithographers came to America first from England and France and, after 1850, from Germany. In 1821 an early American book called *A Flora of North America* was published, which was illustrated using chromolithography. By the 1850s, all major American cities could boast that their local businesses included lithographic companies.[17]

New opportunities for American lithographic firms arose after the Civil War, as America underwent major social and economic changes. Businesses such as seed companies and nurseries expanded rapidly and sought new markets for their products.[18] Though too expensive for newspapers, chromolithography was a popular form of illustration for catalogs and other forms of advertising, such as labels for seed packets and trade cards.

In Rochester, the growth in the nineteenth-century nursery and seed-house businesses offered employment to local printers, artists, and, of course, lithographers. Lithographic businesses such as the Stecher Lithographic Company, which remained in operation for 136 years, were kept busy most of the year with catalogs, advertising, and seed packets. By the late nineteenth century, more than two hundred Rochester printers, employed in eight local printing and lithograph firms, devoted their time almost exclusively to horticulture.[19]

By 1870 the colored lithograph had replaced the black-and-white engraving as the favored type of illustration in ads. The lithograph was called the democratic art because it made colorful art available to the middle class. The pages of catalog seed companies such as Vick's offered sixteen-inch by twenty-inch colored chromos of flowers grown from the seeds that the company sold. The middle-class homeowner could order the lithograph, frame it, and hang it on the wall as an affordable decoration (fig. 6.2).

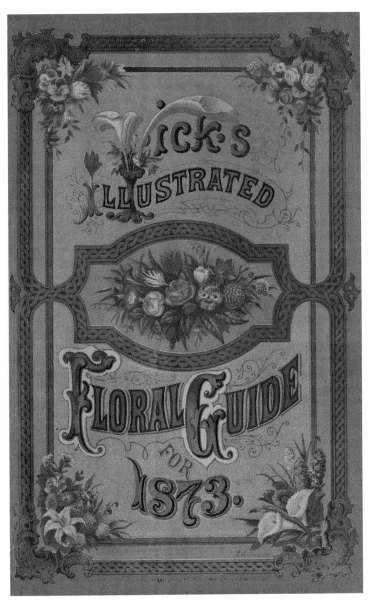

Figure 6.2. James Vick from Rochester was one of the first seedsmen to use color chromolithography, illustrated here in his 1873 catalog, an early use of the art form.

Major businesses around the country used chromolithography for advertising. Beginning in the 1840s, there was not a single chromolithographer of any significance who did not earn part of his income from creating or printing lithographic advertisements.[20]

One of the earliest chromolithographs in a seed catalog appeared in the 1867 autumn catalog of B. K. Bliss. The illustration showed popular garden bulbs, including the hyacinth, the tulip, and the lily. Henry Dreer also included a chromo of bulbs in his own 1867–68 catalog.

In the catalog, the seed company or nursery owner often let the customer know that his business included the latest technology used in producing the catalog's illustrations. Tillinghast, in its 1890 catalog, wrote, "This is not a seed catalogue, but a magnificent volume of elegant colored plates, by far the most extensive, and handsomest collection of floral lithographs ever published in this or any other country."

The D. M. Dewey Company, in Rochester, made chromos of trees, shrubs, and other plants available to the nurseries that employed salesmen who traveled the country to peddle their plants. For such companies, the catalog alone was not sufficient to increase sales. The chromos provided the homeowner a chance to see the plant in full bloom.

A company such as Mount Hope Nurseries, in Rochester, New York, would simply pick a few of the dozens of chromos of trees and shrubs that Dewey made available to form an individual sales book for the company's "tree peddler." Unfortunately, a scam artist—a peddler with a book of chromos but no connection with a nursery—would sometimes knock on a farmer's door, promising quality plants to a gullible homeowner. Because of that fear, Mount Hope eventually discontinued the practice of hiring such agents.

A Dewey illustration for their peddler's book used by the M. V. Johnston Nursery in Ohio in the 1870s showed a scene of the home landscape "as it is" and then another "as it will be," suggesting the final appearance when planted with the trees and shrubs that the peddler had to offer (see fig. 6.3). The chromo presented the English landscape in great detail, including a lawn, vines, evergreens, and curved pathways. Together they embodied the English garden design. That peddler, as a representative of the nursery trade, sold

As It Is. AN UNPLEASANT HOME
BEFORE PATRONIZING THE NURSERYMEN.

As It Will Be A PLEASANT HOME
AFTER PATRONIZING THE TREE DEALERS.

D. M. DEWEY.

Figure 6.3. The M. V. Johnston Nursery from Ohio in the 1870s included this image in the book that their tree peddlers used to sell the nursery's plants. Notice that the dramatic change to the "Pleasant Home" represents the English style of landscape. The D. M. Dewey Company in Rochester produced the lithographs for this collection. *Courtesy of the Newton Historical Society, Newton, Massachusetts.*

his customers not just plants but also an English gardenesque style of home landscape design.

The last quarter of the nineteenth century saw both an explosive growth in commercial promotional lithography and the eventual onset of a rapid decline as competing technology took over.[21] The photograph had arrived.

By the 1890s, photography was replacing both black-and-white engravings and colored chromolithographs for catalog illustration. Johnson and Stokes Seed Company, of Philadelphia, promoted photography in its 1894 catalog: "Putting 'the best foot foremost' in showing one's goods is natural and proper, but in advertising seeds it has led to such wild and absurd exaggeration that confidence in seed catalogue illustrations has been greatly weakened. We have always thought this is a great injury to the business; and to make our catalogues strictly accurate, while still properly showing the real merits of our novelties and specialties, we have adopted the method of photographic illustration from nature." As happened also in many other businesses that issued catalogs, after 1900 photography became the preferred method to illustrate the garden, the landscape, and the plants.

Customers from Coast to Coast

The growth of the nineteenth-century seed and nursery industries was intimately linked to the latest means of printing, illustrating, and delivering the much-anticipated catalog, or as Burpee called it, the "Silent Salesman." The industry tapped important technological and social changes such as the railroad, new post office regulations, cheap printing, and chromolithography and later photography, to build a national business.

As a result, seed and nursery catalogs arrived in more rural homes throughout the country, supporting an ever-growing number of customers. The success of the plant and seed business, especially after the Civil War, coincided with progress in printing, advertising, and transportation. The Childs Company of New York sent out 750 catalogs in 1875, but by 1896 the number had increased to 1,115,000.

The modern marketing of seeds and plants during the late nineteenth century corresponds with the selling of mass-produced household items such as food, cosmetics, clothing, and furniture: multiple copies of the same product, packaged in an assembly line and easily shipped. Gardeners, as part of a new consumer culture, wanted the seeds and plants that came from a modern business that sold a standard product through its catalogs and advertisements in magazines and newspapers.

At the same time the companies published a catalog, they also promoted a certain style of garden, with which the American gardener fell in love: the English garden. The catalogs were modern, informative, attractive, and useful—all qualities that made the reader more open to the style of garden and landscape design presented within its many colorful pages.

Burpee, the Adman

Because Burpee believed in the use of modern advertising as a means to increase his business, he offered a fifty-dollar cash prize for the best advertisement from his customers. The slogan "Burpee Seeds Grow" originated in the competition of 1890 and remained part of the firm's marketing for decades.

In a 1915 interview about his business, Burpee said, "Our catalogue bears the face of a friend, in which our customers have confidence. That confidence is the one thing we are willing to go to any amount of trouble to protect and defend."[22]

He died five months later. After his death, *Who's Who in Advertising* published Burpee's biography, in which these words appeared, "At the age of eighteen [Burpee] founded what has since become the largest mail order seed business in the world. Responsible for its development as a strictly mail order business, he is and always has been, sole author of its one source of development, the 'Burpee Seed Catalogue.'"[23] Burpee found a sense of pride in writing his own catalog and his own ads. He had become a seed company leader, all the while embracing modern advertising. In the year of his death, his company had issued over a million catalogs.

FEATURED PLANT

Clematis recta / Ground Virginsbower

THIS CLEMATIS IS more a shrub than a vine. In my garden it grows at the edge of a raised perennial bed of white flowering plants that I call my "white garden." Its tiny white blooms, hanging over the rocks that form the raised bed, cover the shrub for several weeks in June.

I once saw it in London's Chelsea Physic Garden. Plantsman and writer Phillip Miller (1691–1771) was the garden's director when this plant first came into England in 1753. No surprise, then, that I saw it in the Chelsea Physic Garden that day. Recognized for its medical usages, *Clematis recta* is mentioned in English physician and botanist William Woodville's *Medical Botany,* first published in 1794.

Clematis recta is native to Europe, particularly Russia, Hungary, Austria, and France. It was formerly called *Clematis erecta,* probably because of its shrub-like growth habit.

Though not a vine, it will grow two to four feet high. The leaves are opposite and feather-like. The leaves are also edible. The flowers at the end of the stem are arranged in an irregular, short, flower-like stalk. *Clematis recta* has many tiny, single star-shaped flowers.

This plant is a perennial for us in the Northeast and blooms from early summer on. It does well in full sun or in partial shade and can survive in almost any soil, including sandy and clay soils. *Clematis recta* provides a beautiful show in the garden. This plant is found in forests, valleys, hills, and woodland areas. It needs a medium amount of water and requires little maintenance.

♎ *(facing page)*
Clematis recta, ground virginsbower

Major Themes in the Catalogs

 HEN PETER HENDERSON, a twenty-year-old gardener from Scotland, arrived in America in 1843, he sought work with Philadelphia seedsman Robert Buist. Buist, a fellow Scotsman, took him in and gave him a job, just as Buist had done before for other immigrants from his homeland. Henderson stayed with Buist for a while but wanted his own garden business. America offered him his chance.

After years of growing and selling flowers, Henderson went into the seed business in 1865, opening up a store on Cortlandt Street, in New York City, where he would create his fame as both a seedsman and a writer. Henderson worked long hours each day, sometimes as many as sixteen. His writing he would put off till night. Before the typewriter arrived in 1880, he wrote by hand. He once said, "I am more at home handling a spade than a pen." But the work of his pen would prove to be a major contribution to the growth of horticulture in America.

C. M. Hovey recognized Henderson's writing talent early on. Hovey accepted Henderson's first article, dealing with transplanting large trees, for his publication, *Magazine of Gardening.* Thus began a new garden writer's career.

Henderson also wrote several articles for other popular garden magazines, including *The Horticulturist* and *Gardener's Monthly,* as well as four books. His writing was based on his experience in the garden. That authentic experience made the difference.

Like Burpee, Henderson also wrote the material for his catalog, which he called *Everything for the Gardener,* a name that expressed Henderson's conviction that he could meet any garden need within those pages. More people, however, in the farms and small towns of America knew the owners more through their free catalogs than through their books.

Owners of the major seed companies and nurseries, such as Hovey, Buist, Burpee, and Henderson, became familiar with one another partly through each other's writing and through each company's catalog but also through professional organizations. In 1883, the American Seed Trade Association began as a way for these seed merchants to organize and address common business concerns. The American Association of Nurserymen had already become a trade group for the nursery industry in 1877.

Thomas Meehan, the Philadelphia nurseryman and editor of *Gardener's Monthly,* would often write about the regular arrival of new seed and nursery catalogs at his desk. Sometimes he mentioned company owners such as Vick by name, when he noticed something special in the catalog. In the case of Vick, it was often the illustrations in color that caught Meehan's eye. Usually he simply wrote that a number of catalogs had arrived but that there was no space in the magazine to write about them.

Burpee made a point of saving catalogs from other companies, including Vick's and Maule's, and his company continued that practice after he died. Today the Smithsonian's Division of Horticultural Services oversees the extensive Burpee collection of hundreds of catalogs, which are now stored at the National Museum of American History.

Seed company owners routinely ordered seeds from other seed companies—seedsman James Gregory, from Marblehead, Massachusetts, for instance, ordered seeds from major seed companies including Ferry, Vaughan, Lovett, and Burpee[1]—so they were certainly familiar with their competitors' catalogs. This familiarity would include knowledge of the concerns of the owner in the introduction, the articles, and, of course, the products for sale.

It is no coincidence, therefore, that catalogs frequently discussed topics that also appeared in other seed and nursery catalogs. With authors sharing a mutual interest and familiar with each other's works, the articles and introductory essays reflected common concerns. Company owners' choice of topics gives an insight into the companies and at the same time demonstrates how powerful the companies were in creating a unified voice for the industry. Major themes that the catalogs shared in common, which the writers used to persuade customers to buy seeds and plants, include a wide range of topics, such as progress, novelties, company buildings, awards and premiums, science, and children.

Progress

To be progressive was to be modern. The whole nation was focused on modernity, as expressed in such issues as technology, politics, marketing, transportation, westward expansion, and the growth of the suburbs. Because it was important for any business that its customers know that it was progressive, the seed companies and nurseries wrote about their efforts to keep current. As early as 1862, Bateham, Hanford, and Company, of Columbus, Ohio, highlighted their plans to stay progressive: "It is our intention to 'keep up with the times' in this, as in other departments of our business; hence we shall add to our stock from time to time such new and desirable articles as are brought to notice in this or other countries."

Though long established, Mount Hope Nurseries in Rochester still had to keep its name before the public. In its fruit catalog from the 1880s, forty years after its founding, the company wrote, "On the whole, our patrons and friends will see that we are endeavoring to keep our collections fully up to the times. Neither labor nor expense is spared for our experimental grounds, [for] such varieties as give fair promise of value. Fruit culture is progressive and there can be no progress without experiment."

Improvement in the availability of newer vegetables became a goal for the D. M. Ferry Company. In its catalog of 1884, both celery and the tomato are presented as examples of how the seed industry was truly progressive. Ferry wrote, "We have come to look upon the growth and improvement possible in the seed business as practically without limit. It is but a few years since celery and tomatoes were almost unknown as food plants. Today, in a single country, 300 factories employ 1,500 persons in canning tomatoes; and celery, besides being found in nearly every garden in our land, is grown commercially in immense quantities in certain favorable localities."

Earlier in the century, flowers were not considered an essential in a home landscape; it was a time when farms and orchards played the major role for the gardener. That changed when progress became equated with the planting of certain flowers just then available for sale. The O. M. Richardson Company catalog of 1890 told its customers so: "Every year, as progress in civilization advances, more homes are made beautiful by the addition of flowers. What is more pleasing to the eye than a bed of choice geraniums or verbenas? Each flower is a wonder in itself, the mechanism of which no mechanic can imitate, the color of which no artist can reproduce. Yet such may be had for a small outlay of time and money."

The pulse of the country could be measured by how people demanded plants for the landscape. At least, that was how the seed and plant industries defined progress. The home landscape became the preeminent symbol of the country's development. The George A. Sweet Company, of Dansville, New York, proclaimed in its catalog of 1891, "Nothing better illustrates the progress of our country, the advance in civilization its people are making, and the fact that they are learning to live better, than the greatly increased and continuing demand for nursery stock, both fruit and ornamental."

In 1893, the Landreth Company, of Philadelphia, wrote in its catalog about a progressive spirit that seemed to motivate every American business:

> With Americans progress is the watchword. It enters into every avocation of life—at the mechanic's bench, in the mill, at the workshop, on the rivers and the lakes. The great aim of all imbued with our national spirit is to go ahead and get onward. It is that impulse that has made us as a people what we are, and marked out our future destiny as the ruling power of the world. The American artisan has eclipsed all others in many departments of handicraft, and the mechanical genius of our people is the admiration of mankind. Shall the farmer lag behind?

The seed business, like every other venture, needed to appear progressive in nineteenth-century America. The customer, in turn, wanted to know that he or she was dealing with a progressive company.

No matter what kind of garden the reader had, it was important to be progressive. By 1896, when there were many more seed and nursery catalogs than at midcentury, one of the newer companies, J. T. Huntington, of Indianapolis, continued to maintain the importance of the progressive spirit for the market gardener. Its company catalog urged, "You must not only have your ground in such shape as to bring out all its producing powers, but you must grow products that bring the most money, make the largest yields, and can be cultivated and harvested for the least expense; also something that not only brings quantity, but possesses a rich quality. Times are changing. Old methods will not do. You must have a progressive spirit to successfully meet the demands of the times."

Burpee, in his catalog of 1902, highlighted the importance of being progressive in the gardener's choice of seeds: "The farmer of today who is not progressive cannot long survive his more successful neighbor who casts off the old ways and adopts the new, and is often enriched thereby. In St. Louis, 1903, these marvelous steps in progress will be exemplified in our World's

Fair, where agriculture and its products will be an important feature." The fair, held in St. Louis, exhibited a display from Henry Shaw's garden, which had by then become the Missouri Botanical Garden. As a pioneer in America's botanical garden movement, Shaw would have been happy to show off a progressive St. Louis.

Novelties

The English, beginning in the seventeenth century, treasured foreign plant varieties, and plant collectors traveled the world—including America—to find plants to satisfy that desire. In the early 1800s, an English landscape would often have a garden area called the American garden, which focused on new plant varieties from North America.

The catalogs sometimes encouraged American gardeners to embrace American native plants for their own gardens, but like the English, they sought new exotic varieties. The seed companies and nurseries of America, too, wanted to offer their customers new plants each season. Such plants were called novelties and were usually placed in the catalog's opening pages. These novelty pages were frequently printed on a different color of paper stock from the rest of the catalog: a light blue, sometimes a pale yellow, and even a soft pink, while the remaining pages were white. Thus, the novelty pages stood out as soon as the reader opened the catalog. The intent was to make the novelties appear important. They were not like last year's plants, which were old news and appeared in the back pages of the catalog. If the novelty from last year failed to live up to its promises, it simply disappeared from the pages of the following catalog.

Companies sometimes chose to feature novelties within the catalog's regular pages. From Chicago, the John Charles Vaughan Company sold novelty plants, but in 1891 offered them within their regular selection and not at the front of the catalog. Their colorful and thick catalog of that year said, "We no longer classify specialties and novelties in prominence at the front of our list, but retaining only the valuable, have placed all specialties and new seeds and plants in our regular alphabetical list, that they may stand or fall in a fair examination or trial on their merits with all the well known kind."

Regardless of their placement in the pages, novelties formed an important theme in the catalog. They became a must for the gardener who needed to have the latest plant variety, because the seed or plant catalog claimed the newer variety was better.

Different companies frequently sold the same novelty plants, which were often imported from Europe or Asia. Bartram wrote in its 1807 catalog, "We return thanks to our friends for many valuable presents of rare plants, which have served to increase the variety and usefulness of our collection." The G. H. Barr Company, in New York, wrote in 1853, "In addition to the standard and approved varieties, every novelty worthy of note will be added from time to time."

Though they had offered novelties previously, by 1860 catalogs had come to maintain the absolute importance of novelties for the customer. The seed merchant B. K. Bliss wrote that year in his catalog, "We would respectfully invite the attention of all lovers of flowers to the following list of plants, containing, in addition to all the leading varieties of former years, many that are new and rare, now offered for the first time in this country."

Briggs, of Rochester, New York, maintained that the purpose of the seed catalog was to introduce new plants to the gardener. The company wrote in its 1870 catalog, "To do our share in putting these results before the public on a larger scale than we have done heretofore, and to encourage the cultivation of the new and more expensive class of flowers and vegetables, is our object in publishing this descriptive and illustrated catalog. In fact, the increasing public taste has required it of us; it has been called for in various ways by a multitude of friends."

The company sold new plants because the customer wanted them. Yet at the same time the seed and plant trade told the gardener that he or she needed the plants. Did the customer need them because the catalog said so, or because the customer simply wanted the latest in garden fashion?

The seed companies and nurseries did not fear the expense involved in obtaining the latest plant novelty. The Hoopes Company, of West Chester, Pennsylvania, wrote in its 1882 catalog, "Few of our patrons can form any idea of the heavy expense we annually incur in obtaining these new plants. Not only are all the choicest novelties imported direct from leading florists of England, France and Germany, but in our own country, every new plant giving promise of merit is at once procured and tested."

The customer learned from the company what were the important new plants, as well as the importance of adding these to one's plant collection in the garden. In 1884, Meehan wrote in his *Gardener's Monthly* that many were still unfamiliar with the *Weigela* shrub that both Shipley and Shaw had planted thirty years earlier. Meehan wrote, "It is surprising that though it has been known [for] some years it is yet as scarce as though a wholly new plant."[2]

The Hallock and Thorpe Company, of Queens, New York, noted in 1885 how the cultivation of new plants had spread throughout the country: "We are reminded of what an interest has grown during the past ten years in lilies, in roses, in geraniums, in gladioli, in carnations, and in chrysanthemums. We are not wrong when we say that the interest is more than hundred-fold increased. We point with pride to the labor we have done in those fields, to the numerous varieties that are of our origination—we may say, our children." Like the long line of British and American plant collectors, the seed companies and nurseries continued to search out and offer new plants because it was an important part of their business.

The author of the catalog told readers that he kept his eye out for available plants to offer for sale but chose only those that were truly worthwhile. The reader could depend on the results of that vigilance. The Green Nursery in Rochester wrote in 1889, "Through our system of securing most of the new varieties that have merits, and testing them in our sample orchard, vineyards, berry fields and beds before listing them in our catalog and recommending them to our patrons, we have knowledge as to which varieties are best for various localities."

Canna

ONE POPULAR novelty plant in the nineteenth century was the French canna, introduced in the Joseph Harris catalog of 1891. Harris wrote, "The new French cannas are perhaps the most valuable floral novelties of recent introduction. They can be grown from seed and come into flower the first season. The plants are dwarf in habit, growing from 3 to 4 feet high, and are remarkable for the size and brilliancy of their flowers and the beauty of their foliage."

The Vaughan Seed Company, in 1892, also mentioned the French canna as a desirable plant. The catalog listed the offering of varieties by M. Crozy, a Frenchman who had, since 1870, developed 220 cultivars. They wrote, "It is well known to most of our customers that greater improvements have been made in French cannas than any other class of plants. The many beautiful varieties raised and sent out by M. Crozy have made rapid strides in popular favor and the demand for them is everywhere on the increase."

By 1898, the A. Blanc Company, in Philadelphia, had introduced the newly developed American cannas. The catalog said, "It has been conceded by experts that the American cannas, grown by specialists, are preferable for all purposes to the French hybrids." A new canna variety called "Philadelphia" was described in these words: "After three years' trial this has proved to be the best canna grown to any extent up to the present time." The latest plant was constantly replaced by even newer varieties. The ongoing search to offer the most contemporary selections was discussed in every catalog.

The story of the canna was also that of many other plant varieties. A certain plant would appear on the market, offered as a novelty in the catalog. It would be grown for a while, and then replaced by a newer variety.

Even though many companies featured the same novelties, keeping ahead of the competition in obtaining newer plant varieties also became an important theme in the catalogs. The Connecticut-based Hale Company wrote in its 1889 catalog, "In fruits, as well as in every other business, the greatest profits are made by those who lead, or keep very near 'the head of the procession.' There is neither fun nor profit in following along two or three years behind and simply imitating those who have gone before."

If a company was not a leader with a new variety in which customers expressed interest, it might order novelty plants from another firm to satisfy customers' desires for the newer plants. Henry Dreer advertised Burpee's Emerald Gem Melon without mentioning that the plant came from Burpee.

By the 1890s, catalogs were claiming that the customer demanded the novelties. Yet for at least fifty years, the companies themselves had proclaimed that these plants were important for the garden. The Childs Seed Company wrote in 1890, "Customers will look every year for a lot of sterling novelties, which you must provide, and each must prove as worthy as you recommend. These are not easy to get, and usually cost enormously." The company owner assumed that the gardener would be on the constant search for new plants. Of course, the gardener's desire for novelties was fed by the seed and plant catalogs' insistence that novelties formed an integral part of gardening.

After 1850, as the seed and nursery catalogs from West Coast companies appeared, the format of their catalogs resembled those long sent from the East Coast. The Ives Company, of Albuquerque, New Mexico, in 1892 invited its customers to choose new seeds to make the home a more comfortable place. The company wrote in its catalog, "We invite the attention of those who want 'something new' to our well-selected list of novelties. They are of sterling worth, and we believe some will replace old favorites. And those who prefer the old friends, tried and true, will find them in our general list of plants and bulbs. Old and new are all worthy of a careful trial."

Because it was important that gardeners keep up with the newer varieties of plants, the catalog sometimes avoided listing old varieties in favor of the newer ones. In 1897, the owner of the Eaton Company, based in South

LOVETT'S GUIDE to Fruit Culture.

CUTHBERT
MANCHESTER
HANSELL
GOLDEN QUEEN

J. T. Lovett
Little Silver, N.J.

Monmouth

SPRING

1887

Geo. E. Errington Del.

CHAS. HART & SON, LITH. 36 VESEY ST. N.Y.

Figure 7.1. This cover of Lovett's 1887 catalog mentions the 'Manchester' strawberry, though by then its reputation had begun to fade. *Courtesy of the Bailey Hortorium, Cornell University, Ithaca, New York.*

The 'Manchester' Strawberry, the Greatest on Earth

*T*HE CASE of the novelty 'Manchester' strawberry is a good example of a plant that several catalogs listed as a worthwhile new plant but quickly discarded, in this case within five years.

The Lovett Company, of Little Silver, New Jersey, first wrote about the 'Manchester' strawberry in its catalog of 1882: "It is not claimed that the Manchester is a perfect strawberry—but it is believed that it is nearer so than any variety that has yet been disseminated. In fact, it is with complete confidence [that] we make the broad claim that it is 'the greatest strawberry on earth.'" By that time, the 'Manchester' strawberry had already been on the market for one year.

During the years from 1883 to 1885, at least seven catalogs praised the 'Manchester' strawberry as an important new fruit. About the 'Manchester', the Bliss catalog of 1883 wrote, "It is safe to assert that no strawberry introduced within several years has received so many favorable comments from prominent fruit-growers and dealers, and that no other kind combines so many desirable qualities. For family use, as well as for market, it stands preeminent." In the same year, the Crawford seed catalog said that the 'Manchester' "was claimed to be 'the greatest strawberry on earth.'" The Fitts Company that year wrote, "For home use or market it stands pre-eminent. The plant is a strong vigorous grower, free from rust or blight, wonderfully productive, bearing uniformly large fruit of a bright scarlet color, and in quality better than any other very productive variety."

There is, however, little mention of it after that time. Ford, in his 1886 seed catalog, said, "Manchester oh Manchester! A year ago we said thou wert one of our very best, but thy behavior the past season has wrought a great change. Good bye, oh Manchester, good bye" (fig. 7.1).

Sudbury, Massachusetts, wrote, "My list of varieties is much larger this season than last, though not as extensive as that found in many catalogs, as I do not think it advisable to offer the many old varieties which have long been superseded by better ones."

Not every seed company or nursery, however, thought novelties were worth the money. In its 1870 catalog the Knox Company, from Pittsburgh, reluctantly agreed to jump on the novelty bandwagon: "For pecuniary reasons solely, it is an undoubted fact that hundreds of varieties and subvarieties are annually offered in this country and introduced here from Europe as new and greatly to be desired articles, that have nothing but their newness to recommend them, and often times not even that, that are soon discarded as worthless. As a rule, the old established varieties of vegetables are the best, and the new ones are but seldom superior to them, and consequently are well left alone." Knox was one of the few companies opposed to spending on novelties, because they sometimes proved not worth the investment.

The Parker and Gannett Company, of Boston, accused certain seed companies of just filling space in the catalog by offering useless novelties. In 1882, the company catalog included the following precaution: "There may be varieties found wanting in the following pages that figure prominently in more pretentious volumes; but such names as only serve for literary adornment we have carefully expelled, to make room for those whose merits we know will commend them to a place in every collection."

Offering novelties simply meant that the catalog had to be bigger, according to James R. Pitcher, a seedsman from Short Hills, New Jersey. Not all novelties, he argued, were worth the money, because you might not see them offered in the next catalog. Pitcher wrote in 1893, "Not only the trained gardener, but the amateur as well, has doubtless long since observed the misapplication of this title 'novelties' by concerns publishing large editions of gorgeous catalogues, and claiming to present under this heading flowers, plants, and vegetables recently discovered or originated, which are brought into notice by impossible drawings and glowing descriptions, seemingly with but one object—that of selling! To a very great extent this bad practice has lessened the credibility and due appreciation of the gardening public for any really new and desirable article brought before their notice by modest and true representations, many of these so-called and highly lauded novelties having turned out, after testing, to be either complete delusions or mere resurrections of some old and forgotten types, that never had sufficient individuality or merit to deserve continued prominence."

Exotic versus Native Plants

In nineteenth-century America, the search for newer plant varieties often supported an inclination to explore areas outside rather than within the United States. Through most of the nineteenth century, the catalogs considered native plants to be less desirable for the home landscape or garden than exotic or imported plants were. Garden historian Denise Wiles Adams examined American seed and nursery catalogs from 1750 well into the early twentieth century and found that there were 103 plants listed continually in the catalogs. Although there were a number of native plants on the list, the majority were exotic.[3]

Some companies, however, advocated the cultivation of native plants. From the colonial Williamsburg era of the seventeenth century into the next century, the John Bartram Company argued for the importance of native plants in American gardens. In 1870, English garden writer William Robinson, in his book *The Wild Garden,* recommended native perennials rather than the labor-intensive carpet bedding with annual plants. We know that his advice influenced American seed companies and nurseries, because Robinson began to be referenced by seed and nursery catalogs such as that of James Vick, who featured articles on the wild garden in his monthly magazine.

The earliest American mention of the native American plant *Baptisia australis* occurred in 1783, when it first appeared in Bartram's garden. Downing later included notice of it in *The Horticulturist* of 1846, when John J.

Thomas suggested "the combination of blue Baptisia with red and white Dictamnus and Aquilegia Canadensis."[4] By 1899, Peter Henderson's catalog was offering it under the category "Hardy Perennial Plants." By then styles had changed and perennials were becoming more desirable in the garden, including native plants.

The British plant collector and nurseryman Thomas Drummond traveled to America in the 1830s, when he discovered *Phlox drummondii* in Texas; the plant was later named after him. By the 1870s, American seed companies, including Vick, were offering the plant for sale. *Phlox drummondii* is just one of many native plants that came back to American gardens after they proved to be desirable additions to the English garden.

In 1892, the Harlan P. Kelsey Company, of Linville, North Carolina, encouraged the gardener to choose native plants: "It is a notable fact that while our parks, cemeteries, lawns and gardens have been stuffed to overflowing with these costly foreign importations, our most beautiful and easily obtained native ornamentals have been almost entirely excluded."

The focus on native plants shifted the discussion of novelties in the plant catalogs at the end of the nineteenth century. By then the available novelties included native trees, shrubs, perennials, and annuals. In the 1890s, Americans ended their reliance on Europeans for new plants, drawing on native resources and pursuing exotics abroad.[5] Boston's Arnold Arboretum, with the help of English plant explorer E. H. Wilson, collected its own plants in areas outside the United States, including China and Japan. Later, other public gardens in America, such as Longwood Gardens, also sent out plant collectors.

Company Buildings

Another theme that often appeared in catalogs was the important role of the company's facilities, which included offices where orders were received and filled, where seeds were stored, and where one could find greenhouses,

Native Plants Return Home

SOMETIMES A native American plant would come back home from abroad, finding a place in our gardens only after the English had cultivated it for decades.

The following appeared in Philadelphia nurseryman Thomas Meehan's journal, *Gardener's Monthly,* of 1882:

> It is often a matter of surprise that the English should grow what they call "American plants" better than we can. These plants form the greatest attraction of their grounds. Why should not America grow American plants? Now, what they call American plants are only those chiefly which belong to the Ericaceous family. These are Rhododendron, Azalea, Kalmia, and Andromeda, and such well-known beautiful flowering shrubs in which America abounds. But it is not generally known here that they could not grow them there if it were not for the garden art and garden skill at the back of their culture. . . . There is no reason why, with a little study to adapt our circumstances to the wants of these plants, we should not have as good "American plants" as they have in England.[6]

trial gardens, and even box-making factories. This was, after all, a business, and the customer had to be convinced that the seedsman or nursery owner had the most modern buildings. In 1886, Meehan's *Gardener's Monthly* called the new five-story building that William Henry Maule built in Philadelphia "evidence of his success" even though his seed firm was new.[7]

Often illustrated in the company catalog, a business's facilities were represented as having been built in the latest style, as the most equipped and extensive, and as being capable of handling any orders. Owners wanted the catalog reader to understand that the company was current and had the newest in technology to handle the important business of growing and selling seeds and plants. Sometimes illustrations of the facilities where the order was received, filled, and sent out were included within the pages of the catalog, as was the case with Peter Henderson's five-story company building in New York (fig. 7.2).

Illustrations included in the catalog often reinforced the written message. Maule, located in Philadelphia, pointed out his buildings in his 1889 catalog: "Do not the illustrations of my warehouses on this and opposite page, prove beyond question that I have good reasons to be proud of a business requiring such facilities to conduct it? Above cuts are exact representations of my Filbert and Jones St. stores, while [the] illustration opposite is a good interior view of the Filbert St. property. These are not fancy pictures, but represent things just as they are."

Ferry Company wrote in 1881, "The more perfect the facilities for handling a crop of seed, the less the liability of error." A company often boasted that it had the newest or best buildings in the town, the country, or even the world. Ferry made that argument in the same catalog: "We give a representation of our new seed warehouse, one of the largest buildings used for mercantile or manufacturing purposes in the city of Detroit."

The facilities might also include up-to-date greenhouses. Thus, the customer would learn that the company was growing plants year-round and so could provide a quality product. Storrs and Harrison discussed their greenhouses in their 1885 catalog: "Our greenhouses number twenty-one,

VIEW OF THE
SEED WAREHOUSES
OF
PETER HENDERSON & CO.
35 & 37 CORTLANDT ST. NEW YORK.   Frontage 51 feet, Depth 130

🌿 *Figure 7.2.* Peter Henderson had a thriving business at his seed store in New York, an image of which was included in his seed catalog. The upper floors were devoted to receiving and shipping seed orders. *Courtesy of the Warshaw Collection of Business Americana—Seed Industry and Trade, Archives Center, National Museum of American History, Smithsonian Institution.*

averaging over one hundred feet in length, all in perfect order and heated throughout with the best approved hot water apparatus, which makes the most perfect atmosphere for their production of healthy, hardy plants."

It was important, too, that the reader know that the company continued to build facilities to meet the growing demand for its seeds and plants. New construction, therefore, became a theme in many catalogs. Joseph E. Bonsall, from Salem, Ohio, wrote in his 1887 catalog: "The past summer has been a very busy one with me, not only looking often after the plants that I already had, but building more houses to accommodate my increasing trade."

New facilities, combined with experience and strong customer service, made for a dependable company with which one would like to conduct business. The Haines Company, of Philadelphia, described its facilities in 1887 as being situated near all the principal shipping points, both railroads and steamers, and as fitted with the modern improvements necessary for the business. That made it just the kind of company any gardener could trust.

In its 1888 catalog, Ferry described its box factory in these words: "It is a three story building, in the same architectural style as the warehouse, and especially adapted to the manufacture and repair of our boxes, of which we have in use over 250,000. Here, in the busy season, 100 men are at work with various machines designed especially for us, and capable of doing everything from the sawing of the lumber to the sand-papering of the finished boxes. We annually manufacture over 700,000 feet of lumber, much of it black walnut, into about 35,000 boxes." By the end of the century, the Ferry Company had two buildings: an eight-story office building and a six-story box factory across the street (fig. 7.3).

The John Lewis Childs Company claimed to be the best in the country because it had the latest in buildings, heating systems, and machinery. In 1892, the company's bulky, colorful catalog said, "Our principal store was erected in 1890 and is an impressive 4-story and basement structure, built entirely of brick and iron and is therefore absolutely fire proof. It is the finest

D.M.FERRY & CO'S SEED WAREHOUSES AND BOX FACTORY,
DETROIT, MICH.

&& *Figure 7.3.* The facilities of the seed company were often a theme in the catalog, as here in an illustration from the 1897 Ferry Seed catalog. *Courtesy of the Bailey Hortorium, Cornell University, Ithaca, New York.*

seed house in America and is fitted with every convenience for filling orders promptly and correctly. It is heated by steam and is furnished with gas and water, and has a powerful gas engine for running the necessary machinery and elevator."

A discussion of the outstanding facilities sought to win over the customer, who was often far away and would probably never visit the company. Just knowing that the business had such large and contemporary buildings must have made the reader think the business itself was impressive. As was clear in the pages of *Ladies' Home Journal,* standardized products from any industry were important to buyers, mostly women, because such products also represented a sense of what it meant to be progressive and modern. People wanted them.

Awards and Premiums

Nineteenth-century advertising added the attraction of awards and premiums as another marketing strategy in an increasingly competitive environment. Many products, as illustrated in the advertising pages of *Ladies' Home Journal* during the 1890s, saw such promotions as essential. Awards and premiums were sent through the mail, but they were also won at fairs and exhibitions, including local flower or horticultural society shows.

In 1810, Elkanah Watson organized the first county fair where premiums for gardening were offered in Pittsfield, Massachusetts.[8] After that, the display of and the awards for the best fruits, vegetables, and flowers became an important part of the annual state fair around the country. Throughout the century, fairs also became an important vehicle to showcase a seed company's or nursery's seeds and plants. The fact that the companies received awards for their flower or vegetable displays at such fairs and exhibitions became another ad in the catalog to persuade the reader that their product had quality.

Vick's seeds won prizes at various state fairs. In 1872 Vick traveled to Milwaukee for the Wisconsin State Fair, where he received a silver medal for his flower arrangements. An article in the *Milwaukee Sentinel* of 1876 mentioned a premium at the upcoming state fair for the best display of flowers from Vick's seeds.

Recognition for an award appeared often in company catalogs. In his 1877 catalog, Robert Buist reported that "Buist's Garden Seeds were awarded the Grand Prize Medal at the Centennial Exposition." On the back cover of its 1895 catalog, the Dundee Nursery from Illinois included an image of its evergreen exhibit at the World's Columbian Exhibition in Chicago in 1893, where the company also won "the highest and only award for the best collection of hardy evergreens."

Figure 7.4. Mandeville and King Seedsmen of Rochester offered premiums for purchasing their seeds. *Courtesy of the Warshaw Collection of Business Americana— Seed Industry and Trade, Archives Center, National Museum of American History, Smithsonian Institution.*

The seed companies and nurseries often let their readers know that they rewarded customers for their purchase of seed and plants (fig. 7.4). Vick offered a premium to anyone who bought the company's flower seeds, a practice common in other late nineteenth-century industries as well. In the 1890s, the Pabst Brewing Company in Milwaukee offered a premium of colored lithographs, suitable for framing, and also a calendar, in return for purchasing their Malt Tonic beverage, which the company marketed to women and sold in drugstores.

The seed and nursery industries conducted business much like other industries, showcasing awards for their products and offering premiums. The catalogs reflected that message in word and illustration. The practice has not been lost. Today, to make a purchase more attractive, marketers still entice a customer with a reward.

Science

Another theme used to persuade readers to purchase seeds or plants was the focus on science. This theme emphasized the fact that the company employed skilled horticulturists who used the latest scientific methods, such as hybridizing, to produce the best seed or plant. Burpee, a plant breeder from an early age, gave the world several new vegetables and flowers, including the bush lima bean, cabbages, squashes, and, of course, sweet peas.

Hybridizing improved cultivated plants, both culinary and ornamental.[9] It enabled the company to produce a plant that was more valuable to the gardener, thus providing, for example, a better vegetable or a more attractive flower color. Because a gardener needed to know that the seed company or nursery sought hybrids to provide a quality plant, the science of gardening became a theme in the catalog.

The Washburn Company, in 1869, wrote in its catalog about the changes in plant development: "Annuals are not what they were in former days. The skill of the hybridizer in the production of new varieties, and the diligence of the enthusiastic florist in the selection of the finest plants, have entirely changed the character of many of these flowers."

In 1870, Briggs, from Rochester, New York, wrote in that year's catalog, "At no period in the history of the seed trade has such an earnest and intelligent determination been manifested to improve the productions of the vegetable kingdom, as during the past few years, and at the present time. By hybridization and careful cultivation, old and homely flowers have become beautified—the parents hardly being recognized in the children—and many splendid new varieties have been produced. Old garden vegetables have also been much improved, and many and new valuable kinds added to the list."

Using the latest approach to growing and harvesting seeds was important to Ferry. In its 1884 catalog, the company wrote, "Instead of being grown by men who knew little about it, and merely grew a few by accident, or saved such as were self-sown and self-cultivated, nowadays seeds are produced by those who have given seed growing years of careful study, and from stock which has been developed by good culture and judicious selection, to the highest attainable excellence."

The consumer also needed to know that the company tested its seeds before they were listed in the catalog. In 1891, the Cornish Company, based in Newburgh, New York, wrote in its catalog, "We have introduced from Europe a new method of testing, which enables us to detect the immature and badly germinating varieties of seeds. We assert that nothing but seeds of unsurpassed quality, and highly germinating powers pass through the doors of our establishment." Readers of the catalog were assured that they dealt with a company that was truly modern because it kept up with the latest scientific developments in seed and plant propagation.

Children and Gardening

Finally, the role of children in gardening became a common theme in the seed company and nursery catalog. Mention of a child or an illustration of a child in the pages of the catalog (fig. 7.5) was certainly attractive to the customer, who was often a mother.

Edward Bok, editor of *Ladies' Home Journal,* once said that a packet of seeds taught a woman more about beauty than did a Ruskin essay.[10] Bok fostered the view of woman as a homemaker and mother. Because women made the purchases for the home, Bok made his articles attractive to women, including articles about children, in his publication. Before 1900, *LHJ* had the largest circulation of any magazine in the country.

The B. N. Strong Company, based in Connecticut, discussed in 1852 how important it was to teach children how to garden: "Children are frequently led into mischief in the absence of other means of occupying themselves. How different would it be if they were taught to turn their attention to the neatness and productiveness of a garden."

☙ *Figure 7.5.* Children were often illustrated in the catalog, as in B. A. Elliott's 1891 catalog. *Courtesy of the Bailey Hortorium, Cornell University, Ithaca, New York.*

In 1859, the Bloomington Nursery in Illinois wrote in its catalog, "Thousands of our children pine for the want of nature's health-giving luxury, fruit, without doubt the best stomach regulator the world affords. So, too, with their attachments and their sense of the beautiful in nature they dwindle for want of some of their most proper objects—homes and trees, and plants and flowers, and the exercise enjoyed in their cultivation."

The Charles T. Starr catalog of 1882 discussed how much improved society would be if more children gardened. Starr said,

> Would that I could induce everyone who reads this to love and cultivate flowers, if not for their commercial value, at least for their ennobling and refining influence; for this is one of the few pleasures that improve alike the mind and the heart, and make every true lover of these beautiful creations of Infinite Love, wiser and purer and nobler. It teaches industry, patience, faith, and hope. Would that every American child could be brought up under such an atmosphere, and through life be guided by their teachings. We would then have fewer Guiteaus and more James A. Garfields; for the heart and character of the man so depraved surely could never have had any love or association with the beautiful and innocent in nature.[11]

Seed company owners and nurserymen, like others concerned for moral well-being in society, felt that when children worked in the garden, they grew up to become productive citizens. Joseph Harris, from Rochester, in his 1882 catalog wrote about how to start a children's garden:

> The children each have a separate plot. They start many of the plants in boxes in the house. Make it convenient for the children. Do not ask them to make bricks without straw. Let them have all the seeds they want. If they get healthy recreation and some knowledge of vegetable growth—if they grow up to love flowers and take an interest in the garden—if they have something to think about besides dolls and dresses and dancing parties, we can well afford to let them waste a little seed and a little land. In fact, it is far from being a waste. It will pay ten times over.

In 1885, Dreer also recommended giving children a decent plot of soil in the garden and adequate tools. He wrote,

> Given rickety tools that have long been mustered out of service, a piece of ground that even sand burrs would blush to be seen upon, and the relics of last season's purchase of seeds, what wonder is it that children regard gardening as unprofitable.
>
> A few simple tools well made, a plot of ground on which the sun shines and which is ordinarily fertile, seeds that will grow, and plants that are thriving, added to an occasional spurring of the little workers to the fulfilling of their task, will enable them to reap in due season an ample reward.

Children would be better off gardening than having idle time on their hands. That appeal to women was often repeated in the seed and plant catalogs, both in words and in images. Crosman Brothers included a child on the company catalog cover of 1896 (fig. 7.6).

Appeal of the Catalog

The seed companies and nurseries offered seeds and plants in every catalog because the gardener needed them. By the end of the nineteenth century it was clear, however, that the company owner had helped create that need by penning a message that appeared over and over again in nineteenth-century seed and nursery catalogs: "We are here with modern facilities and the newest plants to fill your order." It was a supply-and-demand cycle, with demand created by the industry. The Vaughan Company, of Chicago, summed it up in the motto that appeared in their seed catalogs: "Cultivate a garden with ever-newer plants to show you are progressive."

The common themes in the catalogs meant that the seed and nursery industries had similar concerns but also that the home gardener was hearing the same message over and over again. The gardening public, especially

Within the image: Crosman Bro's

ESTABLISHED
1840.

CROSMAN BRO'S

PLANTS. | TOOLS.

GARDEN | SEEDS.

FLOWER | SEEDS

CROSMAN BRO'S

1896.

Garden & Farm
Annual

OFFICE & SEEDHOUSE,
503 Monroe Ave.

RETAIL STORES.
23 S. Clinton St

Rochester, N.Y.

Figure 7.6. This is a child on the cover of Crosman's 1896 seed catalog.
Courtesy of the Bailey Hortorium, Cornell University, Ithaca, New York.

Peter Henderson

*T*HOUGH SEEDSMAN Peter Henderson's books appeared throughout the late nineteenth century in several editions, his success came because he based his writing on experience in the garden. Boston nurseryman and garden writer C. M. Hovey once went to visit Henderson in Jersey City, New Jersey, where Henderson had his gardens and found him on the top of a manure pile, turning it with a fork.

Henderson, like Robert Buist and Thomas Meehan, was an immigrant British gardener who found a home in America by appealing to the growing interest in the garden and landscape. These immigrant gardeners brought with them professional garden training and the drive to educate others about gardening through their own seed or plant business.

Shortly after Henderson died in 1890, New York florist A. D. Cowan said at a meeting of the New York Florists' Club, "To Peter Henderson will belong for generations to come the credit of popularizing, improving and developing gardening in these United States."[12]

the middle class, would become accustomed to a certain type of landscape, often illustrated in the catalogs or written about, with particular plants, often acquired from abroad but available through national seed and plant industries. Thus the persuasive ability of the catalog was linked to the consistent catalog themes.

Gardening had come to be important for Americans because the seed companies and nurseries in a growing media-dominated culture successfully argued that to be modern, one needed to have a garden. At the same time, the companies extolled their facilities and the importance of buying ever-newer plant varieties, which the company would then offer in the pages of the catalog.

What the company owner wrote about in these recurring themes was a blending of the product, seed or plant, with the cultural values of nineteenth-century America. He sold the garden by selling American values such as progress, technology, science, and family life. That discourse enabled the company to function as a business and the customer to relate to the company. One might conclude that the meaning for American gardening from the catalogs was not given but rather was discursively constructed within a historical context. The garden style that continued to be promoted, however, was that of an English garden, dependent on exotic plants rather than native plants, well into the end of the nineteenth century.

❧ ☙

FEATURED PLANT

Baptisia australis / Blue False Indigo

IN MY FRONT YARD *Baptisia australis* **has a home toward the back of a perennial bed. Its delicate blue flower spikes appear in May and June. The Perennial Plant Association named it the Perennial of the Year in 2010.**

A native plant, *Baptisia australis* is found in much of the central and eastern United States but is common also in the Midwest. It was introduced into England by 1734. The Bartrams included it in their 1784 catalog. In his catalog of 1899, New York seedsman Peter Henderson listed *Baptisia australis* under "Hardy Perennial Plants" at twenty-five cents each, or one dozen for two dollars and fifty cents. This is another case of one of our native plants returning to America after a sojourn of decades in the English garden.

Baptisia australis has blooms of deep bluish purple with foliage of slight gray. The flowers are irregular in shape; they will grow to be one inch in length and consist of flower clusters.

This plant will grow three to four feet high. It prefers full sun to part shade and dry to medium moisture. It can survive in almost any type of soil, including normal, clay, and sandy soils.

&e (facing page)
Baptisia australis, blue false indigo

8

Gardening and
the Middle Class

T HE MASSACHUSETTS Agricultural Club offered Dorchester fruit
grower Thaddeus Clapp (1811–1861) one thousand dollars for the
rights to his pear, which he called Clapp's Favorite. Clapp declined
the offer, and his pear went on to become one of the most famous fruits of
the nineteenth century.

The club had hoped to honor Marshall P. Wilder (1798–1886), a wool
and cotton merchant, by naming the pear after him, in recognition of his
service as president of the Massachusetts Agricultural Club. Wilder's passion
for plants also motivated him to become a founding member and president
of the Massachusetts Horticultural Society.

Wilder cultivated his thirteen-acre estate in Dorchester, purchased in
1832, and rose to become a prominent Boston horticultural authority while
working a few miles away in his textile business in Boston. Over a fifty-year

period, Wilder grew 1,200 varieties of fruits and introduced the Anjou and Bartlett pears to America. His collection of 300 camellias grown in his greenhouses was considered the best in America.[1] In addition, his book *The Horticulture of Boston and Vicinity* details the gardens in and around Boston. Wilder was thus both a practical gardener and a horticultural leader.

Like the English aristocracy, Wilder lived the life of a country gentleman —and Dorchester, which was home to several fruit growers and gentleman farmers during the nineteenth century, was a suitable place in which to do so. At about the same time as Shipley and Shaw were developing their own picturesque gardens, Wilder, too, had his property laid out in the new natural landscape style so popular in England.[2]

When Dorchester, with a population of forty thousand, became part of Boston in 1870, wealthy property owners, including nurseryman Wilder, divided their lots for suburban homes, and the town became more clearly defined as a home for middle-class commuters. By then there was a train station a few blocks away; within twenty years electric cars moved along Dorchester streets. By 1900 there were one hundred thousand residents of Dorchester.

Between 1845 and 1860, the number of Boston workers living outside the city rose from a few hundred to more than ten thousand.[3] Middle-income people (mainly tellers, clerks, and bookkeepers) who could not afford to own property in the city traveled to Boston first by carriage or coach and later by railroad. Cheap transportation of large numbers of people on gradually improved roads and by railroad transformed suburbs such as Dorchester from the fringe society of early nineteenth-century Boston into a new kind of community,[4] which increasingly became the choice of residence for many who worked in the city. By the 1870s, both the direction of future growth and the goals of suburbanites had become more sharply defined: suburbs became the new independent communities of commuters.[5]

Dorchester has not completely forgotten its earlier agricultural roots, however. Today, an eleven-foot bronze pear in Dorchester's Everett Square, near fast food chains buzzing with customers and unending traffic clipping along, commemorates the Clapp family orchard. Eventually the Clapp Farm, like Wilder's, was subdivided, and its new ladder-like streets, which connected Boston Street and Dorchester Avenue, were named after hybrid pears cultivated by the family. You can still see the street signs named after pears: Mount Vernon, Bellflower, Dorset, and Harvest.[6]

Wilder lived long enough to see home gardens become possible for an emerging nineteenth-century middle class. Fruit and ornamental gardening, once a hobby for the wealthy upper class, became possible for the middle-class suburbanite. That message became a marketing tool that helped realtors sell suburban properties, as well as helping seedsmen and nurserymen through the medium of their catalogs sell garden essentials such as seeds, plants, statuary, trellises, urns, and, of course, the lawn mower.

The catalogs supplied seeds and plants but also the style of garden favored for the suburbs: an English style that required a lawn, trees, and groups of shrubs, along with beds of colorful flowers on the lawn. That was the garden in fashion presented in word and image in the catalogs through much of the nineteenth century, and it dominated the new media culture of the 1880s and '90s.

Suburban Gardens

As long as the country was a land of farmers, gardening meant the orchard and the kitchen garden, with the ever-present flower garden as a diversion for the farmer's wife.[7] Horticulture separated from agriculture as the emerging nineteenth-century middle class in America developed a desire for home gardens. As more big cities developed factories, first on the East Coast and then across the nation, factory owners and other professionals began to live on larger city lots or in suburbs. In this setting, a display garden became an important expression of one's position in the community. With the rise of the suburb in the second half of the century, home gardening became a leisure pursuit as middle-class Americans across the country adopted a less utilitarian expectation about residential space. They no longer needed herbs and vegetables from gardens, for the American canning industry provided them new canned products, and thanks to the lawn mower, a new English invention, the lawn replaced rough meadows cut by scythe or grazed down by sheep.

The suburban dream demanded an open vista, no matter how small. In particular, the ideal house came to be viewed as resting in the middle of a manicured lawn.[8] Elements of the English garden style such as rock gardens and carpet beds of flowers in the lawn were seen as possible for the new suburban gardener.

The seed and nursery catalogs voiced personal, moral, and social reasons for having a garden, arguing that gardens promoted the health and well-being of the family. The middle-class home had to have a lawn as well as flowers, vegetables, fruits, foliage plants, bulbs, and perennials. Even the cultivation of shrubs such as the new azaleas became important for the gardener, according to the seed and nursery catalogs.

In 1874, Marshall Wilder presented *Azalea mollis* to the Massachusetts Horticultural Society (fig. 8.1). It was a new Japanese species imported only a few months earlier from English horticulturalist Van Houtte, who had raised it from seed sent to him from Japan. Wilder's plant produced a cluster of ten flowers. "It is hoped it will prove a hardy and valuable acquisition."[9]

That the middle class acted as a new emerging social group became clearer in the ways this group chose to decorate both the inside and the outside of their homes. By 1890 the expectations about residential spaces and the desirability of home ownership had become firmly implanted in middle-class culture.[10]

To be considered middle class, a homeowner had to cultivate a certain type of garden. The middle-class image was not just about gardening but about creating an identity through the arrangement of walkways, plants, and lawn, along with areas of flowers and vegetables. Status could be conveyed through the type of plants grown. For example, the more exotic and expensive varieties of produce—asparagus, broccoli, and German radishes

Figure 8.1. The azalea, especially varieties introduced to England from China and Japan, became popular in American middle-class suburban gardens. Storrs and Harrison featured it in their 1898 catalog. *Courtesy of the Bailey Hortorium, Cornell University, Ithaca, New York.*

—pointed to a presumably more sophisticated palate and the means and skill to satisfy it.[11]

Takoma Park, Maryland, was an early example of a suburb—the first in the Washington, D.C., area. The community was begun in 1884 and was made possible by new modes of transportation, particularly the train. Large numbers of the middle class could, for the first time, escape the disadvantages of urban life and find peace, space, and a healthy environment for raising a family.[12] Sales promotions pointed out that the new lots offered buyers the chance to have a garden.

Garden as Status Symbol

*I*N *1884*, the Vick Seed Company frankly told its readers that home property values would rise with a garden, arguing that this was one reason, out of many the catalogs proposed, for a garden. *Vick's Illustrated Monthly,* the company's magazine, said, "What we do in the gardening way is done for the appearance, the respectability of the thing, done for the same reason that we have a coat of paint put on the house, or renew the wall-hangings."[13] The company thus suggested that a homeowner achieved a middle-class identity through a certain appearance to the house with its cultivated outdoor space with a certain style of garden and landscape.

The Role of the Seed Company and Nursery

In 1845, with most Americans living on farms, the *Genesee Farmer* described the garden first as a means of profit; second, as a source of products for the family's comfort; and last, as an "innocent recreation."[14] With the demographic shift to the suburbs and the rise of the middle class, the meaning of gardening changed. After 1870, the plant and seed catalogs, garden books, garden magazines, and garden advertising preached how essential the garden was in order to enjoy middle-class status. Seed companies and nurseries redefined gardening to a mass audience as they created a new way to sell their seeds and plants using a recognizable form of garden, the English style, as the dominant image in their catalogs, books, magazines, and newspaper ads.

Just the possibility of being outside on one's own land became an important factor in drawing the middle class to the suburbs. If a man could not be a farmer, he could at least be close to nature, on his own plot of ground, in his own house.[15] As early as 1850 the Connecticut-based B. N. Strong Company wrote about the home garden in its catalog:

> A garden is essential to the health, and comfort, and well-being of the mechanic and the day-laborer; and it may also be said to be essential to the comfort and enjoyment of individuals in every class.
>
> In the case of the journeyman, or day-laborer, what can be so delightful as half an hour spent in his garden, with his wife and children around him, after his daily toil? The change from laborious exertion, to the lightest of all out-of-door employments, must be to him a relief.
>
> To the farmer, too, as well as to the professional man, how many broken hours will pass unemployed, and perhaps without enjoyment, if he has not a garden in which to occupy his time, and in which he may occasionally try experiments on a small scale, either for amusement, or for verifying the experiments of others, before carrying them into practice on his farm?

By 1876, social pressure to improve one's home landscape with a lawn, trees, and shrubs had become an important issue for the middle class. The seed companies fueled that need through their claims of the importance of gardening. By the end of the century, seed companies and nurseries would be congratulating themselves on how well they were able to sell gardening to the American public. The L. L. May Company, of St. Paul, Minnesota, wrote in its 1901 seed catalog, "A hundred years ago the 'seedsman' was unknown; today his goods are a necessity, and the humblest cottager, with his little garden patch, as well as the bonanza farmer, with his broad acres, are alike dependent upon the seedsmen for the success which crowns their efforts in tilling the soil."

Despite America's love for the English garden, the D. M. Ferry Company in its 1881 catalog boasted that the American garden was what distinguished the United States from Europe: "There is no country in the world where horticulture, in its vegetable and floral departments at least, is so universally popular as this. It is true that the European countries, with their vast estates which have been the pride of titled families for centuries, can show much finer examples of elaborate gardening than we can, but nowhere do the people take so much interest in it; nowhere is the home garden, the pride and delight of the whole family, so common as here." At the end of the century, English social critics would bemoan the severe cost of industrialization to the country and call the "English cottage garden" the purest form of rural history. So was born the image of a thatched-roof dwelling fronted by a fence enclosing colorful flowers—an ideal that sought to restore what was lost.

The catalogs that came from seed companies and nurseries encouraged the homeowner to cultivate a garden, no matter how small. A garden was a sign of civility and culture for the emerging middle class.

The Rewards of Gardening

As was true for the English garden designers of the eighteenth and nineteenth centuries—such as Capability Brown, Humphry Repton, and John Claudius Loudon—it was important for the American gardener to look at garden design as art. That is how the O'Keefe Seed Company, located in Rochester, New York, spoke about gardening in its 1870 catalog: "Our 'Remarks on laying out flower gardens' will, we hope, not only prove a valuable aid to our customers, but assist in disseminating an increasing taste for gardening art." The seed and plant catalog helped the home gardener develop a sense of gardening as an art form much like painting and music, a view many English gardeners had held during the previous two hundred years.

The audience for the 1874 Long Brothers catalog consisted of gardeners who had developed a taste for better varieties of plants than the ordinary kind. The Long Island–based Long Brothers wrote, "*The Home Florist and Illustrated Catalog of Plants and Flowers* [their catalog] is designed to aid all classes of cultivators, but especially those who aspire to the rearing of a higher and choicer order of plants and flowers than are common at the present time."

The Park Seed Company, in 1888, praised the caliber of its customers, who, the company felt, readily understood gardening. Park wrote in his catalog, "I number among my patrons the most eminent and the most successful amateur florists in the land. They are those who read and reflect, and who use their knowledge. They are constantly searching for new and choice flowers and original information. They are energetic, progressive, and have a genuine love for the true, the good and the beautiful."

In the copy for an 1892 trade card, the C. A. Johnson Company, of Oklahoma, boasted about its contribution to developing a sense of "high culture." The company wrote, "The possession and cultivation of flowering and ornamental plants is not only an evidence of high culture, but is a source of much pleasure and satisfaction to the possessor." Certain plant varieties and styles of landscape design created a sense of status, much as they had in the estates of colonial Williamsburg. A garden, like any fashion, told the world a person's social class.

Among its various attributes, gardening could even keep the homeowner out of trouble with the law. D. M. Ferry wrote in its catalog of 1875, "A garden is not by any means a bad savings bank. Out-door work, so engaging and so remunerative, must likewise induce cheerfulness of disposition, and health of body, and must tend to develop that attachment of the citizen to his home, which is one of the strongest safeguards of society against lawlessness and immorality."

In his 1875 catalog, Joseph T. Phillips, from Pennsylvania, attributed a good home to all who have a garden. He wrote, "The cultivation of the garden, the ornamental planting of our grounds, and the general use of flowers, afford striking proof of the high state of civilization which marks the progress of the present age."

In its catalog of 1891, the California firm Timothy Hopkins Company developed a philosophy of gardening for the middle class. The garden could be understood both as art and as a symbol of social status. The company wrote in that catalog, "The garden is a rare gift to man, a compensation for the troubles and despondencies of life, a place of culture for those higher senses which there alone can find the keenest pleasures. Here there is opened up a world of appreciation and artistic possibilities, which furnishes the mind with most exalted admiration. Withal, the garden brings to man a restfulness of spirit, a satisfaction in living, a broad and charitable view of life, all of which help to make him a more perfect and useful creature."

Gardeners developed a bond with other gardeners, especially when they shared the same neighborhood, as in a suburb. The Childs Company wrote in its 1892 catalog, "Between people who love and cultivate flowers and gardens there is a bond of friendship and sympathy. They are never strangers; they are ever ready to assist each other; they rejoice in the success of each other and deplore each other's failures." The company discussed the bond that exists between gardeners as motivation for gardening. The gardener, the catalog argued, is part of a larger community. The seed company, in this case Childs, wants to be part of that group as well.

What Plants Formed the Garden

The suburban gardener wanted a landscape and plants that were similar to those of the estate owner, though his property would be smaller. The seed and nursery catalogs offered fruits, trees, annuals, vegetables, shrubs, and, of course, lawn seed, thus enabling the suburban garden to echo the property of nineteenth-century wealthy estate owners such as Joseph Shipley, whose landscape design and plant choices at Rockwood mirrored the English style.

Helping Find Suburban Properties

*T*HE *D*WYER Company, of Cornwall, New York, offered its readers assistance to find a suburban property in the town where it conducted its seed business. Its 1894 catalog said, "We have decided to keep a memorandum of all the desirable places offered for sale in this well-known, healthy, and most desirably located town. We will therefore be prepared to answer all communications directed to us in reference to the purchasing of property. Please be sure to say exactly what is wanted, how far from the depot, post office, churches and river you wish to be, how much land is wanted, how large the house should be, what size barn, and out-building is needed." If anyone such as a banker or insurance broker wanted to relocate to Cornwall, the Dwyer Company was there to help make it possible to own a beautiful home and garden in the suburbs.

Fruit

Marshall Wilder, like many English country gentlemen, cultivated hundreds of fruit trees on his property. The new suburban middle-class gardener also wanted fruit trees.

Green's Nursery, a fruit-growing business in Rochester, said in its 1898 catalog,

> What enterprise can you undertake more pleasant and profitable than that of fruit growing? But I desire a word, not only with the man who

plants acres of orchards for profit, but with the villager, the city man, the farmer, the mechanic, the worker in factories who has a small garden and who desires to make his home attractive to his wife and family, as well as to himself, by the planting of a few trees, grape vines, raspberry bushes, or gooseberries in his garden. To you who have this garden, I will say that whatever you expend in making that garden productive of fruit will repay you a hundred fold in pleasure and profit, in watching these things develop their beautiful crops, and in the fruitage thereof.

Seed companies and nurseries considered fruit-growing customers to be ideal citizens, concerned about the welfare of the home. The McWhorter Company, of Illinois, wrote in its 1863 catalog (which they referred to as a "little pomological talk"), "Fruit growing bears an inseparable connection with the health, happiness, and all the delightful relations of our homes. It cultivates the home feeling. Home is the center of our earthly joys. But how desolate a home that supplies not its cooling shade and its health-giving fruits."

H. G. Corney, from New York, wrote in his catalog of 1885 that the demand for fruits was growing and that it was his job to meet that demand: "Small Fruits have become the fruit of the people, almost a necessity of life. Every one who has a country home or a garden wants them and I am trying to grow them in sufficient quantity to supply the constantly increasing demand."

Flowers

In England the interest in filling the flower garden with masses of color had increased since the 1840s. The new annual flowers being introduced from hotter climates yielded much brighter and more emphatic colors than the herbaceous plants that had traditionally been available.[16] The new plants included pelargonium, petunia, verbena, and lobelia. That trend happened in America as well, with landscapes like Shipley's in Delaware, where

1891

Cottage Rose Garden
COLUMBUS, OHIO.

Figure 8.2. The house in the suburbs is improved when it includes a
"Cottage Rose Garden." *Courtesy of the Warshaw Collection of Business
Americana—Seed Industry and Trade, Archives Center, National Museum of
American History, Smithsonian Institution.*

pelargoniums were grown in abundance. The mass planting of annuals in ribbon beds or carpet beds guided by rigid color schemes embodied the English Victorian style of gardening both in England and in America.

The James H. Park Company, located in Brooklyn, painted a beautiful home and garden scene in words when its 1853 catalog said, "If you wish to add a most pleasing and beautiful ornament to your dwelling; to surround your family with one of Nature's most genial and blessed influences; to have one of the purest of earthly pleasures ever within your reach—cultivate flowers, and teach your children to love them" (fig. 8.2).

By 1871, people across the country were cultivating the same flowers because those were the varieties offered in most of the seed and nursery catalogs. This shows the importance of the kind of garden that the catalogs so often discussed. The Phelps and Reynolds Company, which did business out of Rochester, New York, wrote in its catalog of that year, "Flowers have become almost a necessity to persons of taste and culture. The resident upon the prairie of the west, the planter of the south as well as the dweller in the metropolis, must have the grand peony-flowered asters, the brilliant double zinnias, the boldly-marked and rich colored petunias."

Detroit's D. M. Ferry Seed Company wrote in 1872 about the relaxation that cultivating flowers gave to the homeowner: "As a relaxation from the cares of a professional or mercantile life, a light diversion to be enjoyed morning and evening, the culture of flowers is peculiarly desirable." The words spoke to the middle-class worker who could practice the simple and enjoyable act of gardening with flowers.

By 1885, flowers had become a necessity, according to the Paul Butz seed company, located in New Castle, Pennsylvania. The company catalog of that year said, "Flowers beautify your places and make home lovely, and are no longer considered a luxury, but a necessity. Nothing more effectually promotes taste and refinement, and a well kept flower-garden adds hundreds of dollars to the value of any farm or village cottage." Keeping a garden also added to the resale value of the property, a theme in promoting the need for landscape design that has never died in the real estate business.

Pike and Ellsworth, a Florida company, defined the working class and the middle class in their catalog of 1893. The company catalog said, "Believing flowers to be as necessary to the poor as to the rich, and that the choicest and rarest were designed for the cottager as well as the banker and broker, we entered the business with the idea in view of as rapidly as possible placing ferns, palms, orchids, and all such high-priced plants, within the reach of the humblest lover of flowers." The company owners wrote their catalog to appeal to the emerging middle class, composed of the bankers and the brokers who were settling into their suburban homes, perhaps with no elaborate glass greenhouse but surely with a garden. Plants that decades earlier had been available only to the wealthy could now become part of the middle-class plant collection.

Bedding Plants

After the 1860s, the American middle-class garden featured the English carpet-bedding style of planting, where flowers or plants with brightly colored leaves formed a design like sections of an ornate carpet, usually on the lawn. Many seed and nursery catalogs, such as Vick's, included carpet bedding in both essays and illustrations. An article published in Meehan's *Gardener's Monthly* in 1863 stated, "It is fashionable now, in Great Britain, to have the ground of the flower-gardens on grass, and beds of different forms dug out of the sod for small flowers, which are generally planted on the ribbon style. On private establishments the flower-gardens are immediately in front of the mansions; and the very green grass neatly cut short, and the pretty blooms of the flowers make an elegant appearance."[17] Similar to carpet bedding, the ribbon style shows its defining swirls of plants created by the rows of low annuals. The fashion is still replicated today out front of Roseland Cottage, in Connecticut, which was built in the 1850s.

The Victorian interest in bedding plants with colorful leaves and blossoms continued until almost the end of the century, both in England and in America. The tastes of garden owners, especially if they were well-to-do,

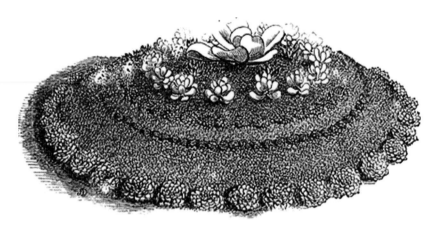

included a fondness for such carpet-like masses of low-growing foliage plants with brightly colored leaves that could be clipped in low geometrical designs (fig. 8.3). These were put in the center of the lawn or, less objectionably, planted as borders along walks or close to the house. Plants most commonly used included alternanthera, echeveria, coleus, irisene, ageratum, lobelia, and low-growing feverfews.[18]

Marshall Wilder said, in his address to the Massachusetts Horticultural Society at its fiftieth anniversary in 1879, that the recently introduced subtropical plants such as palms, agaves, musas, dracaenas, caladiums, and similar plants "and the multitude of ornamental foliaged plants, both hardy and tender, which now enrich our gardens, is the most characteristic feature of the present era in horticulture."[19]

Vegetables

Through proposing a garden with vegetables, W. Atlee Burpee wanted to help the homeowner both save money and feel a sense of relaxation and at the same time help the country move forward. In 1894, he wrote in his catalog, "It is our purpose simply to emphasize a self-evident fact, that proper economy suggests more attention to the garden. The butcher's and grocer's bills can be reduced to the health of both person and purse by a greater care and forethought in cultivation of the vegetable garden."

No matter how perfect the outside of the home may have seemed, a garden without vegetables was no garden. The Robert Buist Company wrote in its seed catalog of 1896, "No country home can be complete without a vegetable garden."

Water Lilies

The Florida-based Pike and Ellsworth Company encouraged the use of exotic plants such as water garden varieties that earlier in the nineteenth century had been accessible only to the wealthy, who usually had a conservatory or greenhouse for such plants. In 1890, they wrote in their catalog,

> The greatest charm of a collection of plants lays in its variety; palms, orchids, ferns, half hardy shrubs, aquatics, tropical and semi-tropical fruits, etc. are highly ornamental and possess a charm never experienced with most ordinary plants; but we are aware that the possession of such plants has heretofore been possible to the wealthy only. We know only too well what it is to wish in vain for those things which have been kept so far beyond the reach of a limited purse. Our object to place these and all other plants, both common and rare, within the reach of the most humble cultivator of flowers.

Pronouncements of the value of water lilies filled the pages of William Tricker's catalog of 1893. He wrote, "No class of plants have acquired such general appreciation, or occupy the public mind as aquatics do at the present time. No flowers are more fascinating, beautiful or more lovely than water lilies, and the question is often asked how can I grow such charming flowers. A few notes to this query may interest the readers of this catalogue." Then, like a teacher of horticulture, he offered not only the plants but also instructions on their cultivation through the construction of a backyard water garden.

Because of the popularity of glass houses, England had long treasured water lilies. The genus name *Victoria,* assigned to one type of water lily, was given in honor of Queen Victoria. In 1852, the English built a water lily house at Kew Gardens.

Bulbs

Beginning in the early part of the century, so many seed companies and nurseries wrote about the important role of bulbs in the home landscape that they became an integral part of the garden. Boston's Hovey Company wrote in its catalog of 1876, "The Holland or Dutch bulbs have always been admired for their great beauty and brilliant colors; and, for decorating the garden with early spring-flowers, they are indispensable." Vick, in his catalog of 1878, said, "The Bulb Garden is made glorious by the Lilies, Paeonies, Gladioli, and Dahlias, and a score of elegant flowers that have been known and loved for ages."

The English had long traded with the Dutch for their bulbs, especially the tulip. By the turn of the nineteenth century, English tulip growers, after long experience in growing the bulbs, were cultivating their own tulips rather than leaving the enterprise to the Dutch.[20] American seed and nursery businesses, however, continued importing tulips from Holland, especially after 1860, thus increasing the demand for them in the United States.[21]

Perennials

In 1885, Jacob Manning, from Reading, Massachusetts, encouraged the use of hardy perennials rather than bedding plants, which were mostly annuals. His company catalog of that year said, "There is a growing demand for the kind of plants [perennials] offered in this catalogue."

Seed companies wrote about various ways to design the home landscape and often recommended the contemporary English garden, which, by the 1880s, was moving away from carpet bedding toward the more natural "wild garden" with a focus on perennials. The English landscape style—promoted by the earlier writings of Repton and then Loudon and Paxton and still later by the Irish gardener William Robinson—dominated the garden discourse of the seed and nursery industries for the whole century, both in the United States and in England.

Nurseryman William Kenrick, from Newton, Massachusetts, wrote in his book *The New American Orchardist* in the 1835 edition, "The modern style of gardening, in the place of the regular geometric forms, and the right angles, and right lines, has substituted all that is more consistent with nature, and with beauty. Celebrated English writers have ascribed this important change in the style of gardening in England."[22] He recognized the English naturalistic garden style with lawns, scattered trees, and grouped shrubs as the more natural design, long promoted by English garden writers.

In 1889, Fred W. Kelsey, from New York, wrote about the importance of perennials along with hardy trees and shrubs in the landscape, "The paramount advantage in using hardy trees and plants for all kinds of ornamental planting is becoming better appreciated as the more understood. By a careful selection from the many species and varieties now offered, almost any effect desired can be harmoniously produced without the yearly expense and troublesome renewals incident to the use of annuals and tender exotica. While the hardy trees, evergreens and shrubs form the sky lines and ground work for all important and effective planting, the fine herbaceous perennials give a completeness and finish, with a restful 'home-like' appearance, not attainable in any other way."

By the end of the century, Gertrude Jekyll (1843–1932), the English artist turned garden designer, had inspired gardeners to plant large borders of perennials in the landscape. She admired William Robinson's ideas on naturalistic planting, in which native plants often played an important role. Her choice of both native and exotic perennials, which added structure and color to the landscape, would become an element of landscapes across England

House Plants

*D*URING THE Victorian era in late nineteenth-century America, as in England, it was considered important to cultivate plants inside the house throughout the cold winter months to bring a sense of garden even indoors. Lewis Templin wrote in his 1886 annual catalog, "While we are admiring our beautiful gardens, we should not forget to make some preparations for beautifying our homes during the long dreary winter months. Nothing can do more towards making the house cheerful in winter than a few pots of choice flowers in bloom." He then proposed hardy bulbs and winter-blooming plants that the reader could grow in the house.

James Vick, in his 1874 catalog, wrote, "Nothing gives a home a more cheerful appearance than a few plants and flowers, and when they are accompanied with tasteful accessories, the fine effect is much increased." He suggested the use of window brackets, ornamental pots, hanging baskets, and flower stands "of moderate price, and yet of excellent design."

and in America, where she also traveled to design gardens. Today the term "English garden" is sometimes equated with the landscape designs of Jekyll and her friend Sir Edwin Luytens, the architect with whom she worked on many garden projects.[23]

The seed and nursery catalogs promoted gardening and gardens for the middle-class suburban homeowner through a series of arguments. The professional who worked in the city needed the garden to escape the pressures

An English Flower Garden

*T*HE *M. O'KEEFE* Company, of Rochester, New York, discussed laying out an English Victorian style of carpet bedding in its 1870 catalog:

A flower garden should resemble a rich picture, with all the colors nicely contrasted and blended together. We find that the most beautiful flower gardens are those in which there is a continual display of beautiful colors and sweet odors, and the plants all having a neat and agreeable habit of growth. As to the situation, we should prefer a level plot situated near the dwelling-house, and well exposed to the sun and air, with a southern aspect. The soil should be of a deep, rich loam.

We think the modern style of grouping and massing the colors in separate figures, is much neater than the old method of mixing and intermingling the species and varieties in all the beds.

They should be placed in regular beds or figures, neatly cut out in the lawn, and always in circles or ovals, and when well kept, the green turf will add much to the brilliant colors of the flowers, as well as to form a fine contrast to the beds themselves.

The Victorian fashion of the geometric beds of flowers returned garden fashion in both England and America to the era of formalism and moved away from the natural or picturesque garden view.

O'Keefe encouraged flowerbeds but also the presence of a lawn. Thus, the homeowner was expected to establish a landscape that had by then been popular in Victorian England for decades. The bedding-out system was an indispensable part of the high Victorian English style of gardening, first established in the 1850s.[24] Annuals from more-tropical climates, collected by British plant hunters and later sold to American nurseries, formed the major plant variety for such flowerbeds.

In Thomas Meehan's magazine *Gardeners' Monthly* of 1878, C. J. Bjorklund recommended, "Having got our carpet beds planted, let us be attentive to the trimming of the plants . . . not allowing the foliage of two adjoining kinds to intermix with each other, nor allowing any openings whatever."[25]

of the city and the demanding business of insurance or banking. The whole family, including the children, enjoyed the fresh air as a reward for work outdoors. The value of the real estate increased with the addition of a garden in the home landscape. The family ate homegrown fruits and vegetables and enjoyed their own flowers for home decoration. The garden was a source of comfort and a way to bond with others, thus forming a community of gardeners. Finally, the homeowner could be identified as middle class through the garden.

The style of gardening that the seed companies and nurseries recommended was dependent on English garden fashion. In this period it included a lawn, curved walks, trees, shrubs, carpet beds, and, by the final third of the century, perennial borders. In American gardens, the influence of that English landscape design became more dominant, especially after 1870.[26] That was the time when American gardeners became part of a growing mass media culture.

❧

In 1863, Charles Whitmore gave a speech to the Massachusetts Horticultural Society at a gathering to unveil a bust of Marshall Wilder. The world needed to know how grateful the society was to Wilder for his thirty years of service.

Wherever he was needed, Wilder addressed horticultural groups around the country. One of his most famous speeches was delivered after the death of his friend Andrew Jackson Downing. Wilder died in 1886, while preparing a speech for a meeting of the American Pomological Society, the group he had founded.

Boston's Forest Hills Cemetery was built in the 1840s in the naturalistic style of the English park design. It included a pond, lawns, and walkways where Sunday visitors enjoyed a casual stroll. Today you can see the Clapp pear immortalized in the stonework at the Clapp family gravesite. Thaddeus Clapp, like Wilder, was a gentleman farmer whose property became suburban middle-class homes with gardens. When Wilder died, he, too, was buried in Forest Hills.

⚜ *Solenostemon scutellarioides* 'Royal Glissade', 'Royal Glissade' coleus

⚜ ⚜

Solenostemon scutellarioides / Coleus

THIS NEWER coleus variety 'Royal Glissade' grows in a border along the stone walkway leading to my front door. It hangs a bit over onto the walk, but that's all right. I like the colors of red, orange, maroon, pink, and white that come together in this plant. I have also used this coleus in containers.

Coleus was an important plant in nineteenth-century Victorian gardens, both in England and in America, because of its varied leaf color and shape. Plants from warmer climates arrived regularly in England and offered increased opportunities for the English gardener. In the summer they were planted to create intricate designs of carpet bedding on the lawn. When used in carpet bedding, however, coleus had to be clipped regularly to maintain the design of its pattern in the garden.

The Dingee and Conard catalog of 1892 offered a series of coleus plants called Success Coleus with this description: "Everybody admires gorgeous summer bedding coleus, and every flower grower wants a bed, border, or edging of them. In fact, they are indispensable for bright bedding effects."

The John Lewis Childs Seed Company said in its 1897 catalog that coleus was "the most popular foliage plant grown." Vick's catalog, *Floral Guide,* of 1893 said, "Coleus is the best and cheapest ornamental-leaved plant we have for ornamental bedding."

Coleus is an annual, although it is sometimes called a tender perennial. 'Royal Glissade' will grow to a height of ten to sixteen inches and blooms in the late summer. As with any coleus, unless in a carpet bed, it requires little maintenance besides evenly moist soils. Coleus does well in sun, shade, or partial shade, depending on the variety. Some varieties grow upright, while others are low-growing and used in edging.

✿ ✿

The Grandest Rose
of the Century

ARDENERS IN ENGLAND share a long history with the rose. In the monasteries of the Dark Ages, monks cultivated roses, mostly for medicinal purposes. By the eighteenth century, roses were coming into England from China; Chinese roses featured the tendency of repeat blooming, a most desirable trait for rose connoisseurs. Philip Miller, English garden writer and curator of the Chelsea Physic Garden, cultivated the first such rose, called *Rosa chinensis,* in 1752.

Nineteenth-century American seedsmen and nurserymen followed the English tradition of cultivating roses. They not only grew roses, advertised them, and sold them but also imported roses from England.

Seedsman Robert Buist, for example, collected roses, traveling to Europe for new varieties. He, too, hybridized roses of the Chinese species that the English cultivated.[1] In 1844, Buist wrote *The Rose Manual,* the first book in America on roses.

Ten years later, Boston seedsman Joseph Breck, in his book *The Flower Garden,* devoted several pages to the history of roses and their importance in the garden. He wrote, "This well-known and highly esteemed family of plants, or shrubs, embrace many distinct species, which, by the skill of the florist, have multiplied into thousands of varieties."[2]

C. M. Hovey grew 1,400 varieties of roses in his Cambridge nursery.[3] He frequently won awards for his roses at the Massachusetts Horticultural Society's annual flower shows.

On the West Coast, the Los Angeles basin and its environs became the center of commercial rose production in the mid-nineteenth century. The roses came primarily from the East Coast, though some originated in California's mission era.[4] Bernard S. Fox (1816–81), an Irish nurseryman who first worked for Hovey when he came to America, started an early nursery in California, which included thousands of roses.[5]

This is the story of a rose import from England that some called the greatest in the nineteenth century: the climbing rose 'Crimson Rambler'.[6] It became a must-have plant for the middle-class gardener, first in England and then in America.

American Gardening with Roses

Roses have served many purposes—including aesthetic, decorative, and medicinal—for the American gardener. Roses appeared in colonial gardens, such as are represented today in the restored gardens of Williamsburg and the seventeenth-century housewife's garden at the Whipple House, in Ipswich, Massachusetts. The colonists used the flower for healing. Vinegar of roses, for example, was used to treat headaches.

In the nineteenth century, the gardens of wealthy Americans featured rose gardens. Shaw's garden, in St. Louis, displayed roses purchased from the Robert Buist Company. Joseph Shipley's Rockwood included a formal rose garden.

In his 1847 book *The Rose,* American landscape designer and horticulturalist Samuel Parsons called the rose the most beautiful denizen of the floral kingdom.[7] English garden writer Ursula Buchan has said that if there is one genus of plants that can be said to be essential to the English garden, it must be the rose.[8]

The rose, however, was slow to find a place in many American gardens. An article in Downing's magazine *The Horticulturist,* in 1852, lamented that more people did not use roses in the garden: "It has always been a wonder to us, as much as this plant is professedly admired, as numerous as its claims are, and as easy of cultivation as it is, that it has, by the mass of mankind, received no more attention. Will it be uncharitable to suppose that three-fourths of the population of our country have never seen so rare and fascinating a flower?"[9]

Milwaukee's Currie Brothers Seed Company wrote in an 1887 issue of their company magazine, "There is, perhaps, no plant in our gardens which is so much admired, so much talked of and written about, and in the culture of which is so much interest and enthusiasm is displayed, and, at the same time, around which so much mystery hangs as the Rose."[10] In the same issue the enormous demand for this plant is also mentioned. American gardeners wanted roses, but where would they come from?

Storrs and Harrison, in their 1895 catalog, called the rose the essential flower for every garden: "For years the Rose has been one of our leading specialties and the demand has steadily increased from year to year until now it requires upwards of half a million plants annually to supply it."

In the nineteenth century, the American seed and nursery industries listed roses for sale, mainly imported varieties. Unfortunately, most of the nineteenth-century native plants, including native roses, were rarely accepted by the American gardener.[11] Roses offered for sale in the seed and nursery catalogs were usually imports. Although the first famous Noisette rose was found in the early 1800s in South Carolina, it had to travel to France and then back to America before it became acceptable to the American gardener. Garden writer Mabel Osgood Wright said in 1905 that even by that date

America had contributed comparatively few roses to the great list of popular varieties.[12]

In 1880, the nurseryman Henry B. Ellwanger, son of the founder of Rochester's Mount Hope Nurseries, gave a talk to the Western New York Horticultural Society. In the speech he traced the history of America's contributions to roses of his period, which were the 'Prairie' and Noisette roses. He concluded: "In the production of new Roses, instead of having exhausted the field, as a few writers have incautiously observed, we have only just entered it; the future possibilities open to the raiser of new Roses is only dawning upon us."[13] There was interest in roses for American gardens, and gardeners grew them, but the catalogs sold varieties that came from outside the county, particularly from England.

The case of an imported rose, the 'Crimson Rambler', serves as an example of the influence of the seed and nursery catalogs on the promotion of English plants. They wrote about and advertised this rose as the most important rose discovery of the late nineteenth century. It became a rose for every garden; anyone who grew it knew it was an excellent addition to the garden, according to the seed and nursery catalogs. The Peter Henderson catalog of 1899 wrote that the 'Crimson Rambler' rose "is adapted to the entire country, and should be in every garden in America."

The seed and nursery catalog plant choices became the plant choices of the American gardener. Gardeners had long come to trust the catalogs. The seed and nursery industry, however, continued to rely on England for plants. The 'Crimson Rambler' rose was no exception.

History of the 'Crimson Rambler'

Collectors brought many plants, including roses, from Asia to Western Europe in the nineteenth century. One of the most famous roses was the 'Crimson Rambler', which came to America from Japan via Great Britain.

Although the plant arrived in Scotland in 1878, not until 1893 did nurseryman Charles Turner, from Slough, market it—as 'Turner's Crimson Rambler'. It became a sensation almost immediately. Queen Victoria is said to have made a special journey to Slough to see it.[14] In its May 27, 1893, issue, the London journal *Garden* called it "a splendid addition to our hardy Roses."[15]

The parentage of the 'Crimson Rambler' rose is unknown, though Cornell horticulturalist L. H. Bailey classified it as a multiflora species of the platyphylla variety.[16] Those who breed roses have used it to develop newer and better roses. In 1909, Schmidt of Germany used it as a parent for the bluest of all ramblers, 'Veilchenblau'.[17] The flower is a mauve color and is the closest that growers ever came to a true blue until twenty-first-century genetic engineering arrived in the plant world.

The 'Crimson Rambler' was introduced into America shortly after Turner offered it for sale in England. The Ellwanger and Barry firm Mount Hope Nurseries in Rochester, perhaps because the younger Ellwanger was a rose expert, was one of the first in America to list it. The company wrote about this variety in its 1894 catalog: "Turner's Crimson Rambler (Climbing Polyantha) Originally received from Japan and first introduced in England Fall 1893. Described as follows: 'The brightest crimson color, flowers are produced in large trusses of pyramidal form; plant of very vigorous growth, producing shoots 8 to 20 feet long in one season; a grand variety for climbing or pegging down; very hardy, free flowering and continuous bloomer and, in fact, too much that is good cannot be said of this fine new variety.' Small plants, $2.00" (fig. 9.1).

The history of this rambler was told in the English magazine *Gardening* in 1894:

This is a new Japanese rose, a form of Rosa polyantha or multiflora, of free rambling habit, and bearing ample clusters of double crimson roses. During the last two years it has caused quite a sensation in Europe. It is now being "sent out." While we have not yet seen the living rose, it has been exhibited and certificated in Europe, and lauded to such an extent by high authorities that we feel confident of its merits. . . . The editor of the Gardener's Chronicle tells us: "It is the most beautiful hardy rose of its kind introduced for many years. . . ." According to a correspondent of

Ellwanger & Barry
ROCHESTER, N.Y.

"Crimson Rambler Rose."

the London Garden, "The rose was purchased by Mr. Jenner by commission from Japan in the year 1878, along with a number of other plants, through Professor R. Smith, then of Tokio [*sic*], now of Mason College, Birmingham. In the year following its introduction it bloomed so freely and its effect was so striking that it won Mr. Jenner's admiration. After having been grown for eleven or twelve years in a private garden, Mr. Jenner presented all the plants to Mr. John Gilbert, Bulb Nurseries, Bourne, Lincolnshire, and with his consent, Mr. Gilbert sold the stock to Mr. C. Turner of Slough. Mr. Turner gave it with Mr. Jenner's consent, the name of 'Crimson Rambler'. Before this rose came into Mr. Turner's possession it was known under the name of The Engineer."[18]

American Seed Companies and Nurseries Sing Its Praises

From 1894 onward, the 'Crimson Rambler' rose appeared in American seed and nursery catalogs well into the twentieth century. The same details of the plant's origin and qualities were repeated over and over again, so the reader became quite familiar with how the 'Crimson Rambler' had assumed such importance. Each catalog noted its growth habits: can climb ten to fifteen feet, has a flower measuring one and a half inches, and offers a long season of bloom. As one American garden catalog stated in 1895, "Of the many fine garden roses introduced during the past ten years there is not one of greater importance or likely to prove more valuable than 'Crimson Rambler.'"[19]

The flower company Dingee and Conard offered it to every new subscriber to their company magazine, *Success with Flowers*, featured it on the back cover of an 1890s issue, and described it in the June 1898 issue with

&ed *(facing page)*

Figure 9.1. The 'Crimson Rambler' rose appeared in the Ellwanger and Barry catalog of 1895, shortly after this rose was introduced in the country. *Courtesy of the Bailey Hortorium, Cornell University, Ithaca, New York.*

🙠 *Figure 9.2.* Peter Henderson illustrated here in his 1896 catalog how the 'Crimson
Rambler' rose would easily fit in a suburban American home landscape. In this
image, he encouraged the lawn with its flowerbed. *Courtesy of the Bailey Hortorium,
Cornell University, Ithaca, New York.*

these words: "Perhaps no other one variety of Roses has been written of more than has this beautiful climber. . . . Too high praise cannot be bestowed on it."[20] An illustration in the Peter Henderson catalog of 1896 demonstrates how the 'Crimson Rambler' rose would fit into the home landscape, along with the lawn and flowerbed, to create an English design for an American property (fig. 9.2).

By 1895, seed companies in the West, such as Harrison H. Given, of Denver, had also come to feature this rose. The Given catalog of that year said, "A charming pillar rose; for covering trellises or buildings there is nothing finer." The American seed and nursery catalogs of the 1890s prized this rose above all others. In 1897, the 'Crimson Rambler' rose appeared on the front cover of the Wilson seed catalog with these words: "This has been so widely advertised in the past two years that it needs no comment from us. Suffice it to say that it has won more gold medals in this country and Europe from the Horticultural Societies than any flower of recent introduction."

As in Henderson's illustration, the 'Crimson Rambler' appeared in many catalogs, depicted as climbing up a wall of a house or the side of a front porch. The 1899 cover of the catalog *Cottage Rose Garden,* from G. Drobisch of Columbus, Ohio, included such an illustration of this rose, along with other popular roses, including a 'Yellow Rambler' and a 'White Rambler'.

In Delaware, the Buntings Nurseries still listed the 'Crimson Rambler' in 1936. In 1946 Earl Ferris Nursery, of Hampton, Iowa, continued to sell it. The Chase Nursery Company, of Alabama, offered it in 1955. The 1967 catalog of the Krider Nurseries, in Middlebury, Indiana, wrote in its catalog, "For those who want hardy vigorous old-fashioned climbers like grandmother grew, we have the best." First on the list was the 'Crimson Rambler', "the hardiest climbing rose of them all."

From its introduction on, the rose appeared on trade cards as well. The R. D. Luetchford Company, of Rochester, New York, featured it on a card in the late 1890s with these words: "The wonderful new rose Crimson Rambler. 300 blooms on one shoot." The rose's prolific flowering became one of its features heavily promoted in advertising.

In an 1896 issue of the Dingee and Conard's magazine *Success with Flowers,* a reader from Pulpit Harbor, Maine, wrote, "Would the Crimson Rambler Rose be hardy in this section?" The editor responded that no one yet knew. "The only way [to find out] is to try it and report the result for the benefit of the public."[21] The mass marketing of seed and nursery catalogs made gardeners want plants that sometimes might not be appropriate for their growing area. Advertising presented the plant in such a compelling way that a gardener had a hard time saying no. After all, every gardener wanted to buy the latest. Philadelphia nurseryman Thomas Meehan wrote in his *Gardener's Monthly* of 1867, "The *Gardener's Monthly* is sustained by genuine horticulturalists all of whom are buyers."[22]

The promotion for the 'Crimson Rambler' rose paid off because the rose enjoyed an amount of fame for many years. Seed companies and nurseries offered this rose for decades, and today it can still be purchased from specialty growers.

Newspapers, Magazines, and Books

Seed companies and nurseries must have sold the 'Crimson Rambler' aggressively, because it was widely known to American gardeners, appearing in garden magazines and garden books as well. The description of the plant and the numerous accolades from newspapers and magazines were quite similar to the words of the catalogs and, in some cases, exactly the same.

The trade journal *Florist's Exchange* wrote in 1894, one year after the rose was introduced, "At Antwerp the first prize for a new plant in flower was awarded to Turner's rose, Crimson Rambler."[23] In the September issue that same year the writer mentioned that the 'Crimson Rambler' had been planted at the Robert Scott and Sons Model Farm in West Philadelphia: "The Crimson Rambler is making great efforts to sustain its name by rambling up accommodating poles to the tune of several feet."[24]

In the next year's June issue of the same trade journal, the writer said that this rose would live up to the endorsements it had received: "From what we have seen of this rose we are inclined to believe that it will come nearer filling the glowing catalogue descriptions than most of the new varieties which have been figured and portrayed in the past few years."[25]

Born right after the Civil War, and a master printer by profession, J. Horace McFarland wrote several books on gardening, including *How to Grow Roses* (1937), which was highly regarded among rose growers. McFarland, too, endorsed the 'Crimson Rambler' as a must-have rose that was both a vigorous grower and absolutely hardy.[26]

McFarland wrote that the Arnold Arboretum in Boston displayed this plant two years after its introduction into the country. The rose there was judged a "superb sight."[27] That a public garden would feature this plant as a worthy addition to the garden gave even more credibility to the advertising it had received in the garden catalogs, newspapers, and magazines.

The influential English garden designer Gertrude Jekyll wrote that the 'Crimson Rambler' rose took the garden world by storm, for its easy cultivation, its great speed of growth, and its masses of showy crimson blooms.[28] She featured it in several garden designs, especially when it was trained over a wire support. The fact that she would recommend it also made it a rose that gardeners wanted. The emerging consumer culture defined fashion, like gardening, by what appeared in the mass media; Jekyll regularly published articles and books about garden design.

Garden writers included the rose in their books and articles. A founding member of the Garden Club of America, Helena Rutherfurd Ely, wrote in her 1902 book *A Woman's Hardy Garden*, "I have a trellis along one side of a grass walk three hundred and fifty feet long. At each post are planted two Roses, the 'Crimson Rambler' and a Wichuraiana. The Wichuraiana blossoms when the Rambler is done. Imagine the beauty of this trellis when the Roses are in bloom."[29] She wrote as if the 'Crimson Rambler' had found a home in every garden. Certainly the reader would have been familiar with it.

Gardeners Plant the Rose

Vines such as Boston ivy, also introduced to American gardeners from England, were important plants for the nineteenth-century home landscape. Seedsman Peter Henderson, in his book *Gardening for Pleasure,* wrote, "Climbers are indispensable."[30] The 'Crimson Rambler' joined the rank of vines the catalogs offered as quite appropriate for covering a porch railing or climbing up the side of the house, thus adding a vertical element to the landscape.

The catalogs listed the 'Crimson Rambler' as a novelty plant at first; however, it soon became a necessary plant for the American garden and thus found a spot in the back pages of the catalog, where it remained popular for decades. The seed and nursery catalogs, listing this rose with other climbers, continued to promote it as the best rose introduced in years. The catalogs both created and reflected that popularity. Perhaps McFarland was right when he said that this rose swept the country because it was advertised so heavily.[31]

Garden historian Patricia Tice has written that the 'Crimson Rambler' rose was popular in the early twentieth century because it was hardy and required a minimum of care—an important consideration for the busy American gardener.[32] Middle-class gardeners, often garden amateurs, usually did not hire gardeners, so they preferred plants that would not make great demands. They wanted plants that required minimal maintenance.

The 'Crimson Rambler' Rose Becomes a Cultural Icon

Eventually the 'Crimson Rambler' rose appeared in art forms such as music, paintings, and novels; that notice became a sure sign that the culture had accepted this heavily promoted rose variety.

American Impressionist Philip Leslie Hale painted the 'Crimson Rambler' rose under that title in 1908. He taught art at the Museum of Fine

Arts, in Boston, but lived in Dedham, Massachusetts, a suburb of Boston. His white house included a long porch facing the street, where a tall red 'Crimson Rambler' rose grew on a trellis resting against the porch's railing. The rose's crimson flowers cascaded down the trellis to create a colorful display.

In Hale's painting, a woman in a white dress and straw hat sits on the porch railing. She was Rose Zeffler, a woman Hale often employed as a model in his work. Hale captured the bold contrast between the white dress and the red roses in this painting.

Today, Hale's painting hangs in the Museum of American Art of the Pennsylvania Academy of the Fine Arts, in Philadelphia. When the painting made its way to the Carter White House, in 1978, Hale's daughter wrote, "It is said to remind Mrs. Carter of her grandmother's house, rather surprising in view of the distance from Dedham of Plains, Ga.!"[33]

The early twentieth-century American novelist Edith Wharton loved gardening. She once traveled to Italy to visit famous gardens for inspiration to design her own landscape at her property, the Mount, in Lenox, Massachusetts. The trip resulted in her book on Italian gardens.

In one of her novels Wharton wrote, "The tiny lawn was smooth as a shaven cheek, and a crimson rambler mounted to the nursery window of a baby who never cried."[34] A few years later, another of her novels included this line: "He had brought her the Crimson Rambler because she had given up boarding-school to stay with him."[35] The 'Crimson Rambler' had become a climbing rose that everyone, even those who did not garden, easily recognized by name.

At a Paris social function in 1913, women used the flowers of the 'Crimson Rambler' rose as a design feature on their dresses. The *New York Times* called the fashion styles at the event the most daring of the preceding one hundred years.[36] No matter whether it was the dress design that stirred that review, the flower of the familiar 'Crimson Rambler' was the center of the story.

In 1917, the Broadway stage offered a musical called *The Rambler Rose*, written by New York composer Victor Jacobi. The review said it was a "very prettily set piece and the music tuneful."[37] The success of the musical sparked interest in Jacobi's other work.

Interest Diminishes

Not everyone, however, valued this rose. The American writer and historian Alice Morse Earle doubted its longevity when she wrote in 1901, "I wonder whether a hundred years from now any one will stand before some Crimson Rambler, which will then be ancient, and feel as I do before this York and Lancaster goddess."[38] The 'York and Lancaster' rose was an old-fashioned white-and-pink damask rose, dating to the fifteenth century and England's War of the Roses. Earle's words predicted what today most rose experts think about the 'Crimson Rambler' rose: not worth it. Because mildew often appears on the plant and also because this rose variety lacks any scent, eventually most rose gardeners came to consider the 'Crimson Rambler' not worth growing anymore, though it had once been quite popular.[39]

Michael Walsh, born in Wales in 1848, came to America at the age of twenty and worked as a gardener at several estates in the Boston area. He bred several new rambler roses, including 'Excelsa', in 1908. This cultivar quickly replaced the more mildew-prone 'Crimson Rambler'.[40] The largest public collection of Walsh's ramblers in this country is in Elizabeth Park in Hartford, Connecticut. The park, the oldest municipal rose garden in the country, today grows fifteen thousand roses, including ramblers.[41] Some of the original 'Crimson Rambler' roses planted in the early 1900s still bloom there.[42]

The 'Crimson Rambler' has proved more valuable for breeding other roses with stronger qualities. When the more disease-resistant wichuraiana hybrids 'Dorothy Perkins' and 'Excelsa' appeared in 1901 and 1909, the 'Crimson Rambler' fell out of favor.[43] But at one time, and for many years, the 'Crimson Rambler' rose was the novelty sensation for the American garden.

After the introduction of the 'Crimson Rambler', interest in climbing roses increased and numerous hybrids were developed.[44] It started in the early 1890s when a British nurseryman named Turner offered the 'Crimson Rambler' cultivar for sale and gardeners in Great Britain fell in love with it. In this country, the seed and nursery catalogs that called this rose the "sensation of the century" soon sold it to the American gardener, who planted it and continued to grow it for many years.

Early on, the Peter Henderson Seed Company became an advocate for the 'Crimson Rambler' rose. Patrick O'Mara, from Henderson's, planted four 'Crimson Rambler' roses, one on each of the four sides of a house in Hackensack, New Jersey, so that the plant could be tried in every exposure. In 1895, O'Mara reported in *Garden and Forest* magazine, "Both the wood and the buds of these plants are still plump and perfectly sound."[45]

Today roses continue to be important in the garden. Garden writers say that roses form the true basis of any garden.[46] Though the 'Crimson Rambler' is still available, gardeners now prefer newer varieties of the climbing rose, such as the blush pink 'New Dawn' rose.

The story of the 'Crimson Rambler' rose illustrates the influence exerted by seed and nursery catalogs, like Henderson's, when selling American gardeners exotic plants from Britain. It is another example of how nineteenth-century Americans gardened in the English style.

🌹 🌹

FEATURED PLANT

Rosa 'Excelsa' / 'Excelsa' Rose

WHEN WE MOVED into our house twenty-five years ago, I remember a low-flowering red rose with several high canes growing along the driveway. I just left it there. The rose turned out to be the climbing rose 'Excelsa', which had a link to the 'Crimson Rambler' rose.

In the early twentieth century, summer residences dotted Woods Hole, a seaside town on Cape Cod. City dwellers with money built sprawling estates on the water that often included a staff for the house and the garden.

James Story Fay (1812–97), a former cotton broker and businessman, hired Michael Walsh, an Irish gardener who had arrived in America in 1868.

While working on the Fay estate, Walsh introduced over fifty roses. He specialized in climbers, including the 'Excelsa' rose in 1908. 'Excelsa' won the 1914 Gertrude M. Hubbard Gold Medal for the best American rose introduced in the previous five years.

After Fay's death in 1897, Fay's daughter, Sarah (1855–1938), encouraged Walsh to continue to cultivate his roses. By the early twentieth century, the fame of the Fay rose garden had begun to attract visitors from around the country to see the roses at the estate.[47]

Walsh was able to make a business of his climbing roses for himself and for Miss Fay. During the years from 1907 to 1917, Walsh published yearly catalogs of his roses, hydrangeas, and hollyhocks. The roses, especially ramblers, were shipped all over the United Sates and became popular also in England.[48]

Rosa 'Excelsa' is a combination of *Rosa wichuraiana* and 'Crimson Rambler'. The wichuraiana roses were exported from Asia and Japan to Europe in the 1890s and were brought to America in the early 1900s. The wichuraiana characteristics predominate in the 'Excelsa'.[49]

The 'Excelsa' shines with scarlet-crimson cupped flowers on small, glossy green leaves that remind me of a holly. The flowers become pinker as the color fades after blooming in late June.

Pruning this rose is not easy, because the thorns or prickles are sharp. I try to wear gloves when I prune it. Mine is a low shrub, though the canes can reach several feet high. I grow it in partial shade.

When I first saw this rose on my property, I had no idea that it was Walsh's most famous rose introduction and was an improved version of the old 'Crimson Rambler'.[50]

Landscape Design According to the Catalogs

T WAS IN the landscape, rather than in the planting of flowers such as a particular rose, that the fullest expression of the English garden appeared in nineteenth-century America. The home grounds of middle-class America emerged as an American interpretation of the kind of landscape that the English had cultivated since the eighteenth century. The lawn became the signature element of that landscape, though in America the lawn took on a more democratic look in which the green grass of one property flowed into that of the next. Meehan wrote in his magazine *Gardener's Monthly* in 1886, "In suburban landscape gardening there has been a tendency of late years to abolish all line fences and especially those which separate the front yards from the street."[1]

In the first half of the nineteenth century, the seed companies and nurseries set out simply to sell their products in catalogs that were mainly lists of seeds or plants, but by the end of the century the business of selling had changed forever, due to the new communication technologies of the typewriter, the Linotype, photoengraving, and the sextuple printing press.[2] Whether a company sold soap or a patent medicine, the old way of advertising—simply informing the customer about the product and hoping for a sale—was gone. By the 1890s a company had to create a need for the ever-growing number of products on the market and attach an image to that product for the consumer to make a purchase.

For the first time in history, the seed and nursery catalogs, along with any associated advertising, sold a modern, media-inspired garden, promoting an image that included such elements as a lawn, carpet beds, curved walkways, carefully placed trees, groups of shrubs, and one or two urns on the lawn. Thus was born the company owners' version of the English garden. The essays, illustrations, and ads in the catalogs reflected this image, which was easy for customers to recognize because they saw the same image in other publications.

The image worked in the same way as all advertising: capturing a certain look in word and illustration that connected with a product—in this case, garden seeds and plants. By the end of the nineteenth century, the new, modern advertising was characterized, for the first time, by its ability to sell an image along with the product to a mass audience spread across the country. The most powerful image for the seed and nursery industries proved to be their version of the English landscape.

Rochester seedsman James Vick (1818–1882), in his catalog and magazine, presented many essays and illustrations focusing on designing the home grounds or landscape gardening. He is just one of many seed company and nursery owners who saw it as their duty to educate their customers with landscape ideas. The social benefits of landscape gardening appeared in Vick's writing. He said, "As the boy or the girl, the man or the woman, who walks well-dressed among companions is less apt to do a mean act or violate the amenities of social intercourse, so one, who with a laudable pride improves his home and delights in its beauty, is by that means a better citizen himself and a source of virtuous strength to his neighbors."[3]

In the 1870s, Rochester, New York, became known as the Flower City because of the number of nurseries and seed houses that were located in the city. Several of Rochester's nurserymen came from the Old World and were well equipped with the theories and techniques of its way of gardening.[4]

Vick was eighteen when he came to America from Portsmouth, England. His work for several years was in the publishing business, but by the 1860s he had established his own seed company.

Visitors came to see Vick's display of spring bulbs at his home on fashionable East Avenue in Rochester, down the same street from where George Eastman, founder of Kodak, would later build his estate. In 1868, Vick featured five hundred varieties of double and single tulips, with fifty thousand plants. He wrote in his catalog of that year, "Many thousands visited my grounds the past spring, from all parts of the country, and all agreed that they had never before witnessed such a magnificent show. The bulbs I sell are exactly similar to those I plant."

The local newspaper said of Vick, "The enterprising florist and seedsman excels in his specialty—no one approaches him in this country, nor is anyone likely to do so. He obtains the best bulbs and seeds to be procured in Europe, and tests them in his propagating houses and gardens, exemplifies their efficacy and reproduces them for sale throughout the Union."[5] The Vick Seed Company claimed, in its catalogs of the 1870s, that its seeds came from the best growers in France, England, and Germany.

In his seed catalog, and later in his garden magazine *Vick's Illustrated Monthly,* Vick often wrote about the English landscape. He featured images of English gardens. The magazine frequently included articles from a "London correspondent." His travels to England sometimes became a topic in his writing. Vick never forgot his English origin or the English style of gardening, which he clearly preferred.

Vick wrote, in his catalog of 1868,

As many persons are troubled to know how to improve their grounds to the best advantage, and as I am entirely unable to furnish the information needed, in the busy season, and can then only give very meager and unsatisfactory answers to the many letters asking information on this subject, I thought a few suggestions at this time might be profitable to my numerous friends.

In the first place, I would remark that the space in front of the house, and generally the sides exposed to view from the street, should be in grass.

Vick insisted on the lawn as the basis of any landscape around the home, a concept true to the landscape legacy of Humphry Repton, John Claudius Loudon, and, of course, Andrew Jackson Downing.

American gardening, by the end of the nineteenth century, had come to include the creation of an artful, or tasteful, landscape. Plant industry catalogs, such as Vick's, also offered the gardener instructions on landscaping, or landscape gardening, as the English had called it for decades.[6]

Frank Scott and the Lawn

Though American landscapes showed a more democratic view of the lawn, in which a street in the suburbs had the lawn of one property flow into that of another, the lawn still became the symbol of the English garden in the nineteenth century. Thanks to Frank Scott, the lawn would forever link American gardening to the English garden.

Scott, a sketch artist from Ohio, loved landscape design and spent a summer as a student with the foremost landscape designers of the time: Downing and his English associate, architect Calvert Vaux, in New York. In 1870, Scott wrote *The Art of Beautifying Suburban Home Grounds,* a book architect and historian David Handlin calls "the commuter's manual."[7] Scott relied heavily on the English picturesque garden style in his writing. He introduced what would become an influential volume on landscape design with these words: "In the specialty of decorative gardening, adapted to the small grounds of most suburban homes, there is much need of other works than have yet appeared."[8] In that one short line Scott indicated the need for homeowners to learn about landscaping, or what he called "decorative gardening."

Nurseryman Thomas Meehan's magazine *Gardener's Monthly* hailed Scott's work when the book's new edition appeared in 1886 (fig. 10.1). Meehan wrote, "It is a work of which American horticulturalists have cause to be proud. Its influence on landscape gardening must be very great, and now, where there promises to be a revival in the lovely art, its presence is particularly timely."[9]

The Scott book, national garden magazines such as *Popular Gardening and Fruit Growing,* and the seed and nursery catalogs were all sending a similar message about what kind of landscape would show that the homeowner had taste for what was called rural art, using plants in a unified, pleasing, and seemingly natural way. The landscape recommended in word and image was predominantly in the English style, which, throughout the nineteenth century, took several forms. A garden might demonstrate the picturesque or naturalistic view, the gardenesque, a return to a more formal trimmed look, the Victorian carpet bedding, or the William Robinson wild garden. In all cases, however, it would include a lawn.

A Garden Magazine on Landscape Design

Because of the availability of cheap paper, improved printing technology, and favorable postage rates, consumer gardening magazines multiplied in the late nineteenth century. Garden-related magazines wielded significant influence over the country's gardening tastes and practices.[10] A series of articles, entitled "Taste and Tact in Arranging Home and Other Grounds" (published in the 1890–91 volume of the magazine *Popular Gardening and*

⁂ *(facing page)*

Figure 10.1. The 1886 edition of Frank Scott's book *The Art of Beautifying Suburban Home Grounds* included this image that depicted a suburban home landscape, including the lawn that ran seamlessly into neighboring properties. *Courtesy of the Frances Loeb Library, Harvard Graduate School of Design, Special Collections, Cambridge, Massachusetts.*

Fruit Growing) provides a context for the lessons on landscaping that also appeared in the seed and nursery catalogs. Readers of magazines such as *Popular Gardening and Fruit Growing* thus learned how to design a landscape at the same time that nurseries and seed companies extolled decorative gardening as an important part of the middle-class home.

The first article presented the purpose for the series, which was to provide useful articles "on arranging home and other grounds with taste and discernment."[11] There was a growing need for this kind of instruction because of the growth of suburbs around the country. The reader was invited to send in landscape problems that future articles would address.

The next article included a sketch from a nurseryman who wanted a landscape design for his home. The magazine was happy to help and supplied a detailed plan because "if there is one class more than another whom we are glad to see interested in tastefully improving their grounds, it is the nurseryman."[12] The proposed plan included a lawn, a walk with a shrub or rockery screen, a grove of ornamental trees, mixed flower borders, a specimen fruit plat, and masses of evergreens. These were all detailed in the plan, illustrated for the reader. The elements of the design reflected the English Victorian landscape.

Seedsmen and nurserymen needed to be at the forefront of landscape design so that their customers could learn the correct method of landscape gardening. The article said, "They should also undertake by liberal and judicious leadership, to influence public sentiment towards improving the public highways, cemeteries, parks, squares, school grounds etc." The perceived role of the seed trade and nurseries was to change the public's ideas about landscape so that artful landscape design would spread into the public domain.

The third article in the series addressed the problems of a narrow house lot. A plan proposed curved walks on the property, with a view of the lot seen from the front, as well as through the verandas.

In the next article, the reader asked for help in landscaping a home property that was mainly lawn. The argument of the author was that landscaping is what nature does: "What indeed can be more commendable for any resident of this fair earth than to desire to take of nature's beautiful trees, shrubs, flowers, grass, and embellish the place he knows as home. And truly nature meets such a one more than half way, for most lavishly has she placed at man's command the riches of her handiwork in natural growths of most varied character."[13] The author totaled the number of available plants for the landscape at 1,300 varieties that came from the forest and the nursery.

In the same article, the author proposed the English naturalistic view of landscape rather than the symmetrical style. He wrote, "Nature in her delightful landscapes never arranges after straight lines; why should we do so when using of her materials about the home?"[14] Discussion of the two styles of landscape gardening persisted throughout the century.

In another installment of the series, a reader sent the magazine a drawing of his home grounds. The garden, made up of straight lines with square flowerbeds that were uniform in size and shape, was behind the house. The advice given was that the visitor to the garden should not see the garden all at once but gradually: "The mere fact, that in entering a garden such as this, the eye may comprehend its entire plan at a glance, lessens the inducement to a visitor to proceed to examine its parts throughout."[15] The method to achieve that look was to avoid straight lines and design the garden in sections hidden by shrubs, which would also give the garden a more natural look. This advice makes use of the same principles used in the English gardenesque design of Joseph Shipley's landscape in Delaware, where the visitor finally sees the house only after passing several areas of trees and shrubs planted along the side of the long, curved entrance road.

The next article included a drawing of the new suburban property of a New York businessman whose home was an hour's ride from his place of business. He wanted suggestions on improving the grounds. The article recommended "ample lawn areas, extended vistas, graceful walks and drives, and a good assortment of deciduous and evergreen trees, shrubs, flowers, etc. throughout, besides a large vegetable and fruit plat."[16]

The final article in the series focused on a seven-acre property in Kansas, where the owner had planted ten thousand trees on land that had been prairie. The writer praised the property owner for adding the trees: "Our correspondent is so alive to the possibilities of a garden, and has shown so much zeal and good judgment in the beginning he has made to date."[17] The author suggested an English picturesque approach to the landscape, with curved drives and vistas accented with several areas of lawn.

In these *Popular Gardening and Fruit Growing* articles, some common themes emerged. Primary among them were that the landscape should be designed in the English naturalistic or picturesque style and that the property needed curved drives and walkways with groupings of trees and shrubs and, of course, an extensive lawn. The seed companies and nurseries promoted this same view of landscape that consumer garden publications such as *Popular Gardening and Fruit Growing* extolled.

Seed Companies and Nurseries on Landscape Design

The seed and nursery companies took on the role of a reliable source of guidance from whom the middle class could learn how to landscape the home lot, no matter what size. A homeowner who wanted to design and plant his own home landscape could look to the catalog for instruction and support and, of course, the necessary plants.

The Thomas Learmont Company wrote in its 1860 catalog what it called "a few practical remarks to persons about to plant new gardens and pleasure grounds, also to those renovating or replanting old ones, when no professional gardener is employed," cautioning that such a person would have "to superintend preparing the grounds and plants, and it frequently occurs that for the want of a little practical advice, suffers losses and disappointments." Because the homeowner purchased plants from the nursery, the nursery felt it important to make sure the homeowner placed them in an appropriate spot to ensure their survival. Landscape advice followed in articles and drawings.

As early as the middle of the nineteenth century, the seed and nursery companies were writing in their catalogs about the importance of the home landscape for everyone, not only the rich estate owner. Overman and Mann said in 1862, "It is now deemed rational to adorn and beautify the surroundings of house, however humble. And what more sensible idea can the owner of the soil entertain than to draw in his mind from its wanderings, and to surround his family with the cheap comforts and delights of home?"

The home became an important symbol of national identity as the country entered the Civil War. That same Overman and Mann catalog of 1862–63 said, "The foregoing is premised upon the fact that notwithstanding the hard times, and the horrors of war, no former season has been so characterized by the tree planting spirit as the past. Everywhere the prevailing disposition seems to be to circumscribe ambition and concentrate its energies within the domestic circle—to make home what it should be."

Not until after 1870, however, with the advances of print and transportation along with increased industrialization, and with articles appearing more often in the catalogs, did the importance of the home landscape for the middle class take center stage within those same pages. The seeds and plants from a national company enabled a homeowner to create a landscape much like the one pictured in catalogs such as Henderson's, in 1886 (fig. 10.2). Through that process of managing the home grounds, the homeowner felt linked with other middle-class homeowners.

While the wealthy needed gardeners to tend the landscape on what was usually an estate, the middle-class home gardener, who was often referred to in the catalogs as an "amateur gardener," could, without too much demand, maintain the home garden, usually on a much smaller property. The amateur gardener was a middle-class homeowner who, like the wealthy, sought to cultivate a landscape with a lawn.

Like so many other mail-order garden catalogs, the Lovett nursery catalog of 1882 gave the homeowner lessons in landscaping, describing itself as

❧ *Figure 10.2.* Henderson in this catalog cover of 1886 shows the home
landscape with the lawn, a water garden, and carpet beds. *Courtesy of the
Warshaw Collection of Business Americana—Seed Industry and Trade, Archives
Center, National Museum of American History, Smithsonian Institution.*

"a handbook of all that is necessary to aid in improving and adorning the home grounds, with a complete catalogue of species and varieties, naming and describing them so fully and accurately and in such a clear and instructive manner that it is a task of ease and pleasure to make judicious selections and to plan out intelligently the proposed improvements. Nothing has been neglected that will teach the reader how to lay out home grounds to advantage." The middle-class homeowner, in need of a garden and home landscape, had only to consult the seed company or nursery catalog.

Though instruction in how to landscape the home property was important, the customer also had to know that the nurseries and seed companies would supply the necessary plants. Lines and Coe, of New Haven, Connecticut, wrote in 1894 about how necessary the landscape was: "Through the zeal of the collectors [i.e., plant collectors, probably from England, who supplied the nursery], 'nature's scattered excellencies' are now available. Instead of being restricted to the varieties that grow native about us, we have the whole flora, practically, of the world at our command, as well as the greatest number of the varieties that have been fostered into existence by much care and painstaking." The seed companies and nurseries would help their middle-class readers in their suburban homes to enjoy the exotic plants that once only the wealthy could cultivate. Now they could show off their own Chinese shrubs, a Japanese vine clinging to the wall of the house, or that South American alternanthera plant in the container or carpet bed on the lawn, all displayed in true Victorian garden style.

In 1898, Joseph Breck highlighted the importance of the home landscape during a time when members of the middle class were becoming wealthier. He wrote in his catalog, "As this country grows in taste and wealth, the importance of the house and grounds, which together constitute the home, making an harmonious whole, is becoming more and more apparent, and these remarks are as applicable, if not more so, to the lot containing five or ten thousand square feet, as to the great estate comprising many acres." Breck's company included an image of the English lawn in one of its catalogs, in an ad for grass seed (fig. 10.3).

Figure 10.3. A grass seed advertisement, also including the newly introduced lawn mower, that appeared in Breck's 1886 seed catalog. *Courtesy of the Worcester County Horticultural Society, Tower Hill, Boylston, Massachusetts.*

The front cover of the Storrs and Harrison Company seed catalog of 1898 featured a home with a circular path to the house, shrubs lining the house, a few trees, and a carpet bed of flowers on the front lawn. It was the image of the gardenesque English landscape style, with its Victorian bedding of flowers. Thus, the seed companies and nurseries, through such images as well as articles, promoted the English landscape to an American audience.

Essentials in the Landscape

The English garden style, whether picturesque or gardenesque, demanded first a lawn and then the careful placement of trees and shrubs, so that the lawn would keep its sweeping look and not be lost by too many or too poorly placed trees and shrubs. The seed companies and nurseries pointed that out to the readers of the catalog.

Lawn

Frank Scott dedicated his book to his friend and instructor, A. J. Downing. In his introduction he credited John Claudius Loudon and Edward Kemp with teaching landscape gardening to the English. He saw his task as teaching Americans those same principles. He wrote, "The half-acre of a suburban cottage may be as perfect a work of art, and as well worth transferring to canvas as any part of the great Chatsworth of the Duke of Devonshire."[18]

Although Scott recognized that, compared to the English, the Americans were "yet novices in the fine arts of gardening,"[19] along with the English he considered the well-kept lawn to be the essential element in the landscape. To the English, the lawn was a status symbol by which one's peers judged one.[20] The lawn, Scott suggested, should be open, so that neighbors and passers-by could see and enjoy it. His book presented plans and also a listing of trees, shrubs, and vines suitable for the suburban home landscape. In his book Scott quoted New York seedsman Peter Henderson for the amount of seed needed for a lawn.[21]

The lawn created that parklike look to the landscape, a view that the formal, picturesque, and gardenesque styles each included. The lawn, as Scott discussed it, connected one house to the next by its placement at the front of the property, along the street. One property seemed to flow right into the next, forming a sense of neighborhood, if not community.

Discussion of the English lawn as the basis of the home landscape was quite common in the seed and nursery catalogs. Here is what the seedsman Charles A. Reeser wrote in his 1886 catalog: "A beautiful lawn. It is hardly necessary to say, is one of the most satisfactory and pleasing outside adornments that can be procured, and is rightly deemed a most essential adjunct to rural and suburban homes." The home landscape, according to the nineteenth-century garden catalogs, needed the verdant sweep of a lawn.

Front lawns began as a luxury of wealthy men like Shipley, in Delaware, but later in the century they became a symbol of the middle class as well.[22] The lots in suburban Takoma Park, Maryland, for example, included a large set-back from the street to provide front space for a lawn.

The seed companies generally sold lawn seed. They were happy to recommend the amount of seed needed for the size of a particular property. Downing, in his book, wrote about the lawn in these words: "We advise him who desires to have speedily a handsome turf, to follow the English practice, and sow three to four bushels of seeds to the acre."[23]

Vick, in his 1873 catalog, echoed the words of Scott: "No arrangement of beds, or borders of box, or anything else, will look so neat and tasteful as a well kept piece of grass."

The lawn could be adorned, though. By the end of the century, the cast iron garden vase, or urn, had become a sign of status for the middle class. Vick recommended in his *Floral Guide* of 1873 that on the lawn the owner place two vases, filled usually with annuals:

> Of all the adornments of the lawn, nothing is more effective than a well filled and well kept vase. All the ornamental-leaved plants are appropriate for the top or center of the vase, while a few drooping plants should be placed near the edges and allowed to hang or droop at least half way to the ground. For this purpose the verbena or the petunia will answer.
>
> We often see several small vases scattered over the lawn, but the effect is bad. It is best to have one or two that command attention by their size and beauty.

Figure 10.4 shows two vases, as Vick had recommended, on the lawn of a nineteenth-century middle-class residence in Gloucester, Massachusetts.

The lawn began in the English garden style, came to America, and continued as an essential feature for any home, whether in New England or on the West Coast. Garden historian Thomas A. Brown has observed that nineteenth-century Californians also planted gardens in the predominant English garden style, which included a lawn.[24]

🙠 *Figure 10.4.* This 1870s family from Gloucester, Massachusetts, poses for a portrait outside their home. Two vases were carefully placed on the lawn. *Courtesy of the Portsmouth Athenaeum, Portsmouth, New Hampshire.*

Trees and Shrubs

Ornamental trees in the landscape often became the topic of a catalog's articles. Here is what the E. D. Putney Company, of Brentwood, New York, wrote about evergreen trees to provide an all-year beauty to the property: "Where only deciduous trees are grown there is a lack of tone and character to the landscape. This is particularly so in winter, when the barrenness is really depressing. In bleak localities they are indispensable as wind breaks. Single specimens of Norway spruce, hemlock, juniper and the Retinisporas are very effective in small yards."

As the country expanded into the west, Overman and Mann, of Illinois, wrote in 1860 about the importance of planting trees in the landscape:

> In our heart we pity the man who can dole out a lifetime, and rear a family on the bare prairie, without a vestige of a tree or a shrub, to shield his tenement from the scorching heat of summer, or the howling blast of winter. Such anomalies of the "genus homo" we have seen, and their souls are as desolate as the arid desert their homes so aptly represent.
>
> It is the duty of everyone to plant trees—in the orchard—in the dooryard—in the grove—on the lawn—by the roadside—to tell posterity that he once lived. These treeless plains are to be peopled by a generation of tree-planters such as the world has not yet seen.
>
> Let tree-planting become a passion with the millions that are to overspread these naked plains, and they will be rapidly transformed into a paradise.

Ellwanger and Barry, from their Mount Hope Nurseries in Rochester, wrote in 1875 about how they had contributed to the improvement of the home landscape by introducing important tree varieties to the homeowner. In their catalog of that year they wrote, "That the utility and beauty of ornamental trees and plants are now becoming generally recognized and appreciated, no better proof is afforded than the great demand which has been created for them. They have become a necessity in the garden, and every one who has a garden must have them." Trees and shrubs had become an important part of the landscape because nurseries such as Ellwanger and Barry's continued to offer them and promote their importance. Such nursery owners convinced the middle-class homeowner of the important role of trees and shrubs for home grounds, just as they had done earlier in the century for estate owners such as Joseph Shipley.

In 1875, Joseph T. Phillips, from West Grove, Chester County, Pennsylvania, summed it up when he wrote in his catalog, "In no department of cultivation is improvement of taste to be more distinctly seen than in the decoration of our grounds and the universal love of trees." American gardeners planted trees in the home grounds at the recommendation of the garden catalogs.

Detailed Landscape Instruction
from the Catalog

Discussion of the home landscape for the middle class appeared in the catalogs but became especially prevalent after 1870, the year Scott published his book. Three companies are highlighted here because each gave a detailed treatment of landscape design to their readers.

Franklin Reuben Elliott

Scott's instruction on landscape design may have been more popular, but it was quite similar to that of pomologist Franklin Reuben Elliott. Like Scott, Elliott found his major inspiration for landscape design in Downing. Both Scott and Elliott appealed to the middle-class property owner.

Elliott was a fruit grower and horticulturalist, born in Guilford, Connecticut, in 1817. He opened his nursery, F. R. Elliott and Co., and also a seed store in Cleveland in the 1840s. In 1859 Elliott became secretary and a charter member of the Missouri Fruit Growers' Association. He had also served in 1852 as secretary of the American Pomological Society while Marshall Wilder from Boston was its first president. Elliott's biography in *The Standard Cyclopedia of Horticulture* says that he "was a man of great ability in horticultural matters" and "a valued contributor to the horticultural press at a day when American horticulture most needed advice."[25]

Because Elliott had advised homeowners on landscape gardening for forty years, Elliott's family undertook to publish his book soon after he died; his *Hand Book of Practical Landscape Gardening* first appeared in 1881, three years after his death. Seed and nursery catalogs promoted it. In 1890 the B. A. Craddock Company, of Curve, Tennessee, offered horticultural books including his in its catalog: "I have arranged with the publishers to furnish my customers with . . . *Elliott's Practical Landscape Gardening.* New edition, illustrated, 16 colored plates of trees; giving designs for laying out grounds, with engravings, showing where to set each tree, directions for selecting trees and planting them; also condense[d] instructions as to forming lawns and care thereof; the building of roads; turfing; propagation of trees; pruning and care of trees, evergreens, hedges, screens, etc."

Elliott's book promoted the English picturesque view of landscape: a lawn, with curved paths, groups of shrubs, and well-placed trees.

The type of house dictated what trees should be used in the landscape. Elliott wrote: "If the house is a square character, with a flat roof and standing on nearly level land, then the prevailing character of the trees should be of a round-headed habit; but if the house is of a pointed gothic, or with many broken yet harmonious lines, and its location on some elevated position, then spiral and pointed trees should be largely introduced, and especially near the house."[26] Vick had discussed these same instructions about the choice of trees in his monthly magazine.

Although Elliott wrote for middle-class gardeners with properties smaller than the estates of the wealthy, he recognized his indebtedness to Downing, whose work found more acceptance among wealthy estate owners. Elliott wrote in the preface of his book, "Since the labors of the lamented and talented A. J. Downing, great taste and desires for, and in the improvement of, grounds around our homes, have been developed."[27] The landscape advice of both Downing and Elliott proposed the English style.

Henry Dreer

The Dreer Seed Company defined the purpose of the landscape in its catalog of 1888: "The garden is for comfort and convenience, for luxury even; it is to express civilization and care and design, and to foster the refinement of our natures."

To design a landscape, the homeowner needed to realize that landscape was an art form, and knowledge of the principles of how to shape a landscape was, therefore, important. Dreer used the English meaning of *landscape,* which included both landscape and garden. He said, "Gardening requires talent, the knowledge of the beautiful, the harmony of color, and the ability to grasp ideas and work them out so that the desire may pass from inception to fulfillment."

The Dreer catalog proposed the three styles of landscape design—geometrical, picturesque, and gardenesque, first discussed by Loudon earlier in the century:

> [In gardenesque] are shown varied tastes and methods, the individual preferences which take precedence of style, and which add, after all, the greatest charm to the garden, for they are the most natural. To this class, belong the groupings of small shrubbery, the beds of perennials, which delight by their apparent disorder, the mixed borders which constantly present a change from grave to gay, from beauty of form and color to that which presents an appearance which would be ill-pleasing were it not for the single redeeming feature of fragrance which charms all the senses through one. For this style of gardening perennials are admirably adored, for they combine in a marked degree permanence and beauty.

Having established the need, he then introduced specific perennial varieties of such flowering plants as foxgloves, columbines, and hollyhocks.

Dreer endorsed mainly English garden writer and designer J. C. Loudon's gardenesque view, discussing it in more detail than geometric or picturesque approaches. He sought to instruct the reader about landscape design, as well as sell the appropriate plants from his nursery.

Benjamin A. Elliott

The Pittsburgh seed company owner Benjamin A. Elliott, who began his company in 1840, also gave a considerable amount of space in his catalog to instruction for the homeowner about landscape.

Elliott's company called his catalog a "book," an apt description, because the catalog was as thick as a book. The first 75 pages of the 122-page 1888 edition were devoted to a discussion of landscape art, or "decorative gardening," Scott's term for the landscape. The rest of the catalog listed the plants and seeds for sale. The catalog's title, *A Few Flowers Worthy of General Culture: An Effort to Win for Hardy Plants Recognition of Their Great Wealth of Beauty,* gave recognition to the seriousness of the topic of home landscape. The middle-class homeowner could look to Elliott for help in home landscape design. Elliott did not disappoint.

The goal of the catalog was to help the gardener: "We have endeavored always, by experimenting and traveling, to discover those plants which have the greatest gardening value, and to offer them to our customers." The plants offered in the pages that followed included roses, hardy plants, shrubs, and vines, along with flower seeds and lawn seed.

The catalog was not simply a manual of instructions on how to grow plants but a discussion of the importance of landscape art: "Our object is to show how the most beautiful garden can be made, and indicate the material to be used and the manner of arranging it, giving incidentally such cultural directions as our space will admit of."

His discussion of landscape art was based on the ideas of the Irish-born gardener William Robinson, who was then writing about and designing gardens in England. Robinson, in his book *The Wild Garden,* had proposed hardy plants as an important feature in the landscape. Considered by some a revolutionary, Robinson sought to change the view of gardening from the formal, carpet-bedding look to the more natural wild look, preferring native plants (fig. 10.5).

Elliott mentioned Robinson while discussing the company's objective: "Our main object is to suggest ideas which may tend to the production of beautiful gardens made with hardy plants, and we believe that the persons who become interested in such plants will derive tenfold more pleasure in them than they possibly can in the cultivation of tender ones. Mr. Robinson says there is not a garden of any kind, even in the suburbs of our large cities, in which the flowers of Alpine lands may not be grown and enjoyed."

Elliott's catalog, like Robinson's book, encouraged the use of perennials rather than annuals. Elliott thus portrayed an emerging English garden style as the model for the American gardener. He wrote, "We are indebted to this

great champion of hardy flowers [Robinson] for some of the ideas advanced here, culled from his numerous works on gardening, which have done much to make English gardens what they are—the most beautiful in the world."

The next year's edition of the catalog, in 1889, said in its opening pages, "We desire, as briefly as possible, to point out some of the rules of the art, the observance of which are imperatively necessary to the beautifying of the home grounds, whether it be a country place of many acres or merely a suburban lot." The catalog offered instruction, but it was also a nursery catalog, and its final pages listed the plants for sale that had been discussed earlier in the catalog.

English Garden Writers Inspire American Gardeners

THE COPY EDITOR of *The New Yorker*, Katharine S. White, in the 1950s wrote a series of garden articles for the magazine. After her death her husband, E. B. White, compiled these in a book entitled *Onward and Upward in the Garden.* She attributed the rise of the English garden style in America to both William Robinson and garden designer Gertrude Jekyll. White wrote,

> If in planting any of the shrubs or trees I have mentioned,
> you and I strive to obtain a natural effect, to follow the
> contours of the land, or to study the region we live in so
> as to make our planting suit it, if we naturalize garden
> flowers in our woodlands or bring wild flowers into our
> gardens or strive to make our garden blend gradually into
> a forest or field, we probably owe our ideas, though all
> unconsciously, to two great English gardeners and garden
> writers of the past. They are William Robinson, the au-
> thor of *The English Flower Garden,* which was published
> in 1883 and is still a garden classic, and his younger friend
> Miss Gertrude Jekyll, the formidable lady I referred
> to earlier. It was these two, more than any others, who
> taught Victorian England, and eventually America, to

make a garden, as Mr. Robinson put it, a reflection of "the beauty of the great garden of the world." When he wrote this, most English gardens, except cottage gardens, either imitated the elaborately formal gardens of France or Italy or were devoted to "bedding out"—that is, to planting flowers in scattered small beds to make artificial color patterns or geometrical designs.[28]

White recognized how dependent the American garden had become on the English style, represented at the end of the nineteenth century by Robinson and Jekyll. Robinson discussed native plants that required less water once they were established. The topic of native plants appeared on occasion in American seed and nursery catalogs, but only as it reflected the English style. By the end of the century, American gardeners were returning to perennial borders. When Robinson wrote, America listened.

In Elliott's catalog of 1889, the importance of hardy plants was emphasized: "Many things have transpired since the issue of our fifth and last edition of *A Few Flowers Worthy of General Culture,* to encourage us in believing that hardy plants will take, and are taking the place in our gardens to which they are so justly entitled. Bedding plants are useful, but their place is a secondary one, and they should be so used that they would not exclude the beautiful hardy plants that cheer us from the early morn of spring until December."

In his 1890 catalog, Elliott included a landscape plan for a perennial bed—seventy feet by nine feet—that would bloom from spring until fall. Named varieties of plants that Elliott sold were listed.

A few years later, in his 1894 fall catalog, called *Special Price List of Trees, Shrubs, Bulbs, and Hardy Herbaceous Plants For Fall Planting,* Elliott included an ad for the landscaping services of his company: "The Landscape Gardening Department of our business is in [the] charge of thoroughly capable men, and their work, without exception, has been entirely satisfactory to our customers, many of whom are most critical and exacting. We undertake the improvement of the most extensive suburban grounds, as well as the smallest city lot, and there are no grounds so small that cannot be improved by intelligent and artistic arrangement."

In providing landscape gardening help to his customers. Elliott proposed the English garden as the ideal landscape. By then this was, however, the English garden of the late nineteenth century, which supported Robinson's *Wild Garden* views. Robinson encouraged hardy perennials, native plants, and informality in design—much of what he put into practice at his own garden at Gravetye Manor.

While his was only one of many seed companies and nurseries that offered landscape advice, Elliott gave more-detailed instructions on landscape art. The suburban homeowners who received the catalog by mail could depend on such instruction on landscape design with the English garden as the model.

A Home Landscape Example

The nineteenth-century seed and nursery catalogs wrote about decorative gardening, or landscaping the home grounds. According to the catalogs, which tended to follow predominantly English landscape fashion, a home landscape of that period could be described in the following way:

The house needs to sit some distance from the street, so that as you go by you can see its form: probably Gothic, or maybe even a cottage. Where possible, the building rises up on the property, so that water will drain more easily.

You will see the lawn sweeping down from the house to the street, and even meeting the lawns of the neighbors on the sides. The lawn is kept short and neat throughout the season.

The walkways and driveways on the property need to have some curve to them, rather than consisting of straight lines. The driveway will curve to the front door.

Trees will border the boundaries of the property. You will have some shade trees on the lawn, but not too many. A single tree sometimes gives a perfect look to a spot. You need to have a view through the trees from inside the house, so the trees need to be planted to allow that. Hopefully you were able to use existing trees, as new plantings take years to achieve the desired look. The shape of the tree is quite important. Some will be tall and narrow, as is the case with, perhaps, an evergreen, while others will be more of a round shape. A tree's location in the landscape will dictate the variety of the tree.

Shrubs, both evergreen and deciduous, will be in groups of three around the property. They should not be scattered without some reason but carefully positioned to give a neat appearance from the street and from inside the house. Shrubs might be grouped at select spots as a screen on the landscape to give a visitor a sense of surprise to see what the homeowner has carefully placed in the landscape, perhaps a small garden, perhaps a water feature. (There was no foundation planting until the twentieth century, so no shrubs next to the house.)

Near the front door, perhaps on the lawn, stands a cast iron urn on a base, together reaching four feet in height. The container will have three types of plants: the tallest in the center, the second about half as high as the first, and the third a trailing variety. A vine will cover the porch railing and run up toward the roof and side of the house. This will give shade in the summer and also provide color for the house exterior if the vine has flowers.

Beds of flowers, perhaps carpet beds with intricate designs, will be carefully situated on the lawn. Do not plant too many beds, perhaps only one or two, so that you are simply showing color with leaves or flowers but not overpowering the view of the lawn. The plants need to be low and kept trimmed.

If you do not use carpet bedding but prefer hardy perennials, then in the bed the larger plants should form the center, and shorter plants will then fill out the area to the edge, where the shortest will be found. Be sure to add some annuals to supply color when the blooms of the perennials have passed.

In the back, behind the house but near the kitchen, you could plant a kitchen garden of vegetables, which could include herbs. Also out back, perhaps forming the boundary of the property, some fruit trees will supply blossoms in the spring and fruit in late summer or early fall.

The result resembles an English gardenesque landscape for a nineteenth-century suburban American home according to the recommendations of the seed and nursery catalogs. Figure 10.6, from *Vick's Illustrated Monthly,* illustrates that view.

Nineteenth-Century Landscape Design in America

The landscape, with its lawn and gardens, provided the suburban home with a taste of the country. The well-tended home grounds became a place of both connection and isolation: connection to a rapidly disappearing rural

way of life, and isolation from the city and its disturbing chaos.[29] The image of the English garden discussed and illustrated in the seed company and nursery catalogs guided the homeowner to create that landscape.

Scott's book and popular garden magazine articles about landscaping complemented what the seed companies and nurseries wrote. The landscape was the English garden style as it evolved during the nineteenth century: from the naturalistic or picturesque, to the gardenesque that John Claudius Loudon had encouraged, to Victorian carpet bedding, and by the end of the century to the use of perennials and native plants proposed in books by such authors as William Robinson and Gertrude Jekyll. The prominent American landscape design writers Downing and Scott likewise recognized the English garden as their inspiration. The nineteenth-century American seed companies and nurseries, too, became the voice for the English garden style in the United States.

Vick endorsed Scott's book and used many of its ideas in his own writing about landscape design. He wrote in his magazine *Vick's Illustrated Monthly* of 1878, "We have never seen a plan better than one given from Scott's *Suburban Homes*."[30]

Downing wrote, in the 1850 edition of his magazine *The Horticulturist,*

In England at large, the great wealth of the landed aristocracy, and the enormous size of their establishments, raises the houses and gardens to a scale so far above ours, that they are not directly or practically instructive to Americans. In the Isle of Wight, on the other hand, are numerous pretty cottages, villas and country houses, almost precisely on a transatlantic scale as to the first [in] cost and the style of living. . . . And it is this kind of rural beauty, the tasteful embellishment of small places, for which the United States will, I am confident, become celebrated in fifty years.

Downing would not live to see how much, by the end of the nineteenth century, the United States from coast to coast would take on the English example of landscape garden style. He died tragically in a shipboard fire on the Hudson River two years after that letter. James Vick then bought Downing's magazine to continue its monthly publication. Vick incorporated the magazine's landscape design ideas in his own work and, like other seed merchants and nursery owners, continued the legacy of Downing and the English garden in the nineteenth century.

❧ ❧

FEATURED PLANT

Alternanthera dentata 'Purple Knight' / 'Purple Knight' alternanthera

I HAVE BEEN fascinated with *Alternanthera* since I visited the Berkshire Botanical Garden in western Massachusetts. There, in one bed, a collection of several *Alternanthera* varieties took me by surprise as I walked the garden one summer day. I had no idea there were so many. Later, in my own garden, I planted 'Purple Knight' in a square blue cement container on the lawn. This alternanthera's purple leaves trailed over the edge, while a gold coleus stood tall in the center. It presented a bit of Victoriana in my own garden.

ℜ𝓁 *Alternanthera dentata* 'Purple Knight', 'Purple Knight' alternanthera

If there is one plant that appears over and over again in any discussion of Victorian gardens, it is alternanthera. Gardeners in both England and America used this popular annual in carpet beds on the lawn. In an 1880 issue of Meehan's *Gardener's Monthly,* correspondent William Sutherland described an elaborate landscape in New Jersey: "The flower beds are the glory of the outside, and require hundreds of thousands of plants to fill them, and sixty men or more to take care of them. One very large oval bed of Alternanthera, which is clipped every three days, contained the Shaksperian [*sic*] quotation 'This is an art which does not mend nature but the art itself is nature.'"[31]

Alternanthera is native to Mexico and Brazil, with over two hundred variations. The English plant collector Thomas Nuttall (1786–1859), who spent several years traveling the woods and fields of the United States in search of plants, first mentioned 'Purple Knight' in 1820 as *Achyranthes lanuginosa*. In 1869 the plant was assigned a new name, *Alternanthera lanuginosa*.

'Purple Knight' is a cultivar of the species *Alternanthera dentata*. This plant is used not only in containers but also as a groundcover or in beds and borders because of its beautiful purple leaf color. It will reach a height of sixteen to twenty inches, with a spread of over twenty-four inches. It does well in either full sun or part shade, but in full sun the brightest colors of the plant come through. Once frost appears, 'Purple Knight' can be kept indoors in a greenhouse or in front of a sunny window.

Conclusion

THE DAHLIA has amazed American gardeners with its color, form, and ease of growing, for more than 150 years. Each September, a two-day dahlia show in the town of Wickford on the coast of Rhode Island draws hundreds of visitors to view the form, size, and shades of color of award-winning dahlia blooms, all carefully marked and standing tall in glass vases. But the dahlia's popularity is nothing new. In the 1885 issue of its company magazine, the Currie Brothers Seed Company, of Milwaukee, wrote, "There is at present a very rapidly growing sentiment in favor of the single in preference to the double Dahlias now so long in cultivation. They have for the past few years been exceedingly popular in England, and continue to rise in the estimation of horticulturalists there."[1]

Currie Brothers watched the trends in gardening in England because they were important to the American gardener who wanted to have an up-to-date garden. The point here was not simply the irresistible dahlia but the role the English garden played for its customers; the seed company wrote about the dahlia but also about the importance of the English garden as a model for American gardeners.

This book is an attempt to tell the story of how the catalogs of the nineteenth-century seed and nursery industries sold a particular form of gardening to middle-class Americans, particularly women, who by the end of the century found themselves the major consumers of products for the home. Women preferred advertised goods with a recognizable brand. Gardens are highly important as places and as an idea to thousands of people, yet one might ask why that is so and how a specific garden style came to be so pervasive.[2] The simple answer is that Americans garden in the English fashion because in nineteenth-century America the seed and nursery industries sold the English form of gardening as a way to create social status for a growing middle class. The Italian, Spanish, French, and Dutch gardening styles were certainly not unknown, but the English style was ubiquitous in catalog and magazine articles and illustrations as well as in advertising.

Cultural studies scholar Mikko Lehtonen suggests that to arrive at the meaning of a term, as we might here suggest with the word *garden,* we begin with a text, in this case the nineteenth-century seed or nursery catalog. Then we need to look at the context of the period, and finally at the readers of the text, to understand how discourse on a particular topic enables its cultural expression.[3]

The text here includes primarily American seed and nursery catalogs but also company magazines, independent horticultural journals, books written by industry leaders, newspaper articles, and advertising. In the catalog, the company owner presented a narrative about how important the garden was, what plants should be included, and how the garden should look. Lehtonen argues that such a narrative provides a persuasive voice.[4] The writers of the catalogs did not just sell seeds and plants: they told the story of how and why to design the right kind of garden. Seed and nursery catalogs across the country repeated the same story over and over again.

The catalogs, as advertising for a national audience, became a way for the middle class to create a sense of identity. From the late nineteenth century on, the success of modern advertising has been its ability to enable the consumer to identify with the product. This success derived partly from the sheer pervasiveness of advertising. As an article in Philadelphia nurseryman Thomas Meehan's magazine *Gardener's Monthly,* of 1884, said, "Perhaps in no other country is the press so liberally patronized by seedsmen, florists, and nurserymen as in the United States. In their advertising seasons, which cover most of the months of the year, we can rarely pick up a periodical that does not contain some of their advertisements."[5]

One well-advertised product was the lawn mower. The English lawn mower, introduced in 1830 by Edwin Beard Budding and later sold in American seed and nursery catalogs, enabled the homeowner to showcase a well-trimmed lawn, which came to be viewed as essential for middle-class status. Thus, advertising in the nineteenth century also became a tool for socialization. Selling the garden to a national audience resulted in the same suburban middle-class home landscape that appeared in cities, towns, suburbs, and villages throughout the United States. Its sameness illustrated the success of the seed and nursery industries' media-generated image of what a garden should look like.

Once advertising in a mass-media culture appeared in late nineteenth-century America, marketing a product in the simplest form so that the consumer would experience no problem identifying it became important. Branding resulted from such marketing, in which people recognized the image used to promote the product (as with the familiar face of Quaker Oats, first promoted in 1888).[6]

In the case of the nineteenth-century garden, that meant selling a garden illustrated the same way, whether in a black-and-white drawing or as a chromolithograph, regardless of whether the accompanying text was an article in a seed catalog, in a nursery catalog, or in a garden magazine. The illustration of the garden along with articles on landscape gardening represented the look of an English garden. That garden included elements such as a curved walk, carefully sited trees, a group of shrubs, a lawn, and often carpet beds of annuals on the lawn. The kitchen garden would be behind the house with perhaps some fruit trees in the back.

By buying seeds and plants from the catalog, the homeowner could envision that beautiful lawn or garden of colorful flowers. The same discussion on the garden and landscape in every catalog meant that the seed and plant companies were normalizing the cultural value of a certain form of garden for the middle class. They succeeded so well that landscaping and garden styles remained fairly consistent and homogenous across the continent in the nineteenth century.[7] The only difference was which specific ornamental plants would be chosen for a particular region in the country.

By the 1890s, the result of the persuasive seed and nursery catalogs had become apparent: for the first time in history, what the mass media said inspired gardeners around the country. The catalogs came off the press in the hundreds of thousands. The national readership for the catalogs created a sameness in plant choices and gardening style that America had never seen previously. The gardener, most often a woman, coveted a particular seed or plant and could envision changes the garden would undergo—all made possible by the catalog. The catalog sold dreams and hopes, as does any advertising to this day.

The catalog was not simply a collection of seeds for sale but a vehicle to motivate the middle-class reader to want a garden with a particular form of landscape. That landscape was English in style, based initially on the works of Loudon and later Downing, one in England and the other in America, who both wrote about a similar naturalistic, picturesque, or gardenesque view of nature, and later, at the start of the twentieth century, the English gardener and landscape designer Gertrude Jekyll, who influenced the American garden through her writing on such topics as perennial borders and the mass planting of flowers of a single color. Eventually, garden writers would Americanize the books and articles by such English authors.[8] The model, however, continued to be the English garden.

That model has remained with us. Today, for example, Americans can buy at many newsstands a magazine published in England called *The En-*

glish Garden. According to the magazine's marketing, the audience is simply those who love beautiful gardens. It comes as no surprise that an American readership, long inspired by the English garden, is out there, probably eager for such a publication.

However, the desire for the English garden promoted since the nineteenth century through mass media has become more complicated. Though we may love the English garden, the question of a sustainable landscape now confronts the American gardener. Thirsty lawns drain the supply of water-short communities. Homeowners often use commercial, synthetic fertilizers, which pollute the water around the home. We grow fussy exotic plants even though we know that plants native to each gardening zone require less care and promote habitats friendly to wildlife.

Gardeners still struggle for the perfect lawn; commercial growers continue to search for the perfect hybrid annual and tout the latest variety, just found on the other side of the globe. But perhaps today we do not need the latest plant. Could we be satisfied with a traditional variety or species? Could heirloom flowers and vegetables once again become popular, as a more positive way to fit gardening into the environment? Could lawns be designed to require less maintenance or be made smaller or even be eliminated altogether?

These are all important questions. The American love of the English garden makes talking about them difficult, but the discussion needs to take place so that we can garden in an environment that is safe and will continue for future generations of gardeners.

LOVETT'S GUIDE to Fruit Culture.

CUTHBERT
MANCHESTER
HANSELL
GOLDENQUEEN

J. T. Lovett
Little Silver, N.J.

Monmouth.

SPRING

1887

Geo. E. Errington Del.

Notes

❧ ❧

Preface

1. Miller, *What England Can Teach*, v.
2. Graham, *American Eden*, 376.
3. Pollan, *Second Nature*, 86.

Introduction

1. Meehan, "Ye May Know Him," 373.
2. Stilgoe, *Common Landscape of America*, 345.
3. Adams, *Restoring American Gardens*, 36.

Chapter 1: The British Connection

1. Hovey, introduction, 6. The title of Hovey's publication for the first two volumes in 1835 and 1836 was *The American Gardener's Magazine and Register of Useful Discoveries and Improvements in Horticulture and Rural Affairs*. With volumes 3 (1837) to 34 (1868) he changed the title to *The Magazine of Horticulture, Botany, and All Useful Discoveries and Improvements in Rural Affairs*.
2. Otis, *Grounds for Pleasure*, 85.
3. Slade, *Evolution of Horticulture*, 26.
4. Schermerhorn, "Home and Gardens," 33.
5. Schermerhorn, "Home and Gardens," 36.
6. Martin, *Pleasure Gardens of Virginia*, xxi.
7. Wheelwright, "Gardens and Places," 24.
8. Blane, *Excursion*, 30.
9. Carmichael, *Putting Down Roots*, 63.
10. Wilder, *Address*, 21.

11. Slade, *Evolution of Horticulture*, 157–58.

12. Hovey, "Arboretum Americanum," 195.

13. Harvey, *Early Nurserymen*, 133.

14. Cobbett, *American Gardener*, xxiv.

15. Harvey, *Early Nurserymen*, 33.

16. Hatfield, *History of British Gardening*, 29.

17. Cecil, *History of Gardening*, 90.

18. Cecil, *History of Gardening*, 227.

19. Geoffrey Taylor, *Some Nineteenth Century Gardeners*, 166. Taylor says on that same page, "It is our English, Irish, and Scottish lawns that foreigners most envy, and try ineffectually to imitate."

20. Hovey, "Address," 13.

21. Geoffrey Taylor, *Some Nineteenth Century Gardeners*, 262.

22. Lustig, "Creation and Uses," 46.

23. Cresswell, *Diary*, 15.

24. Pennsylvania Horticultural Society, *From Seed to Flower*, 22.

25. Carr, "Gardening and Gardeners," 667.

26. Cobbett, *American Gardener*, xxvii.

27. Wynne, "Account of Nursery Gardens," 274 and 275.

28. Doell, *Gardens*, 128.

29. Downing, "American versus British Horticulture," 250.

30. Lustig, "Creation and Uses," 23.

31. Thornton, *Cultivating Gentlemen*, 20.

32. Leighton, *American Gardens of the Nineteenth Century*, 74.

33. Hovey, "Address," 9–10.

34. Loudon, "Calls at the London Nurseries," 468.

35. Lustig, "Creation and Uses," 161.

36. Rogers, Eustis, and Bidwell, *Romantic Gardens*, 130.

37. Hovey, "Address," 8.

38. Vick, "Plants for Cemeteries," 163.

39. Lustig, "Creation and Uses," 107.

40. Pauly, *Fruits and Plains*, 201.

41. Pinardi, *Plant Pioneers*, 58.

42. Meehan, Editorial Notes (February 1886), 376.

43. Lustig, "Creation and Uses," 136.

44. Bailey, "Recent Progress," 22.

45. Leuchars, "Notes on Gardens and Gardening," 55.

46. Meehan, Editorial Notes (January 1878), 28.

47. Lindley, *Gardener's Magazine* (1844): 2.

48. Lustig, "Creation and Uses," 38–39.

49. Hovey, "Floricultural Notices," 179–80.

50. Meehan, Editorial Notes (December 1886), 375.

51. Quoted in "Camellia C. M. Hovey," *Gardener's Monthly and Horticulturist* 25 (July 1883): 202.

52. Bailey, "Podophyllum," 3:2725.

Chapter 2: The English Garden Influence at Williamsburg

1. Swem, *Brothers of the Spade*, 21.

2. Swem, *Brothers of the Spade*, 40.

3. Phipps, *Colonial Kitchens*, 135.

4. Brinkley and Chappell, *Gardens of Williamsburg* (1996 ed.), 1.

5. Bullion, "Early American Farming," 39.

6. Wyman, "Introduction of Plants," 12.

7. Leighton, *American Gardens in the Eighteenth Century*, 361.

8. Tishler, *American Landscape Architecture*, 136.

9. Quest-Ritson, *English Garden*, 109.

10. Brinkley and Chappell, *Gardens of Williamsburg* (1996 ed.), 6.

11. Brinkley and Chappell, *Gardens of Williamsburg* (1970 ed.), 47.

12. Brinkley and Chappell, *Gardens of Williamsburg* (1970 ed.), 3.

13. Martin, *Pleasure Gardens of Virginia*, 80.

14. Favretti and DeWolf, *Colonial Gardens*, 146.

15. Newton, *Design on the Land*, 646.

16. Roper, *Seedtime*, 99.

17. Fry, "International Catalogue," 5.

18. Swem, *Brothers of the Spade*, 73.

19. Fitzpatrick, "Overview," 153.

20. Martin, *Pleasure Gardens of Virginia*, 92.

21. Robertson, "English Influences" lecture.

22. Meager, *Compleat English Gardner*, 97.

23. Dumbarton Oaks, *American Garden Literature*.

24. Miller, *Gardeners Dictionary*, xiii.

25. "Rudbeckia" in Miller, *Gardeners Dictionary*, n.p.

26. Pope, "On Gardens," 10:531.

27. Pope, "On Gardens," 10:531.

28. Jacques, review of *Pursuing Innocent Pleasures*, 78.

29. Stetson, "American Garden Books," 347.

30. Bullion, "Early American Farming," 29.

31. Bullion, "Early American Farming," 31.

32. Eliot, *Essays upon Field-Husbandry*, 3.

33. Deane, *New England Farmer*, 3.

34. Beverley, *History and Present State*, 153.

Chapter 3: Early Wealthy Americans and Their English Landscapes

1. Kornwolf, "Picturesque," 103.
2. Parmentier, "Landscapes and Picturesque Gardens," 184.
3. Loudon quoted in Kemp, *How to Lay Out,* 98.
4. Vincent, *Romantic Rockwood,* xiii.
5. Meehan, Seasonable Hints (March 1877), 65.
6. Allen, *Rural Architecture,* 73.
7. Mullin, "Rockwood," 192–95.
8. Lee, "Rockwood."
9. Lee, "Rockwood," 26.
10. Mullin, "Rockwood," 18.
11. Vincent, *Romantic Rockwood,* 30.
12. Vincent, *Romantic Rockwood,* 31.
13. Cothran, *Gardens and Historical Plants,* 74.
14. Downing, *Treatise,* 556.
15. Graptolite, "Trip to Wilmington, Del.," 229.
16. Downing, *Treatise,* 23.
17. Wulf, *Brother Gardeners,* 140.
18. Fry, "International Catalogue," 27.
19. Grove, *Henry Shaw's Victorian Landscapes,* 78.
20. Meehan, "Botanic Garden," 244.

Chapter 4: A Short History of the Nineteenth-Century Seed
and Nursery Industries in America

1. Hibbert and Buist, *American Flower Garden Directory,* iii.
2. Harvey, *Early Nurserymen,* 14.
3. Fitzpatrick, "Overview," 152.
4. Van Ravenswaay, "Horticultural Heritage," 145.
5. Bailey, *Cyclopedia of Horticulture,* 2:1518.
6. *Farm and Garden,* "Seed Trade of Philadelphia."
7. *Practical Farmer,* "Outlook for the Seed Business."
8. Van Ravenswaay, "Horticultural Heritage," 144.
9. Lyons-Jenness, *For Shade,* 54. Others who have used catalogs in their studies of garden history are Thomas Schlereth, Denise Wiles Adams, and Marina Moskowitz.
10. Meehan, "Descriptive Catalogues," 55.
11. Fitzpatrick and Ho, *Bibliography.* The catalogs are part of the collection of seventeen research libraries, including the National Agricultural Library in Beltsville, Maryland.
12. Parks, "Cultivation of Flower City."

13. Brown, *List of California Nurseries*.

14. The garden catalog collections at both the Massachusetts Horticultural Society and Cornell University include many English seed and nursery catalogs from this time.

15. "Fruits and Vegetables," Special Collections, University of Delaware Library website, www.lib.udel.edu/ud/spec/exhibits/sfc/fruit.htm.

16. *Gardener's Monthly*, "Philadelphia Market-Gardening and Seed Growing," 269.

17. Manks, "How the American Nursery," 8.

18. Sloat, "William G. Comstock," 104.

19. Morrison, foreword, xii.

20. Parkman, "Notes on Hardy Perennials," 66.

21. Meehan, "The Rhododendron," 175.

22. *American Florist*, Obituary, 1040.

23. Buist, *American Flower-Garden Directory*, 174.

24. Walpole quoted in Hunt and Willis, *Genius of the Place*, 315.

Chapter 5: Garden Writing from the Seed Companies and Nurseries

1. Hovey, Review of Comstock's *Treatise*, 150.

2. Downing, "Ornamental Trees," 226.

3. Brockway, "Durant-Kenrick House."

4. Woodburn, "Horticultural Heritage," 111.

5. Hedrick, *History of Horticulture*, 475.

6. Kitch, *Girl on the Magazine Cover*, 4.

7. Demaree, *American Agricultural Press*, 28.

8. Mott, *History of American Magazines*, 1:132.

9. Downing, "Ornamental Trees," 225.

10. Bullion, "Agricultural Press," 80.

11. Hovey, introduction to *American Gardener's Magazine*, iv.

12. Pauly, *Fruits and Plains*, 59.

13. Thomas Meehan's garden magazine had a series of titles: *Gardener's Monthly and Horticultural Advertiser*, 1859–75; *Gardener's Monthly and Horticulturist*, 1876–88; and a new publication edited with the assistance of his sons, *Meehans' Monthly*, 1891–1902.

14. Loudon, "Account," 27.

15. Bailey, "List of American Horticultural Books," 1523.

16. Meehan, "Our Correspondents," 15.

17. Tait, "Loudon," 61.

18. Bailey, "Literature of Horticulture," 2:1521.

19. *Thomas Jefferson Encyclopedia*, s.v. "Bernard McMahon."

20. Hedrick, *History of Horticulture*, 477.

21. Fessenden, *New American Gardener*, 10.

22. Fessenden, *New American Gardener*, 184.

23. Hedrick, *History of Horticulture*, 227.

24. Hedrick, *History of Horticulture*, 482.

25. Buist, *American Flower-Garden Directory*, iii.

26. Hedrick, *History of Horticulture*, 453.

27. F. T. Fleisbein to Gregory Seed Company, 1886, Marblehead Museum, letter number 2001.152.107.

28. Loudon, "Account," 114.

29. *Evening Journal* (Jersey City, NJ), Obituary, 60.

30. Bailey, in his discussion of important nineteenth-century American Horticultural Books, lists most of the titles mentioned in this chapter.

31. George Taylor, "Contribution from America," 119.

32. Woodburn, "Horticultural Heritage," 133.

33. Kenrick, *Notes on Ogdensburg*, 8.

34. Hedrick, *Peaches of New York*, 58n1.

35. *Currie's Monthly*, "Mina Lobata," 14.

Chapter 6: The Impact of Social Changes on the Seed and Nursery Industries

1. Manks, "How the American Nursery," 10.

2. *Rochester Union and Advertiser*, "New City Hall."

3. Morrison, *J. Horace McFarland*, 13.

4. Dingee and Conard later became the Conard Pyle Company. Today its name is Starr Roses, a mail order firm.

5. Clissold, *Seed Industry*, 11.

6. Parks, "Cultivation of Flower City."

7. Norris, *Advertising*, 17.

8. Norris, *Advertising*, 50.

9. Lears, *Fables of Abundance*, 70.

10. John, *Spreading the News*, 24.

11. Mack, "Catalog of Woes," 45.

12. Adams, *Restoring American Gardens*, 23.

13. Lyons-Jenness, "Petunias by Post," 10.

14. Meehan, "Post Office Rulings," 86.

15. Barber, "Brief History of Newspapers."

16. Overholser and Jamieson, *Press*, 21.

17. Last, *Color Explosion*, 21.

18. Last, *Color Explosion*, 243.

19. Aeberli and Becket, "Joseph Harris."

20. Marzio, *Democratic Art*, 91.

21. Marzio, *Democratic Art*, 25.

22. *Printer's Ink,* "Personality . . . behind the Business," 12.

23. *Who's Who in Advertising,* 11.

Chapter 7: Major Themes in the Catalogs

1. This was evident in the business records of the James J. H. Gregory Seed Company, which are found in the archives of the Marblehead Museum and Historical Society, Marblehead, Massachusetts.

2. Meehan, "Weigela floribunda," 262.

3. Adams, *Restoring American Gardens,* 297.

4. Thomas, "Grouping Flowers—a Suggestion," 120–22.

5. Pauly, *Fruits and Plains,* 124.

6. Meehan, Seasonable Hints (February 1882), 33.

7. Meehan, "Seed Business in Philadelphia," 28.

8. Hedrick, *History of Horticulture,* 511.

9. Lustig, "Creation and Uses," 56.

10. Quoted in Sullivan, *Our Times,* 4:399.

11. Charles Julius Guiteau shot U.S. President James Garfield on July 2, 1881. President Garfield died two months later.

12. A. Henderson, *Peter Henderson,* 45.

Chapter 8: Gardening and the Middle Class

1. Bailey, *Cyclopedia of Horticulture,* 2:1603.

2. Manks, "How the American Nursery," 9.

3. Binford, *First Suburbs,* 126.

4. Binford, *First Suburbs,* 148.

5. Binford, *First Suburbs,* 219.

6. Anthony Sammarco, Dorchester historian, e-mail message to author, June 24, 2010.

7. McMurry, *Families and Farmhouses,* 59.

8. Jackson, *Crabgrass Frontier,* 55.

9. *Horticulturist* 29 (August 1874): 230. According to the University of Minnesota Extension Service, http://www.extension.umn.edu/distribution/horticulture/DG2386 .html, *Rhododendron x kosteranum* or mollis azalea is often labeled *Rhododendron mollis* in the nursery trade. Mollis azaleas are extremely showy, blooming in late May with flower colors in shades of yellows, oranges, and reds.

10. Jackson, *Crabgrass Frontier,* 46.

11. Tice, *Gardening in America,* 51.

12. Marsh and O'Boyle, *Takoma Park,* 1.

13. Vick, Editorial, 258.

14. *Genesee Farmer,* "Kitchen Garden," 67.
15. Marsh, "From Separation to Togetherness," 509.
16. Elliott, *Victorian Gardens,* 87.
17. Elder, "Arrangement of Flower-Gardens," 169.
18. Hedrick, *Horticulture in America,* 276.
19. Wilder, *Address,* 21.
20. Pavord, *Tulip,* 250.
21. Pavord, *Tulip,* 262.
22. Kenrick, *New American Orchardist,* 20.
23. Helmreich, *English Garden,* 224.
24. Carter, *Victorian Garden,* 131.
25. Bjorklund, "Ribbon Bedding," 164.
26. Marsh, *Suburban Lives,* 6.

Chapter 9: The Grandest Rose of the Century

1. Mullin, "Rockwood," 196.
2. Breck, *Flower Garden,* 207.
3. *Gardener's Monthly,* "Grounds of C. M. Hovey," 248.
4. Gilmer, *Redwoods and Roses,* 128.
5. Brown, *List of California Nurseries,* 42.
6. Initially the rose was called 'Turner's Crimson Rambler', but the name has been shortened over the years to simply 'Crimson Rambler'.
7. Parsons, *Rose,* iv.
8. Buchan, *English Garden,* 30.
9. Bacon, "Rose and Its Culture," 561.
10. *Currie's Monthly,* "Roses," 2.
11. Adams, *Restoring American Gardens,* 59–60.
12. Wright, *Roses,* 165.
13. Ellwanger, "American Roses," 478–79.
14. Harkness, *Rose,* 147.
15. *Garden* (London), "Turner's Crimson Rambler Rose," 434.
16. Bailey, *Cyclopedia of Horticulture,* 3:2985.
17. Beales, *Twentieth-Century Roses,* 87.
18. *Gardening* 2, no. 46 (August 1, 1894): 372.
19. *Gardener's Magazine* (London), quoted in Given's 1895 seed catalog.
20. Dingee and Conard, "Hardy Climbing Roses," 178.
21. Dingee and Conard, "Answers to Correspondents," 150.
22. Meehan, "Subscribing to the Gardener's Monthly," 211.
23. *Florist's Exchange,* "European Notes," 561.
24. *Florist's Exchange,* "Robert Scott & Sons Model Farm," 807.

25. Hill, "Novelties in Roses, 1894," 655.

26. McFarland, *American Rose Annual*, 38.

27. Dimmock, "Rose Crimson Rambler," 260.

28. Jekyll and Mawley, *Roses for English Gardens*, 5.

29. Ely, *Woman's Hardy Garden*, 132.

30. Henderson, *Gardening for Pleasure*, 104.

31. McFarland, *Rose in America*, 30.

32. Tice, "Gardens of Change," 202.

33. Nancy Bowers, letter from the files of the Dedham Historical Society, Dedham, Massachusetts.

34. Wharton, *Gift from the Grave*, 61.

35. Wharton, *Summer*, 266.

36. *New York Times*, "Paris Models Break Record."

37. *Nation*, review of *The Rambler Rose*, 326.

38. Earle, *Old Time Gardens*, 462.

39. Thomas, *Thomas Rose Book*, 235.

40. Cunningham, "Yankee Doodle Roses."

41. Marci Martin, rosarian at Elizabeth Park, e-mail message to author, April 16, 2009.

42. David Wilson, executive director of Friends of Elizabeth Park, e-mail message to author, February 1, 2010.

43. Scanniello and Bayard, *Climbing Roses*, 75.

44. Allen, *Roses for Every Garden*, 47.

45. O'Mara, "Hardiness," 118.

46. Pizzetti and Cocker, *Rosa*, 1128.

47. Witzell, "Gardeners and Caretakers," 18.

48. Witzell, "Gardeners and Caretakers," 20.

49. Scanniello and Bayard, *Climbing Roses*, 117.

50. Quest-Ritson, *Climbing Roses*, 138.

Chapter 10: Landscape Design According to the Catalogs

1. Meehan, Seasonable Hints (April 1886), 97.

2. Clark, *American Family Home*, 139.

3. Vick, "Beautiful Rural Homes," 162.

4. McKelvey, "Flower City," 132.

5. *Rochester Evening Express*, "Where the Rainbows Are Made."

6. For Loudon, landscape gardening always meant the art of laying out grounds.

7. Handlin, *American Home*, 173.

8. Scott, *Art of Beautifying*, 12.

9. Meehan, Editorial Notes (February 1886), 61.

10. Clayton, *Once and Future Gardener*, xiii.

11. *Popular Gardening and Fruit Growing*, "Taste and Tact: First Paper," 25.

12. *Popular Gardening and Fruit Growing*, "Taste and Tact: Second Paper," 44.

13. *Popular Gardening and Fruit Growing*, "Taste and Tact: Fourth Paper," 84.

14. *Popular Gardening and Fruit Growing*, "Taste and Tact: Fourth Paper," 85.

15. *Popular Gardening and Fruit Growing*, "Taste and Tact: Sixth Paper," 124.

16. *Popular Gardening and Fruit Growing*, "Taste and Tact: Seventh Paper," 147.

17. *Popular Gardening and Fruit Growing*, "Taste and Tact: Ninth Paper," 194.

18. Scott, *Art of Beautifying*, 14.

19. Scott, *Art of Beautifying*, 13.

20. Quest-Ritson, *English Garden*, 188.

21. Scott, *Art of Beautifying*, 110.

22. Jenkins, *Lawn*, 5.

23. Downing, *Treatise*, 422.

24. Brown, *List of California Nurseries*, 5.

25. Bailey, *Cyclopedia of Horticulture*, 2:1574.

26. Elliott, *Practical Landscape Gardening*, 56.

27. Elliott, *Practical Landscape Gardening*, iii.

28. White, *Onward and Upward*, 113.

29. Pierce, "From Garden to Gardener," 741.

30. Vick, "Improving Home Grounds," 35.

31. Sutherland, "Hollywood Park," 132.

Conclusion

1. *Currie's Monthly*, "Single Dahlias," 3.

2. Dixon, *Greater Perfections*, xii.

3. Lehtonen, *Cultural Analysis of Texts*, 3.

4. Lehtonen, *Cultural Analysis of Texts*, 80.

5. Silvius, "Advertising," 344.

6. Sivulka, *Soap, Sex, and Cigarettes*, 49.

7. Adams, *Restoring American Gardens*, 36.

8. Seaton, "Gardening Books," 47.

Bibliography

❧❧ ❧❧

Adams, Denise Wiles. *Restoring American Gardens: An Encyclopedia of Heirloom Ornamental Plants, 1640–1940.* Portland, OR: Timber Press, 2004.

Aeberli, William I., and Margaret Becket. "Joseph Harris: Captain of the Rochester Seed Industry." *University of Rochester Library Bulletin* 35 (1982): 69–82.

Allen, Lewis. *Rural Architecture.* New York: Moore, 1852.

Allen, R. C. *Roses for Every Garden.* New York: M. Barros and Company, 1948.

American Florist. Obituary of W. Atlee Burpee. December 4, 1915, 1040.

American Gardener's Magazine 1, no. 1 (1835).

Bacon, Wm. "The Rose and Its Culture." *Horticulturist* 7 (November 1, 1852): 560–62.

Bailey, L. H. *The American Garden.* 1 vol. (numbered 11). New York: Rural Publishing Company, 1890.

———. "List of American Horticultural Books." In Bailey, *Standard Cyclopedia of Horticulture,* 2:1523–52.

———. "Literature of Horticulture." In Bailey, *Standard Cyclopedia of Horticulture,* 2:1520–64.

———. "North American Horticulturists." In Bailey, *Standard Cyclopedia of Horticulture,* 2:1563–603.

———. "Podophyllum." In Bailey, *Standard Cyclopedia of Horticulture,* 3:2725–726.

———. "Recent Progress in American Horticulture." *Science* 21, no. 519 (January 1893): 20–23.

———. "Rosa." In Bailey, *Standard Cyclopedia of Horticulture,* 3:2981–3020.

———, ed. *The Standard Cyclopedia of Horticulture.* [1900]. 2nd ed. 3 vols. New York: Macmillan, 1939.

Barber, Phil. "Brief History of Newspapers." www.historicpages.com/nprhist.htm.

Beales, Peter. *Twentieth-Century Roses.* New York: Harper and Row, 1988.

Beverley, Robert. *The History and Present State of Virginia.* Edited by Louise B. Wright. Chapel Hill: University of North Carolina Press, 1947.

Binford, Henry C. *The First Suburbs: Residential Communities on the Boston Periphery, 1815–1860.* Chicago: University of Chicago Press, 1985.

Bjorklund, C. J. "Ribbon Bedding." *Gardener's Monthly and Horticulturist* 20 (June 1878): 163–64.

Blane, William Newnham. *An Excursion through the United States and Canada during the Years 1822–23: By an English Gentleman.* London: Baldwin, Cradock, and Joy, 1824.

Breck, Joseph. *The Flower Garden*. New ed. Boston: John Jewett and Company, 1856.

———. "On the Selection of Hardy Herbaceous Plants, Suitable for Ornamenting the Parterre, Border or Shrubbery." *Horticultural Register and Gardener's Magazine* 2 (1836): 21–27.

Brinkley, M. Kent, and Gordon W. Chappell. *The Gardens of Williamsburg*. Williamsburg, VA: Colonial Williamsburg Foundation, 1970.

———. *The Gardens of Williamsburg*. 2nd ed. Williamsburg, VA: Colonial Williamsburg Foundation, 1996.

Brockway, Lucinda A. "The Durant-Kenrick House and Property: A Brief Landscape History." Historic Newton website, http://apps.newtonma.gov/jackson/durant-kenrick/index.asp.

Brown, Thomas A. *A List of California Nurseries and Their Catalogues, 1850–1900*. Petaluma, CA: Thomas A. Brown, 1993.

Buchan, Ursula. *The English Garden*. London: Frances Lincoln, 2006.

Buist, Robert. *The American Flower-Garden Directory*. 6th ed. New York: A. O. Moore Agricultural Book Publisher, 1858.

Bullion, Brenda. "The Agricultural Press: 'To Improve the Soil and the Mind.'" In *The Farm: Annual Proceedings of the Dublin Seminar for New England Folklife* (1986), edited by Peter Benes, 74–94. Boston: Boston University, 1988.

———. "Early American Farming and Gardening Literature: 'Adapted to the Climates and Seasons of the United States.'" *Journal of Garden History* 12 (January–March 1992): 29–51.

Carmichael, Marcia. *Putting Down Roots: Gardening Insights from Wisconsin's Early Settlers*. Madison: Wisconsin Historical Society Press, 2011.

Carr, Robert. "Gardening and Gardeners in America." *Gardener's Magazine* 7 (December 1831): 666–68.

Carter, Tom. *The Victorian Garden*. London: Bell and Hyman, 1984.

Cecil, Evelyn [Alicia M. T. Amherst]. *A History of Gardening in England*. London: John Murray, 1910.

Clark, Clifford Edward, Jr. *The American Family Home, 1800–1960*. Chapel Hill: University of North Carolina Press, 1986.

Clayton, Virginia Tuttle. *The Once and Future Gardener*. Boston: David R. Godine, 2000.

Clissold, Edgar J. *The Seed Industry*. New York: Bellman Publishing, 1946.

Cobbett, William. *The American Gardener*. London: C. Clement, 1821.

Conan, Michel. "From Vernacular Gardens to a Social Anthropology of Gardening." In *Perspectives on Garden Histories*, edited by Michel Conan, 181–204. Washington, DC: Dumbarton Oaks Research Library and Collection, 1999.

Conzen, Michael P., ed. *The Making of the American Landscape*. Boston: Unwin Hyman, 1990.

Cothran, James R. *Gardens and Historical Plants of the Antebellum South*. Columbia: University of South Carolina Press, 2003.

Cresswell, William. *Diary of a Victorian Gardener*. Swindon, UK: English Heritage, 2006.

Cunningham, Patsy. "Yankee Doodle Roses: New England Roses and Breeders." Rhode Island Rose Society website, www.rirs.org/yankeedoodleroses.htm.

Currie's Monthly. "Mina Lobata." Vol. 4 (January 1888): 14.

———. "Roses." Vol. 3 (August 1887): 2.

———. "Single Dahlias." Vol. 1 (April 1885): 3.

Deane, Samuel. *The New England Farmer; or, Georgical Dictionary.* Worcester, MA: Isaiah Thomas, 1797.

Demaree, Albert Lowther. *The American Agricultural Press, 1819–1860.* Philadelphia: Porcupine Press, 1974.

Dimmock, A. "Rose Crimson Rambler." *Florist's Exchange* 8, no. 12 (March 21, 1896): 260.

Dingee and Conard Company. "Answers to Correspondents." *Success with Flowers* 6, no. 76 (April 1896): 150.

———. "Hardy Climbing Roses." *Success with Flowers* 8, no. 9 (June 1898): 178.

Dixon, John Hunt. "Approaches (New and Old) to Garden History." In *Perspectives on Garden Histories,* edited by Michel Conan, 77–90. Washington, DC: Dumbarton Oaks Research Library and Collection, 1999.

———. *Greater Perfections: The Practice of Garden Theory.* Philadelphia: University of Pennsylvania Press, 2000.

Doell, M. Christine Klim. *Gardens of the Gilded Age: Nineteenth-Century Gardens and Homegrounds of New York State.* Syracuse, NY: Syracuse University Press, 1986.

Downing, Andrew Jackson. "American versus British Horticulture." *Horticulturist* 7, no. 6 (June 1, 1852): 249–52.

———. "Mr. Downing's Letters from England." *Horticulturist* 6 (June 1, 1851): 281–86.

———. "Ornamental Trees." *New England Farmer* 12, no. 29 (January 29, 1834): 225–26.

———. *A Treatise on the Theory and Practice of Landscape Gardening, Adapted to North America.* New York: A. O. Moore, 1859.

Dumbarton Oaks. *American Garden Literature in the Dumbarton Oaks Collection (1785–1900).* Washington, DC: Dumbarton Oaks Research Library and Collection, 1998.

Dutton, Joan Parry. *Plants of Colonial Williamsburg.* Williamsburg, VA: Colonial Williamsburg Foundation, 1979.

Earle, Alice Morse. *Old Time Gardens.* New York: Macmillan, 1901.

Elder, Walter. "Arrangement of Flower-Gardens." *Gardener's Monthly and Horticultural Advertiser* 5 (June 1863): 169–71.

Eliot, Jared. *Essays upon Field-Husbandry in New-England: As It Is or May Be Ordered.* Boston: Printed by Edes and Gill, 1760.

Elliott, Brent. *Victorian Gardens.* Portland, OR: Timber Press, 1986.

Elliott, Franklin Reuben. *Hand Book of Practical Landscape Gardening.* Rochester, NY: D. M. Dewey, 1881.

Ellwanger, H. B. "American Roses." *Journal of Horticulture, Cottage Gardener and Home Farmer* 38 (June 17, 1880): 478–79.

Ely, Helena Rutherfurd. *A Woman's Hardy Garden.* New York: Macmillan, 1903.

Evening Journal (Jersey City, NJ). Obituary of Peter Henderson. January 17, 1890.

Farm and Garden. "The Seed Trade of Philadelphia." November 1, 1882.

Favretti, Rudy, and Gordon P. DeWolf. *Colonial Gardens.* Barre, MA: Barre Publications, 1972.

Fessenden, Thomas G. *The New American Gardener.* Boston: J. B. Russell, 1828.

Fitzpatrick, John T. "An Overview of American Nursery and Seed Catalogues, 1771–1832." In *Plants and People: Annual Proceedings of the Dublin Seminar for New England Folklife* 20 (1995), edited by Peter Benes, 152–62. Boston: Boston University, 1996.

Fitzpatrick, John T., and Judith Ho. *A Bibliography of American Nursery and Seed Catalogues, 1771–1832.* New York: New York Historical Society Library, 1995.

Florist's Exchange. "European Notes." Vol. 6, no. 29 (June 16, 1894): 561.

———. "Robert Scott & Sons Model Farm." Vol. 6 (September 15, 1894): 807.

Florists' Review. "W. Atlee Burpee." December 2, 1915.

"Fruits and Vegetables." Special Collections, University of Delaware Library website, www.lib.udel.edu/ud/spec/exhibits/sfc/fruit.htm.

Fry, Joel T. "An International Catalogue of North American Trees and Shrubs: The Bartram Broadside, 1783." *Journal of Garden History* 16, no. 1 (Spring 1996): 3–66.

Fuller, Andrew S., ed. *Woodward's Record of Horticulture for 1866.* New York: George E. and F. W. Woodward, 1867.

Garden (London). "Turner's Crimson Rambler Rose." Vol. 43 (May 27, 1893): 434.

Gardener's Monthly and Horticultural Advertiser. "Descriptive Catalogues." Vol. 2 (February 1860): 55–56.

———. "Grounds of C. M. Hovey." Vol. 5 (August 1863): 248.

———. "The Rhododendron." Vol. 12 (June 1870): 175–77.

Gardener's Monthly and Horticulturist. "Camellia C. M. Hovey" [the short article is taken from *Garden,* a London magazine]. Vol. 25 (July 1883): 202.

———. "Philadelphia Market-Gardening and Seed Growing." Vol. 25 (September 1883): 268–71.

———. "The Science of Advertising." Vol. 26 (September 1884): 284.

Gardening 2, no. 46 (August 1, 1894): 372.

Genesee Farmer. "Kitchen Garden." Vol. 6 (May 1845): 67.

Gilmer, Maureen. *Redwoods and Roses.* Dallas: Taylor Publishing, 1995.

Graham, Wade. *American Eden.* New Haven, CT: Harper Collins, 2011.

Graptolite. "Trip to Wilmington, Del." *Gardener's Monthly and Horticultural Advertiser* 3 (August 1861): 228–29.

Grove, Carol. *Henry Shaw's Victorian Landscapes.* Amherst: University of Massachusetts Press, 2005.

Handlin, David P. *The American Home: Architecture and Society, 1815–1915.* Boston: Little, Brown, 1979.

Harkness, Peter. *The Rose: An Illustrated History.* Toronto, ON: Firefly Books, 2003.

Harvey, John. *Early Nurserymen.* London: Phillimore and Co., 1974.

Hatfield, Miles. *A History of British Gardening.* London: John Murray, 1960.

Hedrick, U. P. *A History of Horticulture in America to 1860.* 2nd ed. Portland, OR: Timber Press, 1988.

————. *The Peaches of New York*. Albany, NY: J. R. Lyon, 1917.

Helmreich, Anne. *The English Garden and National Heritage*. Cambridge: Cambridge University Press, 2002.

Helphand, Kenneth. "'Leaping the Property Line': Observations on Recent American Garden History." In *Perspectives on Garden Histories*, edited by Michel Conan, 137–60. Washington, DC: Dumbarton Oaks Research Library and Collection, 1999.

Henderson, Alfred. *Peter Henderson: Gardener, Author, Merchant*. New York: Press of McIlroy and Emmet, 1890.

Henderson, Peter. *Gardening for Pleasure*. New York: Orange Judd, 1883.

Hibbert, Thomas, and Robert Buist. *The American Flower Garden Directory*. Philadelphia: Printed for the authors by Adam Waldie, 1832.

Hill, E. G. "Novelties in Roses, 1894." *Florist's Exchange* 7, no. 29 (June 15, 1895): 655.

"History of Education in America, The." Chesapeake College Library website, www.chesapeake.edu/library/EDU_101/eduhist_19thC.asp.

Horticulturist 29 (August 1874): 230.

Hovey, Charles Mason. "Address." In *Proceedings on the Occasion of Laying the Corner-Stone of the New Hall of the Massachusetts Horticultural Society, August 18, 1864*. Boston: Henry W. Dutton & Son, Printers, 1864.

————. "Arboretum Americanum." *Gardener's Monthly and Horticulturist* 18 (July 1876): 194–98.

————. "Floricultural Notices: New Hybrid Coleus." *Magazine of Horticulture* 34 (June 1868): 179–80.

————. Introduction to *American Gardener's Magazine* 1, no. 1 (January 1835): 1–6.

————. Review of *A Practical Treatise on the Culture of Silk*, by F. G. Comstock. *American Gardener's Magazine* 2 (1836): 149–50.

Jackson, Kenneth T. *Crabgrass Frontier: The Suburbanization of the United States*. New York: Oxford University Press, 1985.

Jacques, David. Review of *Pursuing Innocent Pleasures: The Gardening World of Alexander Pope*, by Peter Martin. *Garden History* 14, no. 1 (Spring 1986): 77–80.

Jekyll, Gertrude, and Edward Mawley. *Roses for English Gardens*. New York: Charles Scribner's Sons, 1902.

Jenkins, Virginia Scott. *The Lawn: A History of an American Obsession*. Washington, DC: Smithsonian Institution Press, 1994.

John, Richard R. *Spreading the News: The American Postal System from Franklin to Morse*. Cambridge, MA: Harvard University Press, 1995.

Journal of Antiques and Collectibles. "Kitchen Gardens, Hearth to Hearth." May 2002. www.journalofantiques.com/May02/hearthmay02.htm.

Kemp, Edward. *How to Lay Out a Garden*. London: Bradbury and Evans, 1858.

Kenrick, William. *The New American Orchardist*. 2nd ed. Boston: Russell, Odiorne, and Metcalf, 1835.

————. *Notes on Ogdensburg*. Boston: Dutton and Wentworth, 1846.

Kitch, Carolyn. *The Girl on the Magazine Cover: The Origins of Visual Stereotypes in American Mass Media*. Chapel Hill: University of North Carolina Press, 2001.

Kornwolf, James D. "The Picturesque in the American Garden and Landscape before 1800." *Eighteenth Century Life* 8 (1983): 93–106.

Last, Jay T. *The Color Explosion: Nineteenth-Century American Lithography.* Santa Ana, CA: Hillcrest Press, 2005.

Lears, Jackson. *Fables of Abundance: A Cultural History of Advertising in America.* New York: Basic Books, 1994.

Lee, Lawrence Elliott. "Rockwood: A Victorian Gardenesque Landscape." M.A. thesis, University of Delaware, 1987.

Lehtonen, Mikko. *The Cultural Analysis of Texts.* London: Sage, 2000.

Leighton, Ann. *American Gardens in the Eighteenth Century: "For Use or for Delight."* Boston: Houghton Mifflin, 1976.

———. *American Gardens of the Nineteenth Century: "For Comfort and Affluence."* Amherst: University of Massachusetts Press, 1987.

Leuchars, R. B. "Notes on Gardens and Gardening in the Neighborhood of Boston." *Magazine of Horticulture* 16, no. 2 (1850): 49–60.

Lindley, John. *Gardener's Magazine* 17 (1844): 2.

Loudon, Jane. "An Account of the Life and Writings of John Claudius Loudon." In Dumbarton Oaks, *John Claudius Loudon,* 27–114.

Loudon, John Claudius. *An Encyclopedia of Gardening.* London: Longman, Rees, Orme, Brown, and Green, 1827.

———. "Calls at the London Nurseries, and Other Suburban Gardens." *Gardener's Magazine* 9 (1833): 467–83.

Lustig, Abigail Jane. "The Creation and Uses of Horticulture in Britain and France in the Nineteenth Century." Ph.D. diss., University of California, Berkeley, 1997.

———. "Cultivating Knowledge in Nineteenth-Century English Gardens." *Science in Context* 13, no. 2 (2000): 155–81.

Lyons-Jenness, Cheryl. *For Shade and For Comfort: Democratizing Horticulture in the Nineteenth-Century Midwest.* West Lafayette, IN: Purdue University Press, 2004.

———. "Petunias by Post." Paper presented at the M. Blount Symposium on Postal History, Smithsonian National Postal Museum, Washington, DC, November 4, 2006.

MacDougall, Elisabeth B., ed. *John Claudius Loudon and the Early Nineteenth Century in Great Britain.* Washington, DC: Dumbarton Oaks, 1980.

Mack, Richard N. "Catalog of Woes." *Natural History* 3 (March 1990): 44–53.

Manks, Dorothy S. "How the American Nursery Trade Began." In *Handbook on Origins of American Horticulture,* edited by Dorothy S. Manks, 4–11. Brooklyn, NY: Brooklyn Botanical Garden, 1968.

Marsh, Ellen R,, and Mary Anne O'Boyle. *Takoma Park: Portrait of a Victorian Suburb, 1883–1983.* Takoma Park, MD: Historic Takoma, 1984.

Marsh, Margaret. "From Separation to Togetherness: The Social Construction of Domestic Space in American Suburbs, 1840–1915." *Journal of American History* 76, no. 2 (September 1989): 506–27.

———. *Suburban Lives.* New Brunswick, NJ: Rutgers University Press, 1990.

Martin, Peter. *The Pleasure Gardens of Virginia*. Princeton, NJ: Princeton University Press, 2001.

Marzio, Peter C. *The Democratic Art*. Fort Worth, TX: Amon Carter Museum of Western Art, 1979.

Massachusetts Horticultural Society. *History of the Massachusetts Horticultural Society, 1829–1878*. Boston: Rand, Avery, for the Society, 1880.

McFarland, J. Horace, ed. *The American Rose Annual*. Harrisburg, PA: American Rose Society, 1916.

————. *The Rose in America*. New York: Macmillan, 1923.

McKelvey, Blake. "The Flower City: Center of Nurseries and Fruit Orchards." In *The Rochester Historical Society Publications* 18, Part II, *Nurseries, Farm Papers, and Selected Rochester Episodes*, edited by Blake McKelvey, 121–69. Rochester, NY: Rochester Historical Society, 1940.

McMurry, Sally. *Families and Farmhouses in Nineteenth-Century America: Vernacular Design and Social Change*. New York: Oxford University Press, 1988.

Meager, Leonard. *The Compleat English Gardner: or, A Sure Guide to Young Planters and Gardners*. London: M. Wotton, 1710.

Meehan, Thomas. "The Botanic Garden, St. Louis, Mo." *Gardener's Monthly and Horticultural Advertiser* 10 (August 1868): 244.

————. "Descriptive Catalogues." *Gardener's Monthly and Horticultural Advertiser* 2 (February 1860): 55–56.

————. Editorial Notes. *Gardener's Monthly and Horticulturist* 20 (January 1878): 26–29.

————. Editorial Notes. *Gardener's Monthly and Horticulturist* 28 (February 1886): 60–62.

————. Editorial Notes. *Gardener's Monthly and Horticulturist* 28 (December 1886): 375–77.

————. "Our Correspondents." *Gardener's Monthly and Horticultural Advertiser* 16 (January 1874): 15.

————. "Post Office Rulings." *Gardener's Monthly and Horticultural Advertiser* 15 (March 1873): 86.

————. "The Rhododendron." (Unsigned.) *Gardener's Monthly and Horticultural Advertiser* 12 (June 1870): 175–77.

————. Seasonable Hints. *Gardener's Monthly and Horticulturist* 19 (March 1877): 65–66.

————. Seasonable Hints. *Gardener's Monthly and Horticulturist* 24 (February 1882): 33–34.

————. Seasonable Hints. *Gardener's Monthly and Horticulturist* 28 (April 1886): 97–99.

————. "The Seed Business in Philadelphia." Editorial Notes. *Gardener's Monthly and Horticulturist* 28 (January 1886): 28.

————. "Subscribing to the Gardener's Monthly." *Gardener's Monthly and Horticultural Advertiser* 9 (July 1867): 211.

———. "Weigela floribunda." *Gardener's Monthly and Horticulturist* 26 (September 1884): 261–62.

———. "Ye May Know Him by His Garden." *Gardener's Monthly and Horticultural Advertiser* 2 (December 1860): 372–73.

Miller, Philip. *Gardeners Dictionary.* 8th ed. London: privately printed, 1768.

Miller, Wilhelm. *What England Can Teach Us about Gardening.* Garden City, NY: Doubleday, Page, and Company, 1911.

Morrison, Darrel G. Foreword to *American Plants for American Gardens*, by Edith A. Roberts and Elsa Rehman. Athens: University of Georgia Press, 1996.

Morrison, Ernest. *J. Horace McFarland: A Thorn of Beauty.* Harrisburg: Pennsylvania Historical and Museum Commission, 1995.

Mott, Frank Luther. *A History of American Magazines, 1741–1850.* 5 vols. Cambridge, MA: Harvard University Press, 1938.

Mullin, Timothy J. "Rockwood: Joseph Shipley's English Estate in Brandywine Hundred, Delaware." *Delaware History* 31, no. 3 (Spring–Summer 2006): 179–210.

Nation. Review of *The Rambler Rose*, by composer Victor Jacobi. No. 105 (September 20, 1917): 326.

Newton, Norman T. *Design on the Land: The Development of Landscape Architecture.* Cambridge, MA: Harvard University Press, 1971.

New York Times. "Paris Models Break Record for Daring." June 28, 1913, 3.

Norris, James D. *Advertising and the Transformation of American Society, 1865–1920.* New York: Greenwood Press, 1990.

Oberle, Stephanie Ginsberg. "The Influence of Thomas Meehan on Horticulture in the United States." M.A. thesis, University of Delaware, 1997.

O'Mara, Patrick. "The Hardiness of the Rose Crimson Rambler." *Garden and Forest* 8 (March 20, 1895): 117–18.

Otis, Denise. *Grounds for Pleasure: Four Centuries of the American Garden.* New York: Harry N. Abrams, 2002.

Overholser, Geneva, and Kathleen Hall Jamieson, eds. *The Press.* New York: Oxford University Press, 2005.

Parkman, F. "Notes on Hardy Perennials." *Gardener's Monthly and Horticultural Advertiser* 17 (March 1875): 66–67.

Parks, Dan. "The Cultivation of Flower City." *Rochester History* 45, nos. 3 and 4 (July and October 1983): 25–47.

Parmentier, André. "Landscapes and Picturesque Gardens." In Thomas Fessenden, *The New American Gardener*, 184–87. Boston: J. B. Russell, 1828.

Parsons, Samuel. *The Rose.* New York: Wiley and Putnam, 1847.

Pauly, Philip J. *Fruits and Plains: The Horticultural Transformation of America.* Cambridge, MA: Harvard University Press, 2007.

Pavord, Anna. *The Tulip.* New York: Bloomsbury, 1999.

Pennsylvania Horticultural Society. *From Seed to Flower: Philadelphia, 1681–1876; A Horticultural Point of View.* Philadelphia: Pennsylvania Horticultural Society, 1976.

Phipps, Francis. *Colonial Kitchens, Their Furnishings, and Their Gardens*. New York: Hawthorn Books, 1972.

Pierce, Joanna Tapp. "From Garden to Gardener." *Women's Studies* 29, no. 6 (December 2000): 741–61.

Pinardi, Norman J. *The Plant Pioneers: The Story of the Reasoner Family, Pioneer Florida Horticulturalists and Their Nursery*. Torrington, CT: Rainbow Press, 1980.

Pizzetti, Ippolito, and Henry Cocker. *Rosa*. Vol. 2 of *Flowers: A Guide for Your Garden*. New York: Harry N. Abrams, 1968.

Pollan, Michael. *Second Nature*. New York: Delta, 1991.

Pope, Alexander. "On Gardens." Article in *The Guardian,* September 29, 1713. Reprinted in *The Works of Alexander Pope,* 10:530–33. Edited by John Wilson Croker. New York: Gordian Press, 1967.

Popular Gardening and Fruit Growing. "Taste and Tact in Arranging Home and Other Grounds." Vol. 6, no. 2 (November 1890): 25–26; no. 3 (December 1890): 44; no. 4 (January 1891): 61; no. 5 (February 1891): 84–85; no. 6 (March 1891): 104–5; no. 7 (April 1891): 124–25; no. 8 (May 1891): 146–47; no. 9 (June 1891): 166–67; no. 11 (1891): 194.

Practical Farmer. "The Outlook for the Seed Business the Coming Year." November 14, 1882.

Printer's Ink. "The Personality That Is Behind the Business." Vol. 91, no. 12 (June 17, 1915): 3–12.

Quest-Ritson, Charles. *Climbing Roses of the World*. Portland, OR: Timber Press, 2003.
———. *The English Garden: A Social History*. Boston: David R. Godine, 2003.

Robertson, Ian. "English Influences on American Gardens." Lecture at Colonial Williamsburg, Virginia, April 12, 2007.

Robinson, William. *The Wild Garden*. London: J. Murray, 1870.

Rochester Evening Express. "Where the Rainbows Are Made." June 3, 1867.

Rochester Union and Advertiser. "The New City Hall—Laying of the Corner Stone." May 28, 1873. Rochester 1873 Time Capsule Homepage, http://www3.rmsc.org/capsule/news%20article.html.

Rogers, Elizabeth Barlow, Elizabeth S. Eustis, and John Bidwell. *Romantic Gardens: Nature, Art and Landscape Design*. Boston: David R. Godine, 2010.

Roper, Elinor M. C. *Seedtime: The History of Essex Seeds*. Shopwyke Hall, Chichester, UK: Phillimore, 1989.

Scanniello, Stephen, and Tania Bayard. *Climbing Roses*. New York: Prentice Hall, 1994.

Schermerhorn, Richard, Jr. "Homes and Gardens of Old New York." In American Society of Landscape Architects, *Colonial Gardens: The Landscape Architecture of George Washington's Time,* 33–43. Washington, DC: United States George Washington Bicentennial Commission, 1932.

Scott, Frank J. *The Art of Beautifying Suburban Home Grounds of Small Extent*. New York: D. Appleton, 1870.

Seaton, Beverly. "Gardening Books for the Commuter's Wife, 1900–1937." *Landscape* 28, no. 2 (1985): 41–47.

Sivulka, Juliann. *Soap, Sex, and Cigarettes: A Cultural History of American Advertising.* Belmont, CA: Wadsworth Publishing, 1998.

Slade, Daniel Denison. *The Evolution of Horticulture in New England.* New York: G. Putnam's Sons, 1895.

Sloat, Caroline. "William G. Comstock, or How America Went to Seed." *Nineteenth Century* 4, no. 1 (Spring 1978): 102–5.

Smith, Mary Riley. *The Front Garden: New Approaches to Landscape Design.* Boston: Houghton Mifflin, 1991.

Spectator. "Fashion in Gardening." September 10, 1898.

Stetson, Sarah Pattee. "American Garden Books Transplanted and Native, before 1807." *William and Mary Quarterly* 3, no. 3 (July 1946): 343–69.

Stilgoe, John R. *Common Landscape of America, 1580 to 1845.* New Haven, CT: Yale University Press, 1982.

Sullivan, Mark. *Our Times: The United States, 1900–1925.* 6 vols. New York: Charles Scribner's Sons, 1926–35.

Sutherland, William. "Hollywood Park." *Gardener's Monthly and Horticulturist* 22 (May 1880): 132–33.

Swem, E. G. *Brothers of the Spade: Correspondence of Peter Collinson of London, and of John Custis, of Williamsburg, Virginia 1734–1746.* Barre, MA: Barre Gazette, 1957.

Tait, A. A. "Loudon and the Return to Formality." In MacDougall, *John Claudius Loudon,* 61–76.

Taylor, Geoffrey. *Some Nineteenth Century Gardeners.* Essex, UK: Anchor Press, 1951.

Taylor, George. "The Contribution from America to British Gardens in the Early Nineteenth Century." In MacDougall, *John Claudius Loudon,* 105–23.

Thomas, Graham Stuart. *The Graham Stuart Thomas Rose Book.* Sagaponack, NY: Sagapress, 1994.

Thomas, John J. "Grouping Flowers—a Suggestion." *Horticulturist* 1, no. 3 (September 1846): 120–22.

Thornton, Tamara Plakins. *Cultivating Gentlemen: The Meaning of Country Life among the Boston Elite, 1785–1860.* New Haven, CT: Yale University Press, 1989.

Thomas Jefferson Encyclopedia. S.v. "Bernard McMahon." Jefferson Monticello website, http://wiki.monticello.org/mediawiki/index.php/Bernard_McMahon.

Tice, Patricia M. *Gardening in America, 1830–1910.* Rochester, NY: Strong Museum, 1984.

———. "Gardens of Change." In *American Home Life, 1880–1930,* edited by Jessica H. Foy and Thomas J. Schlereth, 190–208. Knoxville: University of Tennessee Press, 1992.

Tishler, William H., ed. *American Landscape Architecture.* Washington, DC: Preservation Press, 1989.

Uglow, Jenny. *A Little History of British Gardening.* New York: North Print Press, 2004.

University of Delaware Library Special Collections. "Fruits and Vegetables." www.lib.udel.edu/ud/spec/exhibits/sfc/fruit.htm.

Van Ravenswaay, Charles. "Horticultural Heritage—The Influence of the U.S. Nurserymen: A Commentary." In *Agricultural Literature: Proud Heritage—Future Promise, a Bicentennial Symposium, September 24–26, 1975,* edited by Alan M. Fusonie and Leila Moran, 144. Washington, DC: U.S. Department of Agriculture, in conjunction with Associates of the National Agricultural Library, 1977.

Vick, James. "Beautiful Rural Homes." *Vick's Illustrated Monthly* 4 (June 1881): 162–64.

———. Editorial [on bedding out]. *Vick's Illustrated Monthly* 7 (September 1884): 257–58.

———. "Improving Home Grounds." *Vick's Illustrated Monthly* 1 (February 1878): 35–38.

———. "Plants for Cemeteries." *Vick's Illustrated Monthly* 1 (June 1878): 161–63.

Vincent, Gilbert T. *Romantic Rockwood: A Rural Gothic Villa near Wilmington, Delaware.* Wilmington, DE: Friends of Rockwood, 1998.

Walpole, Horace, "The History of the Modern Taste in Gardening." In *The Genius of the Place: The English Landscape Garden, 1620–1820,* edited by John Dixon Hunt and Peter Willis, 313–16. Cambridge, MA: MIT Press, 1988.

Wharton, Edith. *A Gift from the Grave.* London: John Murray, 1901.

———. *Summer.* New York: D. Appleton, 1917.

Wheelwright, Robert. "Gardens and Places of Colonial Philadelphia." In American Society of Landscape Architects, *Colonial Gardens: The Landscape Architecture of George Washington's Time.* Washington, DC: United States George Washington Bicentennial Commission, 1932.

White, Katherine S. *Onward and Upward in the Garden.* Edited by E. B. White. New York: Farrar, Straus, Giroux, 1979.

Who's Who in Advertising. S.v. "Burpee, W. Atlee." Detroit: Business Service Corporation, 1916.

Wilder, Marshall. *Address Delivered at the Semi-centennial Anniversary of the Massachusetts Horticultural Society, September 12, 1879.* Boston: Franklin Press, 1879.

Witzell, Susan Fletcher. "Gardeners and Caretakers of Woods Hole." *Spritsail: Journal of the History of Falmouth and Woods Hole* 19, no. 2 (Summer 2005): 2–42.

Woodburn, Elisabeth. "Horticultural Heritage: The Influence of U.S. Nurserymen." In *Agricultural Literature: Proud Heritage—Future Promise, a Bicentennial Symposium, September 24–26, 1975,* edited by Alan M. Fusonie and Leila Moran, 111–33. Washington, DC: U.S. Department of Agriculture, in conjunction with Associates of the National Agricultural Library, 1977.

Wright, Mabel Osgood. *Roses and How to Grow Them.* New York: Doubleday, Page, 1905.

Wulf, Andrea. *The Brother Gardeners.* London: William Heinemann, 2008.

Wyman, Donald. "The Introduction of Plants from Europe to America." *Handbook on Origins of American Horticulture* 23, no. 3 (1968): 12–16.

Wynne, William. "Some Account of the Nursery Gardens and the State of Horticulture in the Neighborhood of Philadelphia." *Gardener's Magazine* 8 (June 1832): 272–76.

Index

ﭹ   ﭹ

Black, Joseph H., 73
black Austrian pine, 55
black-eyed Susan, 33, 36, 40–41
Blanc, A., 130
Blenheim, 44
Bliss, Benjamin K., 67, 86, 109, 116, 133
Bloomington Nursery, 147
blue false indigo, 151, 153
B. N. Strong Company, 145, 160
Bok, Edward, 145
Bonsall, Joseph E., 140
Book of Fruits (Manning), 92
book publishing, as marketing tool, 90–91
books, gardening
    American Flower Garden Directory, The
      (Buist), 59, 92
    American Gardener, The (Gardiner and Hep-
      burn), 38
    American Gardener, The (Cobbett), 7–8
    American Gardener's Calendar, The
      (M'Mahon), 91
    American Orchardist, The (Kenrick), 172
    American Silk Grower's Guide, The (Kenrick),
      81, 96
    Arboretum Britannicum (Loudon), 43
    Art of Beautifying Suburban Home Grounds,
      The (Scott), 199–201
    Book of Fruits (Manning), 92
    Cabbages and How to Raise Them (Gregory),
      93
    Carrots, Marigold Wurtzels, and Sugar Beets
      (Gregory), 93
    Compleat English Gardener, The (Meager), 36
    Cottage Residences (Downing), 93
    Elliott's Hand Book for Fruition Growers (El-
      liott), 95
    Elliott's Practical Landscape Gardening (El-
      liott), 95
    Encyclopedia of Gardening, An (Loudon), 48
    English Flower Garden, The (Robinson), 218
    Essays upon Field Husbandry (Eliot), 37–38
    Every Man His Own Gardener (Abercrombie
      and Mawe), 37, 91
    Family Kitchen Gardener, The (Buist), 92
    Fertilizers (Gregory), 93
    Flora of North America, A, 114
    Flower Garden, The (Breck), 180

    Flowers for Every Home (Darlington), 94
    Fruit and Fruit Trees (Downing), 95
    Fruit Culturalist (Thomas), 95
    Fruit Garden, The (Barry), 93, 95
    Garden and Farm Topics (Henderson), 94
    Gardeners Dictionary (Miller), 36
    Gardening for Pleasure (Henderson), 5, 94,
      190
    Gardening for Profit (Henderson), 94
    Handbook of Plants (Henderson), 94
    Hand Book of Practical Landscape Gardening
      (Elliott), 213
    History and Present State of Virginia, The, in
      Four Parts (Beverley), 38–39
    Horticulture of Boston and Vicinity, The
      (Wilder), 155
    How the Farm Pays (Henderson), 94
    How to Grow Roses (McFarland), 189
    How to Lay Out Home Gardens (Kemp), 46,
      47
    Manual of Roses (Prince), 92
    New American Gardener, The (Fessenden), 92
    New American Orchardist, The (Kenrick), 81
    New England Book of Fruit, The (Manning),
      81, 92
    New England Farmer, The (Deane), 38
    Observations on Modern Gardening (What-
      ley), 36
    Onion Raising (Gregory), 93
    Onward and Upward (White), 218
    Practical Floriculture (Henderson), 94
    Rose, The (Parsons), 181
    Rose Manual, The (Buist), 92, 179
    Short Treatise on Horticulture, A (Prince),
      91–92
    Squashes and How to Grow Them (Gregory),
      93
    Standard Cyclopedia of Horticulture, The
      (Bailey), 89
    Treatise on Fruit and Ornamental Trees and
      Plants, A (Prince), 91
    Treatise on Gardening (Randolph), 38
    Treatise on the Theory and Practice of Land-
      scape Gardening, A (Downing), 48, 51, 93
    Wild Garden, The (Robinson), 6, 23, 135, 216
    Woman's Hardy Garden, A (Ely), 189
Booth, William, 65

catalogs, seed and nursery (*cont.*)

Crawford Seed Company, 133

and the 'Crimson Rambler', 183, 185, 187–88, 190, 193

Crosman Brothers, 148

Currie Brothers Seed Company, 227

David Landreth Seed Company, 66, 67, 71, 126

D. Hill, 69–70

Dingee and Conard Company, 104, 113, 178,185–87, 188

D. M. Ferry Company 67, 70, 125, 138, 144, 162

Dundee Nursery, 142

Dwyer Company, 164

Earl Ferris Nursery, 187

Eaton Company, 131, 134

educational role of, xviii, 65, 75–76, 82–84, 213–17, 220, 228

exotic plants in, 68–69, 135

Everitt Company, 72

E. W. Reid, 75

facilities as theme in, 136, 138, 140–41

Fitts Company, 133

flowers in, 84

Frank Finch, 68

F. R. Elliott and Company, 213

fruit trees in, 83

G. Drobisch, 187

George A. Sweet Company, 125

George Thompson and Sons, 107

George W. Park, 83

G. H. Barr Company, 128

G. M. Richardson Company, 125

Good and Reese Company, 110

Goodell Seed Company, 72

Grant Thorburn, 83

Green's Nursery, 75, 88, 103, 129

Gregory Company, 109

Haines Company, 140

Hale Company, 131

Hallock and Thorpe Company, 129

Harlan P. Kelsey Company, 69

Harrison H. Given, 187

Henry Dreer Seed Company, 116, 214, 215

H. G. Corney, 165

H. G. Hastings and Company, 103

Hoopes Company, 129

illustrations in, 66, 67, 114, 116, 138, 187

Ives Company, 131

Jacob Manning, 171

James H. Park Company, 167

J. M. Phillips Sons, 106–7

John Charles Vaughn Company, 127–28, 130, 148

John Lewis Childs Company, 63, 86–88, 110, 118, 140–41, 163, 178

Johnson and Stokes Seed Company, 118

Joseph Breck and Company, 207

Joseph E. Bonsall, 140

Joseph Harris, 89, 110, 130, 147

Joseph T. Phillips, 162–63, 212

J. T. Huntington, 126

Knox Company, 134

Krider Nurseries, 187

Lewis Templin, 173

Lines and Coe, 68, 207

L. L. May Company, 160

Long Brothers, 162

Lovett Company, 113, 133, 205–7

as marketing tool, 60, 61–62, 66–68, 70–72, 73, 75–76

Maule Seed Company, xviii, 110, 138

McWhorter Company, 165

Michael Walsh, 194

Miller and Hunt, 103

M. O'Keefe, Son and Company, 82, 174–75

Morrison and Ball, 66

Mount Hope Nurseries, 93, 109, 125, 183, 212

native plants in, 69, 127, 135–36, 219

novelty plants as theme of, xviii, 127–29, 131, 134–35

O. M. Richardson Company, 125

Overman and Mann, 205

Parker and Gannett Company, 134

Park Seed Company, 85, 162

Paul Butz and Son, 167

Peter Henderson Company, 67, 74, 123, 136, 138–39, 182, 187

Phelps and Reynolds, 167

Pike and Ellsworth, 170

photographs in, 118

Prince Nursery, 34, 60

progress as theme of, xviii, 102, 112, 116, 124–27, 148, 151

Deane, Samuel, 38
Delaware Horticultural Society, 50
Delaware Railroad Company, 49
Dewey, D. M., 116
Dingee and Conard Company, 104, 108, 113, 178, 185–87, 188
D. M. Dewey Company, 116
D. M. Ferry Company: facilities of, 138, 140; and flowers, 167; and garden as safeguard of society, 162; and introduction of new vegetables, 125; and merits of catalog marketing, 67, 70; and plant science, 144
dooryard gardens, 3
Dorchester (Massachusetts), 155
Downing, Andrew Jackson: appeal to upper class, 48, 214; *Cottage Residences,* 93; and English garden style in America, 223–24; *Fruit and Fruit Trees,* 95; and ha-has, 51; and *Gardener's Magazine,* 88; and *The Horticulturist,* 12, 49, 86, 135–36, 223–24; as inspiration to other landscape designers, 213, 214; and lack of professional gardeners in America, 12; and lawn, 199, 210; and *The New England Farmer,* 84; and park movement, 15; and picturesque style, 37, 93, 96; *A Treatise on the Theory and Practice of Landscape Gardening,* 48, 51, 93; and *Weigela rosea,* 49; writings of, 48, 51, 93, 95
Dreer, Henry, 109, 116, 131, 214–215
Dreer Seed Company. *See* Henry Dreer Seed Company
Drobisch, G., 187
Drummond, Thomas, 1136
Dundee Nursery, 142
Dutch gardens, 3
Dwyer Company, 164

Earle, Alice Morse, 192
Earl Ferris Nursery, 187
Eaton Company, 131, 134
E. D. Putney Company, 211
Elgin Botanic Garden, 22
Eliot, Jared, 37–38
Elizabeth Park, 192
Elliott, Benjamin. *See* Benjamin A. Elliott Company

Elliott, Franklin Reuben: as contributor to *Gardener's Monthly,* 90; *Elliott's Hand Book for Fruition Growers,* 95; *Elliott's Practical Landscape Gardening,* 95; F. R. Elliott and Company, 213; *Hand Book of Practical Landscape Gardening,* 213–14
Elliott's Hand Book for Fruition Growers (Elliott), 95
Elliott's Practical Landscape Gardening (Elliott), 95
Ellwanger, Henry, 16, 22, 93, 183. *See also* Mount Hope Nurseries
Ely, Helen Rutherford, 189
E. M. Sherman Company, 74
Encyclopedia of Gardening, An (Loudon), 48
Englischer Garten, 10
English Flower Garden, The (Robinson), 218
English garden style: annuals in, xvi, xx, 6, 167, 168, 175, 222; carpet bedding in, xvi, 102, 157, 167, 168–69, 174–75, 178, 197, 208, 222; exotic plants in, xvi, 6, 13, 43, 151, 170; flowers in, 6, 8–9, 36, 125; lawn in, xvi, 9–10, 102, 197, 199, 201; perennials in, xxi, xx, 171–72, 213, 216, 222, 223; role of seed and nursery catalogs in introducing to America, xx, 23, 116–17, 119, 159–60, 172, 197, 208, 223, 228; trees and shrubs in, xvi, xx, 36, 197, 208, 221; walkways in, xx, 197, 208, 214, 221
English ivy, introduction to America, 30
Essays upon Field Husbandry (Eliot), 37–38
Euphorbia poinsettia, 76
Everitt Company, 72
Every Man His Own Gardener (Abercrombie and Mawe), 37, 91
exotic plants: in English garden style, xvi, 6, 13, 43, 151, 170; in seed and nursery catalogs, 68–69, 135; at Woodlands, 4

fairs, county and state, 142
Family Kitchen Gardener, The (Buist), 92
Farm and Garden, 61
Fay, James Story, 194
Fay, Sarah, 194
fences, in English formal style, 29
Ferris, Earl, 187
Ferry Seed Company. *See* D. M. Ferry Company

Fertilizers (Gregory), 93
Fessenden, Thomas, 92
Finch, Frank, 68
firecracker vine, 97–99
Fitts company, 133
Floradale Farms, 100
Floral Magazine and Botanical Repository, 85
Flora of North America, A, 114
Florist's Exchange, 188, 189
Flower Garden, The (Breck), 180
flowers: in American gardens, 165, 167–68; in
    English garden style, 6, 8–9, 36, 125; at
    Rockwood, 50; at Shaw Estate, 52
Flowers for Every Home (Darlington), 94
Fordhook Farm, xv, 101
Forest Hills Cemetery, 17, 176
formal style, gardens, xvi, 4, 6, 32
Fortune, Robert, 21, 49, 57
fountains, in gardens, 3, 9
Fox, Bernard S., 180
F. R. Elliott and Company, 213
French formal gardens, 3
Frotscher, Richard, 82
fruit: in American gardening, 164–65; in Eng-
    lish gardening, 9; introduction of Euro-
    pean varieties to U.S., 31–32
Fruit and Fruit Trees (Downing), 95
Fruit Culturist, The (Thomas), 95
Fruit Garden, The (Barry), 93, 95

Garden, 47, 183
Garden and Farm Topics (Henderson), 94
Garden and Forest, 97, 193
gardeners, amateur, 67, 190, 205
gardeners, American: dependence on seeds and
    plants from England, 27–28, 30, 33; intro-
    duction of native American plants to, 31
gardeners, professional: early lack of in Amer-
    ica, 11, 12; as familial occupation, 10; at
    Rockwood, 50; role in promoting English
    landscape garden in America, xvi, 11; role
    of in English gardening, 8, 9, 10, 11
Gardener's Chronicle, 20
Gardeners Dictionary (Miller), 36
Gardener's Magazine, xvii, 2, 45, 88
Gardener's Monthly: and carpet bedding, 168,
    175, 225; and catalogs and other advertis-

ing, 62, 229; contributors to, 90, 123; focus
    on specific plants, 70, 71, 129, 137; and
    garden as cultural symbol for middle
    class, xix; and gardening books and jour-
    nals, 20, 47, 86; and important horticul-
    turists, 7, 23, 201; and lack of professional
    gardeners in U.S., 12; and Landreth Com-
    pany, 63; and large estates, 51, 55–56; and
    lawn in U.S. landscape gardening, 196;
    and subscribers as plant purchasers, 188
gardenesque style: elements of, xvi, 6, 7, 45, 52,
    203; exotic plants in, xvi, 6; flower beds
    in, 6,8–9, 52, 215; lawn in, 208; origin of
    term, 45; and plant collecting, 48, 49;
    promotion of by seed companies and
    nurseries, 49
gardenias, 4–5
Gardening, 183
Gardening for Pleasure (Henderson), 5, 94, 190
Gardening for Profit (Henderson), 94
garden phlox, 33
gardens: annuals in, xvi, xx, 6, 167, 168, 175, 222;
    as art form, 43, 45, 52, 161, 163, 214; bulbs
    in, 83, 171; and children, 145, 147–48, 176;
    colonial style, 5; cottage, 6; display, 156;
    dooryard, 3; Dutch, 3, 228; estate, 3–5;
    exotic plants in, xvi, 6, 13, 43, 151, 170;
    flowers in, 6, 8–9, 36, 45, 125, 156, 165–68;
    formal style, xvi, 4, 6, 32; fountains in, 3,
    9; French, 3, 228; fruit in, 164–65; geomet-
    ric, 3, 7, 28, 32, 215; herb, 5; influence of
    seed company catalogs on form of, 5;
    Italian, 6, 228; kitchen, xvi, 5, 9, 50, 62,
    156, 222, 230; knot, xvi; middle class, 3,
    5–6, 156–59, 167, 168, 173; native plants in,
    6, 34, 54, 69, 70, 127, 172; naturalistic, 3, 4,
    43, 172, 203; perennials in, xvi, xx, 6, 33,
    136, 171–72, 215, 216, 219, 220, 222; and
    property resale value, 167, 176; rock, 157;
    roses in, 179, 180; as source of food and
    medicine, 30, 43, 157; Spanish, 2–3, 228;
    standardization in form of, xviii, 101–2,
    229, 230; statuary in, 9; as status symbol,
    xix, 5, 30, 156–58, 159–61, 162–63, 176, 228;
    styles of in America, 2–7; trees and shrubs
    in, xvi, xx, 9, 36, 45, 157; upper class, 3–5,
    10, 30, 48; vegetables in, xvi, 5, 169–70;

gardens (*cont.*)
vista, 3; walkways in, xx, 3, 9; water elements in, 3; water lilies in, 170–71; wild, xvi, 172. *See also* gardenesque style; picturesque style
Gardiner, John, 38
Genesee Farmer, 84, 93, 159
geometric gardens, 3, 7, 28, 32, 215
George A. Sweet Company, 125
George Thompson and Sons, 107
G. H. Barr Company, 128
goldenrod, 33
Good and Reese Company, 110
Goodell Seed Company, 72
Governor's Palace (Williamsburg), 28, 32
Graham, Robert, 77
Gravetye Manor, 220
Gray, Asa, 18
greenhouses, xvii, 6, 14, 20, 55, 138
Green's Fruit Grower, 88
Green's Nursery, 75, 88, 103, 129, 164
Gregory, James J. H., 93–94: advertising of, 106; *Cabbages and How to Raise Them,* 93; *Carrots, Mangold Wurtzels, and Sugar Beets,* 93; *Fertilizers,* 93; and introduction of hubbard squash to America, 93, 106; and Massachusetts Horticultural Society, 14; *Onion Raising,* 93; ordering from competitors, 124; *Squashes and How to Grow Them,* 93
Gregory Company, 109, 111
grottos, in English garden style, 44
ground virginsbower, 121

ha-ha, 4, 50–51
Haines Company. *See* S. Y. Haines Company
Hale, Philip Leslie, 190–91
Hale Company, 131
Hallock and Thorpe Company, 129
Hamilton, William, 4
Hampton Court, xvi, 8
Handbook of Plants (Henderson), 94
Hand Book of Practical Landscape Gardening (Elliott), 213
Harlan P. Kelsey Company, 69
Harris, Joseph, 89, 110–11, 130, 147
Hastings, H. G., 86, 103
Hawkins, John, 31

Hedrick, Ulysses P., 83
hemlock, 55
Henderson, Peter: as contributor to gardening journals, 90; and 'Crimson Rambler' rose, 182, 187, 193; facilities of, 138, 139; *Garden and Farm Topics,* 94; *Gardening for Pleasure,* 5, 94, 190; *Gardening for Profit,* 94; *Handbook of Plants,* 94; *How the Farm Pays,* 94; and lawn, 209; and *Mina lobata,* 99; *Practical Floriculture,* 94; seed company of, 122; writing of, 5, 94, 122–23, 150. *See also* Peter Henderson Company
Henry Dreer Seed Company, 214, 215
Hepburn, David, 38
herb gardens, 5
H. G. Hastings and Company, 86, 103
Hibbert, Thomas, 59, 60
Hill, D., 69–70
Hiram Sibley Seed Company, 106
History and Present State of Virginia, The, in Four Parts (Beverley), 38–39
holly, American, 49
home landscape, xix–xx
Hoopes Company, 129
Hopkins, Timothy, 163
horticultural societies: Delaware Horticultural Society, 50; development of in America, xvii; exhibitions of, 13, 15; Horticultural Society of London, 10, 13,14; Massachusetts Horticultural Society, 2, 6, 14, 17, 65, 81, 154, 157, 169, 174, 180; members of, 13, 14; middle class, appeal to, 13, 14; New Bedford Horticultural Society, 56; New York Horticultural Society, 14; Pennsylvania Horticultural Society, 14, 15; Royal Horticultural Society, 13, 14, 81; Western New York Horticultural Society, 182
Horticultural Society of London, 10, 13, 14
Horticulture of Boston and Vicinity, The (Wilder), 155
Horticulturist: contributors to, 123; founding of, 86, 89; information about specific plants in, 49, 135–36, 181; and lack of professional gardeners in America, 12; transfer of ownership of, 93
Hosack, David, 22
house plants, 173

Hovey, Charles Mason: and *American Gardener's Magazine,* xvii, 21, 80, 85–86; and bulbs, 171; and cemetery movement, 2, 17; first interest in gardening of, 1; and *Gardener's Monthly,* 90; greenhouses of, 20; and improvement of plants, 19–20; and increasing speed of delivery, 101; and the lawn, 10; and *Magazine of Gardening,* 123; and *Magazine of Horticulture,* 2, 22; and the Massachusetts Horticultural Society, 14; and Peter Henderson, 123, 150; and picturesque style, 42–43; plants grown by, 15; and public parks movement, 2; as resource for fruit growers, 31; role in promoting English garden style in America, 2, 8, 12, 23, 43, 96; and roses, 180; and silk industry, 80

Hovey, Phineas Brown, 1

'Hovey' strawberry, 20

How the Farm Pays (Henderson), 94

How to Grow Roses (McFarland), 189

How to Lay Out Home Gardens (Kemp), 46, 47

hubbard squash, introduction of to American gardens, 93

Hunnewell, Horatio Hollis, 56

Huntington, J. T., 126

hybridizing, 144

Hyde Park, 15

illustrations, use of by seed companies and nurseries, 66, 67, 114–18

Ipomoea lobata, 97–99

islands, in English garden style, 44

Italian gardens, 6

Ives Company, 131

Jacobi, Victor, 191–92

James H. Park Company, 167

Jefferson, Thomas, 4, 7, 31, 34, 35, 36

Jekyll, Gertrude: and 'Crimson Rambler' rose, 189; and perennial borders, 6, 172–73, 223, 230; and rise of English garden style in America, 218–19

J. M. Phillips Sons, 106–7

John Charles Vaughn Company, 127–28, 130, 148

John Lewis Childs Company: and coleus, 178; and community among gardeners, 163; facilities of, 140–41; mail-order business

of, 111, 118; and *Mayflower,* 86–88; and novelties, 131

Johnson, C. A., 162

Johnson and Stokes Seed Company, 118

Joseph Breck and Company, 65, 207

journals, farm, 37

journals, gardening

   Agricultural Museum, 84

   American Garden, 86

   American Gardener's Magazine, xvii, 80, 85–86

   American Gardening, 89

   British, 20–21

   Cultivator, 85

   Currie's Monthly, 97

   Curtis's Botanical Magazine, 58

   development of in U.S., 84

   Farm and Garden, 61

   Floral Magazine and Botanical Repository, 85

   Florist's Exchange, 188, 189

   Garden, 47, 183

   Garden and Forest, 97, 193

   Gardener's Chronicle, 20

   Gardener's Magazine, xvii, 2, 45, 88

   Gardener's Monthly

      and carpet bedding, 168, 175, 225

      and catalogs and other advertising, 62, 229

      contributors to, 90, 123

      focus on specific plants, 70, 71, 129, 137

      and garden as cultural symbol for middle class, xix

      and gardening books and journals, 20, 47, 86

      and important horticulturists, 7, 23, 201

      and lack of professional gardeners in U.S., 12

      and Landreth Company, 63

      and large estates, 51, 55–56

      and lawn in U.S. landscape gardening, 196

      and subscribers as plant purchasers, 188

   Gardening, 183

   Genessee Farmer, 84, 93, 159

   Green's Fruit Grower, 88

   Horticulturist

      contributors to, 123

      founding of, 86, 89

      information about specific plants in, 49, 135–36, 181

novelty plants, as theme of seed company and nursery catalogs, xviii, 127–29, 131, 134–35

nurseries. *See* seed companies and nurseries, U.S.

Nuttall, Thomas, 225

Observations on Modern Gardening (Whatley), 36

O'Keefe Seed Company. *See* M. O'Keefe, Son and Company

Olmsted, Frederick Law, 15, 16, 23, 46, 47, 48

O'Mara, Patrick, 193

O. M. Richardson Company, 125

Onion Raising (Gregory), 93

Onward and Upward (White), 218

orchards: in English gardening, 9, 156; at Rockwood, 50; at Shaw Estate, 52

Overman and Mann, 205, 212

Paca, William, estate of, 4

Palm House, 22

Park, George W., 83, 162

Park, James H., 167

Parker and Gannett Company, 134

parks: Birkenhead Park, 15, 46; Central Park, 15, 16, 46; Hyde Park, 15; Mount Hope Park, 16; movement for development of, 15–16; Prince's Park, 46; Regent's Park, 15; St. James Park, 15, 16

Park Seed Company, 85, 162

Parmentier, Andre, 44, 92

Parsons, Samuel, 181

parterres, 32

Paul Butz seed company, 167

Paxton, Joseph: and Birkenhead Park, 15; and Chatsworth, 10, 20, 52; and the English landscape style, 172; and *Garden,* 47; and Prince's Park, 46

pears, 30–31, 55, 154, 155

Penn, John, estate of, 4

Pennsylvania Horticultural Society, 14, 15

penny press, development of, 112

Père Lachaise Cemetery, 17

perennials: American additions to English gardens of, 33; in borders, xvi, xx, 6, 172, 219; in "cottage garden" style, 6; in English garden style, xxi, xx, 171–72, 213, 216,

222, 223; as novelties, 136; resurging interest in, 136; in wild garden, 6, 220, 223

Perry, A. D., 68

Peter Henderson Company, 67, 74, 136, 153, 182, 193

Petre, Lord, 26

petunia, 55

Phelps and Reynolds, 167

Philadelphia, Wilmington and Baltimore Railroad, 49

Philadelphia Flower Show, 15

Phillips, J. M., 106–7

Phillips, Joseph T., 162, 212

Phlox drummondii, 136

photographs, use of by seed companies and nurseries, 118

picturesque style, gardens: curved drives in 204, 214; lawn in, 204; as more natural style, xvi, 7, 9, 42–44; trees and shrubs in, 9, 42–43, 214; unexpected element in, 56

Pike and Ellsworth, 168, 170

pines, 70, 77–79

pinetum, 13, 56

Pinus strobus, 70, 77–79

Pitcher, James R., 134

plant collecting, xvii, 4, 14, 18–20, 45, 48, 49, 55

Platt, Charles A., 48

Podophyllum peltatum, 23–25

Poinsett, Joel, 76

poinsettia, 76–77

Poinsettia pulcherrima, 77

ponds, in English garden style, 44

Pope, Alexander, 36–37, 44

Popular Gardening and Fruit Growing, 201

postal service, importance of to seed and nursery industry, 108–12

Post Office Act of 1792, 108

potato, introduction of to U.S., 31

Practical Farmer, 61

Practical Floriculture (Henderson), 94

Pratt, Henry, 4–5, 59

premiums, use of by seed companies and nurseries, 143

Prince, William, 22, 60; Linnaean Botanic Garden, 22; *Manual of Roses,* 92; *A Short Treatise on Horticulture,* 91–92; *A Treatise* on *Fruit and Ornamental Trees and Plants,* 91

Prince Nursery, 33, 34, 60, 91–92

Prince's Park, 46

printing: advances in, 113, 114–18, 197; importance of advances in to seed and nursery industry, 113, 114–18

professional organizations, horticultural, 123

progress, as theme of seed companies and nurseries, xviii, 102, 112, 116, 124–27

public parks movement, 2, 15–16

Putney, E. D., 211

quince, introduction of to America, 31

railroads: Delaware, 49; expansion of, 49; importance of to seed companies and nurseries, 102–4; Long Island, 101; Philadelphia, Wilmington, and Baltimore, 49; role in development of suburbs, 155, 158

raised beds, 32

Rambler Rose, The (Jacobi), 191–92

Randolph, John, 38

Rawson, W. W., 89

R. D. Luetchford Company, 187

Reasoner Nursery, 19

Reeser, Charles A., 209

Regent's Park, 15

Reid, E. W., 75

Repton, Humphry, 9, 43, 161, 172, 199

rhododendrons, 69, 71

rhubarb, introduction of to U.S., 31

Richardson, O. M., 125

ribbon beds, 167, 168

Riverside Nurseries, 103

Robert Buist Company: awards won by, 142; founding and expansion of, 59–60, 62, 65–66; and *Rudbeckia hirta,* 40; as source of plants for large estates, 48, 55, 56; and vegetable gardening, 170

Robert Buist's Seed Store, 60

Robert Manning Company, 92

Robinia hispida, 49

Robinson, William: *The English Flower Garden,* 218; and the English landscape style, 172, 218–19; and the mayapple, 23; and use of native plants, 135, 216, 223; and use of

perennials, 6, 135, 216, 223; *The Wild Garden,* 6, 23, 135, 216

rock gardens, 157

Rockwood, 42, 46, 48–49, 50, 51, 56, 163, 180

Rosa chinensis, 179

Rosa 'Excelsa', 193–95

Rosa wichuriana, 195

Rose, The (Parsons), 181

rose acacia, 49

Roseland Cottage, 168

Roseland Nursery, 77

Rose Manual, The (Buist), 92

roses: in American gardens, 179–82; Chinese, 179; 'Crimson Rambler', xix, 180, 182–93; 'Dorothy Perkins', 192; in English gardens, 178; 'Excelsa', 192, 193–95; native varieties of, 181–82; 'New Dawn', 193; Noisette, 181, 182; 'Prairie', 182; *Rosa chinensis,* 179; at Shaw estate, 55; shipping of, 104; 'Veilchenblau', 183; *wichuriana,* 195; 'York and Lancaster', 192

Rotch, William, Jr., 56

Rousham, 9, 10, 44

row planting, 5

Royal Botanic Garden, Edinburgh, 59, 76

Royal Botanic Gardens, Kew, 18, 22, 58, 171

Royal Exotic Nursery, 23

Royal Horticultural Society, 13, 14, 81

Rudbeck, Olav, 41

Rudbeckia hirta, 33, 36, 40–41

Rural Free Delivery Act, 111

salesmen, use of by seed companies and nurseries, 116, 118

Salisbury, Robert, 50

Scott, Frank: *The Art of Beautifying Suburban Home Grounds,* 199–201, 209; role in teaching landscape gardening to Americans, 209

seed companies and nurseries, U.S.

A. Blanc Company, 130

A. D. Perry and Company, 68

advances in printing as important to, 113, 114–18

advertising by, 104–8

A. R. Whitney Company, 95

Ashton Nurseries, 49

Phlox drummondii, 136; prizes won by, 142; use of premiums, 142, 143; and vegetable gardening, 83; and the wild garden, 135

Vick's Illustrated Monthly, 85, 88, 159, 198, 213, 224

vinca, introduction of to America, 30

vista gardens, 3

von Weigel, Christian, 58

walks, curved, in English garden style, xx, 197, 208, 214, 221

Walpole, Horace, 77

Walsh, Michael, 192, 194

Ward Hill, 56

Washburn Company, 67, 144

Washington, George, 39

Washington, Martha, 39

water lilies, 170–71

W. Atlee Burpee Company, 94, 101, 118, 119, 126, 169–70

Watson, Elkanah, 142

Webster, Pelatiah, 105

Webster, William, 48

Weidenmann, Jacob, 48

Weigela shrub, 49, 55, 57–58, 129

Western New York Horticultural Society, 182

Weymouth pine, 70, 77

Wharton, Edith, 191

Whatley, Thomas, 36

Whipple House, 3, 180

White, E. B., 218

White, Katharine, 218, 219

white pine, 70, 77–79

Whitmore, Charles, 176

Whitney, A. R., 95

Wilder, Marshall: and American Pomological Society, 213; and *Azalea mollis*, 157; estate of, 154–55, 156, 163; *The Horticulture of Boston and Vicinity*, 155; and Massachusetts Agricultural Club, 154; and Massachusetts Horticultural Society, 14, 154, 157, 176; and picturesque style, 155; and subtropical plants, 6, 169

Wild Garden, The (Robinson), 6, 23, 135, 216

Williams, George, 46

Williamsburg: as example of early colonial landscape design, 27; as example of English formal style, 27–28, 32–33; fences required in, 29; gardens at, 32; and geometric style, 3; roses in, 180; varieties of plants grown at, 31–32

willow, 49

Woman's Hardy Garden, A (Ely), 189

Woodburn, Elizabeth, 82

Woodlands (Philadelphia), 4

World's Fair, St. Louis, 126–27

Wright, Charles, 69

Wright, Mabel Osgood, 181

W. W. Rawson Seed Company, 89

Wyman, David, 30

Wyncote, 45, 48, 50

Wynne, William, 11

Zeffler, Rose, 191

Thomas J. Mickey is Professor Emeritus of Communication Studies at Bridgewater State University, Bridgewater, Massachusetts. He is a graduate of Boston University, the University of Iowa, and the Landscape Institute at the Boston Architectural College, and has been a garden columnist for the *Brockton Enterprise, Quincy Patriot Ledger,* and Portsmouth, New Hampshire's *Seacoast Media.* His other books include *Best Garden Plants for New England* (with Alison Beck, 2006), *Deconstructing Public Relations* (2003), and *Sociodrama: An Interpretive Theory for the Practice of Public Relations* (1995).